# The Promise of the Third Way

*Also by Otto Newman*

GAMBLING: Hazard and Reward

THE CHALLENGE OF CORPORATISM

THE AMERICAN DREAM IN THE INFORMATION AGE (*with Richard de Zoysa*)

*Also by Richard de Zoysa*

THE AMERICAN DREAM IN THE INFORMATION AGE (*with Otto Newman*)

# The Promise of the Third Way

## Globalization and Social Justice

Otto Newman
*Adjunct Professor of S*
*San Diego State Unive*
*USA*

and

Richard de Zoy
*Senior Lecturer in Poli*
*South Bank University*
*London*



palgrave

First published 2001 by
PALGRAVE
Houndmills, Basingstoke, Hampshire RG21 6XS and
175 Fifth Avenue, New York, N. Y. 10010
Companies and representatives throughout the world

PALGRAVE is the new global academic imprint of St. Martin's Press LLC Scholarly and Reference Division and Palgrave Publishers Ltd (formerly Macmillan Press Ltd).

ISBN 0–333–79285–8

This book is printed on paper suitable for recycling and made from fully managed and sustained forest sources.

A catalogue record for this book is available from the British Library.

Library of Congress Cataloging-in-Publication Data
Newman, Otto.
The promise of the third way : globalization and social justice / Otto Newman, Richard de Zoysa.
p. cm.
Includes bibliographical references and index.
ISBN 0–333–79285–8
1. Mixed economy. 2. Globalization. 3. Post-communism.
4. Social justice. I. De Zoysa, Richard, 1944– II. Title.
HB90 .N484 2001
337—dc21
2001021867

10 9 8 7 6 5 4 3 2 1
10 09 08 07 06 05 04 03 02 01

Printed and bound in Great Britain by
Antony Rowe Ltd, Chippenham, Wiltshire

# Contents

# Acknowledgements

In the course of writing this book Richard de Zoysa would like to extend his appreciation to Mike Hickox, formerly Principal Lecturer in Politics, for his critical comments on Chapter 10 and to Jane Franklin, Senior Research Fellow at South Bank University, for her helpful advice given in Chapter 7. He would also like to extend his appreciation to Penny Dole at Palgrave for her editorial assistance. More generally, he would like to acknowledge the assistance given by South Bank University to facilitate the research undertaken to complete this book. Finally, he would like to give his utmost thanks to his family, to Tom and Eleanor, and to his wife Alison for their unstinting support and encouragement.

Otto Newman wishes to express heartfelt thanks to all who, over the many years, have helped him sustain his faith in social progress, first and foremost to June, his better half.

# Introduction

The Third Way in Britain is currently in the doldrums, battered by critics from both left and right and disappointing its supporters by its inability to translate its ideas into a coherent programme of reform understandable to the wider electorate. Acclaim follows blame and self-recrimination, not least in the revealing leaks seeping out of government indicating unease and uncertainty among the leadership of the Party in finding it difficult to convey its core message. And all this at a time when commanding a 179-seat majority in the 1997 election and still polling positively among the wider electorate.

The roots of the Third Way lay in a post-Keynesian intellectual climate and more specifically in the formative years surrounding the economic recession of the early 1990s, at a time when the left had faced many forlorn years in opposition. Left-of-centre leaders, not just in the United Kingdom but also in Europe, needed to regain electoral respectability by abandoning outworn socialist rhetoric, and offering voters policies that would command widespread support among an electorate vastly different from when many of them had last held power. An early indicator of the intellectual shift this implied was witnessed by the reform struggles occurring within the Democratic Party in the USA in the late 1980s, following the success of Ronald Reagan in targeting working-class support. The Democratic Leadership Council wanted modernization of the party programme to make it more appealing to a fast growing suburban constituency. New Labour, in particular, watched these developments with interest.

With an unequivocal call for reform, the Third Way promises to modernize social democracy, currently on the defensive in the light of neo-conservative criticisms that portray its past spending programmes as inflationary and premised on high penal rates of tax, destructive of enterprise and individual initiative. The Third Way eschews the traditional leftist approach to pump-priming the public sector and accepts much, though by no means all, of the preceding Conservative years of reform, re-establishing the primacy of the market. It is pro-business, positive towards free trade and globalization, while cautious in making *a priori* commitments to its traditional constituency. The Third Way embraces the idea of modernizing the public sector by advancing new forms of public–private cooperation and seeking private sector inputs where necessary. The state will monitor and set various performance criteria to ensure high standards are obtained. However, past inadequacies revealed by an over-reliance on private sector mechanisms exclusively (especially in run-down inner cities and older industrial areas lacking adequate investment), will be tackled by New Deal initiatives focused on combating social exclusion, at a time when at least one in five children remain mired in poverty.

Much has been inspired by the example of the USA. The flexibility of its labour market in generating employment and its success in developing innovative technology has built a lauded 'New Economy', where readily available venture capital and an absence of restrictive red-tape are seen as vital to new company formation and success. Central to New Labour's programme is a remodelling of the welfare state by targeting funding and emphasizing the rights people enjoy being commensurate with their responsibilities to their families and wider society. Much remains uncertain, and many see in the Third Way an abandonment of Labour's traditional concern with social justice and universal citizenship rights, while conceding far too much to powerful conservative interests in the media and business. New Labour responds by pointing to the flourishing service sector economy, made secure by a combination of economic prudence and macroeconomic stability, and the need to keep on board its new-found middle-class support. The recourse to private insurance is beyond the means of many, so voting Labour is a way of hastening improvements in public sector provision – in state schools where their children are educated and in NHS hospitals their health care is dependent upon. The underpinning to these changes is not just a policy conversion but also marks a new intellectual terrain mapped by think tanks and academic advisers.

While for the moment domestic debate seems stilled, internationally many newly elected premiers or rivals for office of varying political persuasions claim allegiance to Third Way values, and see in Tony Blair an inspirational figure. Thus a report in *The Independent* of 4 July 2000 was headed 'Mongolian ex-communists win a landslide for their "Third Way"', while a few weeks later the same paper reported that Socialists pin their hopes on a 'Spanish Tony Blair'. Indeed supporters of some variety of a Third Way or new progressive politics extend beyond the confines of Europe and the USA to include the presidents of Chile, Argentina and Brazil, while Thabo Mbeki, the newly elected leader of South Africa also claims to be a follower.

What gives credence to the growing chorus of critical commentary? The range of opposition to New Labour and its Third Way ranges from traditional core supporters both inside and outside parliament who see it as something of a 'sell-out' of key socialist values, to those who argue more dispassionately that the project lacks a coherent political economy since abandoning Keynesianism. Furthermore, its support for globalization and modernization are in crucial respects naïve and ill-informed as to the true nature of modern corporate capitalism. On the right the critique is equally dismissive, viewing it as a covert means to 'raise taxes by stealth', while imposing further regulatory controls on private capital which has demonstrated its munificence by creating, once again, near full employment. Uniting both critiques is the charge that New Labour is over-dependent on spin, focus groups and direct democracy, and is by-passing the traditional representative function of parliament with its right to scrutinize the executive. Power is based on a 'command' model, and is too over-centralized within an emerging presidential style of leadership lacking adequate countervailing checks and balances.

There is, it must be admitted, some truth in these allegations. But there is a distinct promise to the Third Way: a sense of it trying to grapple with a very different emergent social structure, where the old certainties of class formation and hierarchy have long gone in a far more socially fluid landscape, characterized by high levels of female employment, differing family structures and new questions posed by a multicultural society – all transformations that need addressing. A new political repositioning towards the problems and opportunities posed by globalization is becoming evident, be it in developing new international regulatory controls with other similarly minded states, or in dealing with international non-governmental organizations (NGOs) and their pressures to alleviate global concerns. New Labour is decidedly not 'Thatcherism in trousers'. The commitment to the House of Lords reform has seen the elimination of the hereditary principle. Devolution has altered the balance of power between Westminster and the constituent national units that make up the UK. The introduction of the minimum wage and the New Deal offering support to unemployed and underprivileged youngsters and now extending to older workers is significant. Finally, the massive boost to public services awarded under the Comprehensive Spending Review in the Summer of 2000, is a vote of confidence in modernizing and improving the public delivery of services, marking a genuine difference of approach from that of a Conservative administration. New Labour is renewing its pledge to a genuine form of equality of opportunity by a socially inclusive programme of action. The contention that political parties offer little choice is facile.

However, what continues to worry supporters of the Third Way's alternative route to political management, is the timidity and apparent lack of a core conviction to the whole project, thereby diminishing its prospects of success. Thus, the House of Lords reform has produced the stupefying spectacle of a non-elected second chamber countervailing the will of the elected Commons, yet at the same time providing one of the few effective checks on government itself. A nagging feeling persists that government only introduces some reform retroactively not positively. The adoption of the minimum wage was set at a very low level; the introduction of a Freedom of Information Act is lacking teeth; a policy of 'tough on crime', rather than its causes, has taken precedence, while adopting the European Social Charter into English law appears as grudgingly half-hearted as ever. The adherence to tight public spending limits, inherited from the previous administration, has retained the confidence of the City that Labour would be prudent in its custody of the nation's finances, and has been given further reinforcement by granting operational control over interest rates to the now independent Bank of England. However, this resulted in an initial squeeze on public finances, demoralizing many working within the public sector, while promising more than it could deliver, thus dashing expectations of New Labour's capacity to honour its pledges. Questions are asked whether boosting public spending so dramatically in the short term (though much constitutes a catching-up exercise), can be coupled with adequate promises to modernize and improve existing services, thereby re-legitimizing claims that government can work satisfactorily. New thinking as to what exactly comprises modernization, though spelt out in various publications, indicates little by way of concrete results to date. Similarly on Europe, the vital debate on joining the euro, sees government hesitant, vacillating and disunited, thereby departing from its promise to secure a leading European role.

Beyond the United Kingdom, the influence of Third Way ideas was apparent in Germany with the Schröder government and even earlier still with Bill Clinton, the latter visibly under the spell of the Democratic Leadership Council and its proposal to distance the Democrats from their more traditional 'tax and spend' programmes. Clinton needed to connect to newer, more suburban voting constituencies, previously put off by the traditional sectional appeals of the party. This resulted, prior to the 1996 presidential election, in a policy known as triangulation – a defence of existing Social Security and Medicare programmes from Republican encroachment by depicting them as tax-cutting zealots, while at the same time promising welfare reform and avoiding new commitments to big government programmes. The DLC philosophy of opportunity, responsibility and community implied an enabling role for government based on balancing the budget and was heralded as a new form of progressive politics. It certainly helped secure the president's re-election, along with his stewardship of a booming US economy now benefiting from globalization. This occurred despite the evident disapproval of many ordinary working families, worried by the negative consequences they attributed to more open free trade for downsizing their jobs plus significant opposition from one key traditional ally, namely the AFL-CIO labour organization.

In Germany, the Neue Mitte has similarly been ambivalently received. Schröder has cut taxes significantly and deregulated, while promising to secure pension rights for workers in a careful balancing act as the economy opens up to the rigours of Anglo-Saxon shareholding. In France meanwhile, the Jospin government remains deeply suspicious of this modernizing agenda as it seems so overtly corporate friendly, and so the need to temper the destructive potential of market activity is pronounced widely. Yet quietly, the privatizing of industry has proceeded at a rate beyond that of its liberal-conservative predecessors. On the other hand, the French government has experimented with an innovative 35-hour working week, despite big business opposition. Though fewer new jobs have been generated than once were anticipated, it has unintentionally boosted employee flexibility – another key Third Way mantra – to maintain international competitiveness.

All leaders now subscribe to a new brand of social democracy, supportive of free trade and globalization, yet seek in their different ways to moderate the harsher effects of the unfettered market. All are cost conscious, mindful of the need to keep government taxation low and subject to internal and external competitive constraints. The emphasis is on pragmatism, progressivism and modernization, while for many European leaders reform is not viewed simply as a synonym for deregulation and cutting the role of government, but rather implies a commitment to workers' rights, and emphatically is not a race to the bottom in order to remain competitive.

This book charts the development, critique and possible revitalization of the Third Way as a programme of modernization and as a political movement in the United Kingdom, USA and Europe. The text is organized in the following way: Part I – The Background to the Third Way – develops the political, social and economic context out of which this new form of revisionism emerged. The first chapter explores the emergence of capitalism and socialism as rival ideological protagonists. Chapter 2 examines the specific development of social democracy from within the socialist tradition, including its post-war triumphs and slow retreat from the 1970s, when its underlying Keynesian assumptions were undermined and its performance questioned by the advent of globalization. Chapter 3 – The End of Socialism? – explores the regime and ideological crisis of Gorbachev's Soviet Union prior to investigating the problems of the 'transition' – the rebuilding of a market system and securing democratic legitimacy in Russia. Parallel developments in central and eastern Europe, both preceding and following the fall of the Berlin Wall are assessed, including analysis of the possibility of reviving socialism today.

In Part II – The Post-Cold War Era – the initial focus in Chapter 4 is given to why the market economy has been so successful and triumphant, and to the air of invincibility it was able to project before examining its limitations. Chapter 5 sets out the Third Way alternative, in terms of its key ideas and policies, by explicating its intellectual origins and identifying the influence its ideas and analysis have generated within Europe. Chapter 6 offers a critical review of the Third Way, initially from a more sympathetic moderate/centrist position then extending to the New Right/ conservative disposition, before finally examining Left adversarial rejection of its assumptions and practice.

Part III – New Times: the Way Ahead – starts in Chapter 7 by focusing on Labour's flagship Third Way programme – the New Deal, with its commitment to ending social exclusion, while also giving attention to the early influential ideas of Communitarianism and Stakeholding as possible alternative models. In Chapter 8, the divisions in Europe, the emergence of the euro and Britain's uneasy relationship with its partners are explored, before moving on to outline a possible case for Third Way convergence. Chapter 9 switches direction by examining political developments across the Atlantic, especially the influence of the Democratic Leadership Council and its Third Way repositioning of the Democratic Party. The political heritage bequeathed by President Clinton is assessed before addressing the issues and ideas infusing the run-up to the presidential election and the wider influence of an American Third Way. Finally in Chapter 10 – The Promise of the Third Way – an overview is offered of the critical commentary and internal contradictions of the Third Way, including the ever-present pull to the right, before arguing the case for Third Way cooperation as a means to modernizing European social democracy when set against the serious challenge of globalization. US style triangulation is rejected as insufficient in scope and philosophy, so new initiatives are necessary to ensure that the effectiveness and promise of the Third Way are realized.

In opening up the Third Way to critical scrutiny and locating it within its intellectual and contemporary setting, the text has been designed to interest the informed general reader and equally to engage the specialist concerned about the future direction of social democracy and the Third Way in particular. What emerges out of such a debate has the capacity to affect us all for good or ill. Our hope is that we have offered both a guide and some positive suggestions for future deliberation amongst our readership.

# Part I

# The Background to the Third Way

# 1
# Capitalism and Socialism

For the past one and a half centuries, capitalism and socialism have been the principal global protagonists. Capitalism came first. Constituting the motive force behind industrialization and modernization, its role was supreme. The call for freedom (and equality), first enunciated during the English Civil War against monarchical absolutism and later made memorably evident by the French Revolution, served as common sources of ideological inspiration. For Britain – well to the forefront for the first hundred years – Adam Smith's *The Wealth of Nations*, together with the theories of Edmund Burke, John Stuart Mill and Jeremy Bentham set the framework. Divergent as these were in their basic philosophy, the opportunities and freedom from tyranny that the capitalist system provided, reflected the best possible vision for a secure and happy future life.

Socialism traces its ideological roots to the earliest forms of social existence when, it alleges, communal life was solidaristic and untainted by competitive strife. Early philosophical traces are discernible in Plato's *Republic*. The guardians or philosopher kings, hold no property, nor do they live in family units. They selflessly rule in the interests of the wider community. At the time of the Peasants' Revolt in England, led by the redoubtable John Ball in 1381, the sentiments expressed were captured in the witticism of 'When Adam delved and Eve span who was then the gentleman?', implying a society where class division was absent. Thomas More's *Utopia* dreamt of a classless utopia, where the organized societal conspiracy of the rich against the poor would finally be ended. The Levellers and Diggers of the English Civil War threatened the sanctity of private property, but were quickly repudiated by Cromwell's New Model Army. More recently, early criticism of nineteenth-century *laissez-faire* market capitalism and disappointment with the failure of the French Revolution to link political with economic equality led to widespread critique. In England the idealistic communitarianism of Robert Owen echoed similar developments associated with Fourier in France. Until 1848, the wave of popular uprising that surfaced in most western states as yet hardly constituted a political movement, being more a collection of disparate theories. After 1848, a practical movement whereby socialist ideas were transformed into action, prominently reflected the values of dialectic materialism that Karl Marx and his followers had widely proclaimed.

Capitalism, by its very nature, brought in its wake social inequality, exploitation and immiseration. Power – not only material, but equally political, social and cultural – was passing from the landed interest into the hands of the bourgeoisie, who made use of their position to enhance class privilege and personal wealth, while inflicting suffering and alienation on the majority. That the system, at the same time, was wasteful and inefficient would, it was claimed, lead to its eventual demise. Though a necessary stepping stone towards the threshold of material affluence, capitalism was destined to make way for the socialist future where injustice, oppression and exploitation would no longer reign. Communism, with its total removal of the cursed evil of private property and the money economy, was perceived as the ultimate outcome amongst more radical circles. Socialism, acknowledged as a legitimate interim state of transition, would serve as a useful staging post. But only the withering away of the oppressive state apparatus to make way for a process of mere administration would ensure that material scarcity, now thanks to capitalism's bounty, would be finally overcome resulting in peace and plenty for all.

Capitalism and socialism have stood shoulder to shoulder in their historic conflict to become the standard-bearers of the good life. Wherever one established a foothold, the other stood close behind. Politically, industrially and ideologically in their struggle for the allegiance of the majority throughout all parts of the globe, they have competed, denouncing each other while insisting that only they, and they alone, held the key to the good life. The apogee of the struggle arose in the aftermath of the Second World War. The half-century of the Cold War represented an era of intensified rivalry and militant confrontation. For a while, the momentum of the march of time seemed decidedly to have moved in a leftward direction. Radiating from Soviet Russia, and soon after, China, while taking root throughout the developing world, communism was gaining unquestioned ascendancy. In South-east Asia, the Gulf region, Africa, South America and the

Caribbean, successive radical left-wing regimes, implacably opposed to the West, were gaining the upper hand. The West championed above all by the USA, as the pre-eminent capitalist power and leader of NATO, was not beyond geopolitical setback. America's defeat in the Vietnam war, proved a serious ideological blow to its policy of containment, although one quickly moderated by growing *détente* with China. Moreover, criticism of the Vietnam war within the US fed into massive student protest and radicalism. Government economic policy became destabilized through growing inflationary pressures arising from the costs of the conflict, while the Bretton Woods system and dollar convertibility were aborted.

The contagion spread and inspired youth protest in Europe against the managerial state and its corporate supporters. Well into the late 1960s in France and Italy nearly one-third of the electorate regularly supported the communist ticket, allying themselves with the Soviet cause. Generally, in Western societies (the USA being the partial exception), the reality was social democracy. From Britain, France and the Netherlands to Italy, Spain, Scandinavia and the Austrian Republic left-oriented parties publicly committed to a programme of progressive socialization and containment of working-class demands, occupied office most of the time. Capitalism, overtly in most parts of the world had its back to the wall. In the eyes of many observers from all schools of thought, its era of dominance was close to an end as it was subject to ever more state management. New experiments in state corporatism involving both capital and labour as equal partners with state regulation of wages and prices seemed to offer a new panacea during the 1970s. In reality they were more a desperate form of crisis management, as inflation and a lack of growth ended the long post-war boom, and placed additional pressures on maintaining extensive welfare state commitments within a large and growing public sector.

The early 1980s heralded a period of market resurgence with a restatement of capitalist principles in the wake of the failed Keynesian panacea. Stagflation was to be soundly repudiated by the Thatcher/Reagan critique of post-war statism and management demand, replacing it with both monetarism and supply-side economics. A thoroughgoing dismantling of the state-controlled public sector followed. Then, unexpectedly in utter defiance of the informed consensus, came the fateful events of 1989. The year when the Berlin Wall crumbled, communism appeared bankrupt and discredited once and for all, and the Soviet Empire dissolved into a multiplicity of separate unstable units. Dissidents came to the fore, and Marxism, in all its various guises, was authoritatively pronounced to be in its irreversible final demise. As Christopher Pierson observes: 'Scarcely one hundred years after Lord Harcourt's declaration that "we are all socialists now"' had ushered in the collectivist age, political commentators were queuing to bear witness that 'the Socialist Age was coming to an end'. Characteristically David Marquand argued that 'the epic struggle between capitalism and socialism is over; and capitalism has won', while Ralf Dahrendorf insisted quite simply that 'socialism is dead' (Pierson, 1995: 1).

The New World Order had no place for discontent or dissension. The market, universally enshrined and benign, would provide plenty for everyone. Collectivism had been shown up as fraudulent. Capitalism not only proved stronger and more resilient, but ushering in an era of boundless abundance made ideological dichotomy and confrontation a thing of the past. In the USA during the 1990s a new economic paradigm was recognized, based on consistent growth, low inflation and most importantly jobs in abundance. Even *The End of History*, as Francis Fukuyama proclaimed it, stood within sight (1992). When all were pulling in a single direction and keenly subscribed to the winning logic of the market, the zero-sum confrontations of the past became obsolete, as there is now more than enough to satisfy everyone.

It is already apparent that this has not occurred. The system of unfettered capitalism destined to be the key to success, has fallen well short of its promises. For all its material abundance, the West is apprehensive, divided and riven with problems of joblessness, polarization and social decay. The economic miracle of the South-east Asian societies is only just emerging from recession and gloom. Russia, as is equally true of its former national peers, is beset by crises of ill-governance, criminality and incapacity to manage resources – and the contagion has spread to South America. Rootless transnationals have in many instances superseded state power without putting anything else in their place. Massive waves of speculative capital – much of it of dubious origin – circle the globe in search of easy profit, unsettling currencies and disrupting trade. Altogether, the lure of quick riches and dubious gain has become so dominant that, in all aspects of global affairs, trust and integrity seem irrevocably redundant.

One hesitates to exaggerate the reaction. Socialism, since the spectacle of Soviet deceit and oppression was revealed to all, has a long struggle to gain redemption. On the other hand, material well-being has effectively advanced on a global scale by leaps and bounds to an extent that capitalism's imminent demise clearly flies in the face of objective reality. Yet undercurrents, however preliminary, cannot be ignored. A brief decade after its trumpeted terminal demise, socialism is showing some signs of rising from the dead, admittedly in a much modified form, and committed to programmes that were recently considered taboo. In Russia, as well as in several former state partners, there is virtual total disenchantment with the capitalist experiment, with 'reform communists' again forming a parliamentary majority. China, courted by all for its population advantage of more than one billion inhabitants, is clearly in a state of ascendancy in global affairs. Even within the United States, there are calls for moderation and triangulation. And perhaps most significantly, at the start of the last year before the Millennium, in 13 of the 15 European Union member states, left-wing administrations were in control.

It would be mistaken to underestimate the changes that have occurred within the 'New World Order's' initial decade. Both capitalism and socialism have trimmed their sails to a notable extent, while rival ideologies have made their way to the forefront in many parts of the world. Extreme nationalism, fundamentalism and brands of neo-Nazism that mirror the racial and militant orientation of the notorious Hitler era, demand recognition as significant forces in world affairs. Yet, for all their virulence wherever dominant, for all their threat to security, these rank more in the order of regional manifestations, erupting at times, of untoward disturbance, than as universal philosophies comparable to belief systems that surmount the limitations of location and time. Quite possibly, both capitalism and socialism are equally distinctive for the strength of their pliability and their capacity to adapt to changed circumstances as they arise (Schumpeter, 1943).

Remarkably, they are once again in a process of endogenous change. Liberalism, with its emphasis on untrammelled free trade plus minimal government, has for some time held centre stage, and is gradually ceding its prominence to a new type of conservatism which, while balancing the demands of globalization and the nation state, equally acknowledges the need to moderate the market's deleterious effects by government action. Socialism's internal transformation is even more drastic. Uniformly, commitment to public ownership of the means of production plus central management have been put aside. Under a variety of titular changes, such as 'New Labour', market socialism is becoming the norm. Pragmatism rules over ideology. Class allegiance is modulated, while a new, distinctly professional middle-class leadership has moved to the fore. Not least, the horrors of the Soviet regime have not been forgotten. In reorientation, there is a lot of ground to make up. Yet, in contrast to its rival ideology which is profoundly sceptical about human perfectibility, socialism still offers a vision of a better society in which egotism and acquisitive greed have given way to the values of amity and cooperation to the benefit of the entire community rather than merely a privileged few. The release from defending the indefensible practice of those 'socialistic' regimes consigned to the dustbin of history after 1989, has itself become a liberation for much of the left.

Yet the era of stability that the New World Order projected, has failed to materialize. What appears as monolithic American power on closer examination seems a mirage. Regional peace initiatives brokered by the US come and go and somehow seem incapable of final resolution. Yet for all the setbacks and uncertainties in the international relations between states, capitalism remains well entrenched in the saddle. As was true in the past, its closest rival remains an updated form of socialism, suitably trimmed to fit modern times and making a comeback within nations of leading account in global affairs. We will critically elaborate the principal characteristics of both capitalism and socialism in the rest of this chapter. Apart from elucidating the prime forces at work in current conditions, this should equally foster an understanding of the endeavours and characteristics associated with the Third Way.

## 1. Capitalism

As is also true of socialism, capitalism is by no means a unitary philosophy. Variants range from the implacably anti-authority libertarianism to a new-conservatism which, though economically conformist advocates a considerable amount of intervention within the public sphere. In general terms, all adhere to the supremacy of the market as the optimal arbiter in resource allocation, with free trade, opportunity, self-regulation, and individual enterprise providing a sure means to reward everyone. Libertarianism, most prevalent amongst marginal groups in the United States, has never made any meaningful impact on public affairs. Its propensity to be seized upon by right-wing extremists as a convenient vehicle to act out their violent militant dreams, has not endeared them to the public at large. Outrages such as the Oklahoma bombing of a federal building, the Unabomber or the dozens of armed-to-the teeth militiamen in mountain retreats has understandably given the Libertarian movement a bad name. It is often overlooked that behind such extremism, there is a serious coherent philosophy that represents the yearnings for a simpler, less competitive and regimented way of life on the part of millions of citizens throughout the world. According to Ansell, 'to be right wing means to support the state in its capacity as an enforcer of order and to oppose the state as distributor of wealth and power downwards' (Ansell, 1998: 19). Libertarians vehemently reject the first part of this equation.

Anarcho-libertarianism, which comprises most of the popular elements, moves from the presumption that 'no man or group of men may aggress the person or property of anyone else' (Rothbard, 1978: 23), to the assertion that 'War is Mass Murder, Conscription is Slavery, and Taxation is Robbery' (Ibid.: 24–5). Denouncing the state, irrespective of its 'outward appearance' as essentially a 'central, dominant aggressor' defines both a desire to resist unwonted intrusion into personal liberty, while equally tending to legitimate illicit activities from, say, tax refuseniks to those such as the Unabomber who feel justified, in defence of their liberties, in committing murderous acts. However, even the milder version denies government interference beyond the management of exchange, personal security and self-ownership. Taxation is regarded as analogous to legalized theft, public schooling is likened to 'prison without bars', while law enforcement becomes a means of covert oppression. Similarly, all 'victimless crimes' such as pornography, sexual deviation or drug abuse should be removed from public intervention, where all too often they fall into 'busy bodies' self-seeking hands, (Rothbard, 1978; Friedman, 1978). Authority in matters of law enforcement, in the view of some groups, is to be vested in none but the 'sheriff's posse', a customary practice in 'the good old days'.

For more critically worked-out scenarios, one needs to turn to such philosophers as Robert Nozick or Ayn Rand (Nozick, 1974; Rand, 1964). Nozick's major criticism of the egalitarian view of distributive justice was that in ignoring the means by which goods were produced in society they assumed they could be easily allocated to us all on the basis of our needs. For both, their watchword is 'objectivism', implying notions of natural justice both in private and public affairs. This is a mindset that closely approximates Bentham's utilitarian calculus of 'maximum pleasure and minimum pain', though it needs to be added that leading libertarians perceive the prescription in a different way. Rand, in particular, claims that her formulation equips *laissez-faire* capitalism with an ethical base. 'Since reason', she argues, 'is man's basic means of survival, that which is proper to the life of rational beings is good; that which negates, opposes or destroys it is evil' (Rand, 1964: 23). Hence, individuals' capacity to apply rational judgment to all aspects of social existence confines government's role to no other acts than personal protection. With the trade nexus providing the 'only ethical principle for human relationships', all that could lead to coercion is basically wrong. One is forced to observe that much as this might inspire benevolent thought, when it comes to action as such, it appears a long way removed from the actuality of the real world. Libertarianism might well be construed as a convenient cover for the exercise of the extremists' own ends, rather than as a programme for empirical implementation.

In historical terms, conservatism and liberalism throughout the nineteenth century indisputably held centre stage. In virtually all western societies, they vied during this period for dominant power. Embracing the ideals of the French Revolution while equally advancing the cause of free trade, liberalism effected a real contrast with conservatism's values of family life, the national state and religious observance. As the century moved to its end, socialism, which was gradually gaining strength through the teachings of Marx and the events of 1848, was making its way to the front. By the early 1900s, and especially in the aftermath of the First World War, socialism had taken the place of liberalism as the major rival. Liberalism's record of a boom and bust cycle was discrediting, while at the same time the rising level of self-consciousness of the industrial working class had altered the face of political life. The group (or social class) rather than the individual became the basis of organized political life and action. The challenge of totalitarian Fascism/Nazism apart, the Left and the Right counterposed against each other in varying degrees of confrontation continued until 1989.

As a realistic and independent socio-political force the liberal alternative has still only limited appeal, its basic values subtly co-opted by Left and Right. Liberalism's inherent refusal to fundamentally compromise the pre-eminence of the free market has turned into a mantra that few dared question until recently. The *laissez-faire* model of untrammelled free trade is embraced by all, including Third Way proponents who have been amongst the first to suggest a modified course – that is, still within a market paradigm, but suggesting the necessity of a moderate level of intervention at the same time. Yet for all that, even then the Third Way has been dubbed as a subliminal return to the liberal values of the past (Marr, 1998).

Conservatism and liberalism have a great deal in common. For both, the concept of the market economy is a central presumption. Free markets, unhampered terms of voluntaristic exchange, free enterprise and rewards according to effort and merit are heralded as the best –

indeed the only – means to achieve justice and freedom for all. Closely connected, is the aversion to public coercion and central control. Insistence on minimal government, with least interference in civic society and personal life goes hand in hand. Optimal capacities are exercised in producing, buying and selling. People of diverse backgrounds, talents and perceptions interact, if not directly, then in common pursuit. All become enabled and motivated, and each will freely contribute to the common weal. None are excluded, and while the most meritorious will rise to the top, all have an equal chance to succeed. Concomitantly, the few who fall by the wayside will, free of ill-regard or compulsion, be aided until they are fit to recoup.

Beyond this shared concept, their ways tend to part. As terminologically implied, conservatism believes in gradualism, slow and limited change, in national pride and in patriotism, in hierarchy, order as well as tradition. It takes a decidedly sceptical view of human natural inclination towards benevolence, disdains presumptions of perfectibility, and by and large subscribes to the constraining effect of original sin. Being weak and prone to temptation, individuals need continuity, guidance and role models who can inspire them and to whom they can look up. The natural candidates are the persons of good birth and good breeding who, thanks to their personal qualities of independence and autonomy, will be prudent and wise, while at the same time, impartially free of self-glory and corruption. Their dedication to common interest and service, will set norms that others can follow. Rights must be balanced by duties, while the pursuit of personal gain and private success is legitimate concern for public interest and must be of equal account. While none are too mighty to dictate the terms or to evade accountability, at the same time none are too humble to be ignored. Character, honour, integrity and, last but not least, faith in the strength of tradition will moderate the deleterious effects that market forces inflict on individuals and communities. The traditions of value and experience will do the rest.

Liberalism is distinctly secular. Implicitly, its assertion of progress and human will confronts the notion of an omnipotent deity. As a meta-ideology it provides the ground for debate with others, and consequently others have borrowed its clothes. Today, its very pluralism and tolerance gives it exceptional flexibility. The focus on human thought and initiative, capable through rational action of transforming the social and physical environment removes the necessity to rely on divine intervention. The individual precedes the formation of society, but liberals now insist that all of us have social responsibilities as well.

Stability is approved and accepted, but continuous progress towards perfection expresses the essence of the human condition. Uniquely endowed with reason and foresight, *homo economicus* will unerringly choose the best path. Rationally able to balance costs against benefits, to surmount potential hurdles and to follow the optimal path to one's goal, all that is needed is freedom of action. Freedom is vital. The utility calculus will do the rest. What is to one person's advantage, will equally benefit all. The rational weighing of costs against benefits will ensure a proper reward. The key to success is minimal government, untrammelled free trade, equal opportunity for all to pursue their best ends, together with expectation of fair reward. Equality is understood as one of both opportunity and moral worth. It implies political equality in terms of one person one vote, but not social equality, instead proclaiming that skills are unequally distributed and so produce unequal outcomes of income and wealth. In practice, it provides a mixture of both negative freedom (limits on external constraint from the state) with some positive freedoms, such as social support for self-development and maximization of individual skill. Exactly where the line is drawn is debatable.

Government is most effective if restricted to a 'night watchman role': personal protection plus the safeguarding of national security, the currency and little else. With government limited from intervention in private and public affairs, trade will flourish while justice is bound to prevail. The market's 'invisible hand' knows no distinction of privilege or class. The criterion for making the grade is effort and enterprise. Whoever will bring to the market the cheapest and best and remains sensitive to changing demand is set to succeed. Producers' benefit – be it individuals, associations or agglomerates – will equally promote the interest of the consumer. Goods will be cheap, varied and plentiful and will always, in the long term, reflect demand. As soon as glut threatens, there will be a balancing market response. Fashions will alter prices, adjustments be made, and production will turn in different directions and the equilibrium will soon be restored. Producers' self-interest dictates adaptation. Diversification or innovation will constantly stimulate new waves of demand which rising incomes will satisfy. However, whoever disregards or abuses the nexus of market conditions – be it through idleness, disregard of the market dictate or defective quality of work, invites the sanction of failure. The remedy nevertheless lies in their own hands. Rational conduct allows access to the goods things in life to each and to all. As Seldon puts it: 'The market sublimates the energies of the people as they are good, bad or indifferent: all other systems coerce, cajole or distort them, with disastrous results' (Seldon, 1990: 106). Bentham's utility principle to the effect that rationality dictates the preferment of pleasure as against pain, lays down the social context.

The socialist assertion that people endowed with political office will selflessly use it for the common good is mere presupposition and disproved by empirical evidence. Even when not motivated by cupidity or the seduction of power, how can ordinary mortals conceivably foresee future exigencies that might subvert their plans, accurately pre-guess the multitude of diverse demands, regulate production to exactly the point where in quality, quantity and diversity they precisely reflect demand. How can they ensure that consignments of goods or services will arrive at the right place at the right time, that there will be no hold up in transport, that the public's changed tastes are reflected in changes at the producing end, that accounting will honestly and promptly be made, and that resources will be directed to the sources where returns become optimized. The task is gargantuan and so far beyond human capacity that experiments at wholesale planning have immutably been destined to fail.

While an individual entrepreneur or even a large company is but a cog in the wheel, the state apparatus handling the plan is all-encompassing and omnipotent. There is no scope for spontaneous reaction or for initiatives of damage control. Collectivization in the early days of the Soviet Union is estimated to have cost some twenty million lives; the Chinese collectivizing famine, together with the ravages of the Cultural Revolution had an even greater negative impact; The Cambodian Pol Pot regime's fantasy of turning the clock back on urbanization resulted in a Killing Fields campaign that exterminated close to one-fourth of the national population; and Stalin's successive purges plus the Gulag monstrosities made Soviet society into a dysfunctional prison camp, stifled talent and popular initiative, while wiping out millions in horrendous circumstances (Pipes, 1994; Conquest, 1990). That is how socialist planning on a national scale was implemented and how it utterly and miserably failed in every way. Such excesses, characteristic of dogmatic dictatorships, have mercifully not been visited upon western democracies. Yet, even there, limited parallels cannot be set aside, Britain's notorious 1979 'winter of discontent' being a prime example. Margaret Thatcher's prime ministerial election and her subsequent draconian measures of privatization and deregulation were in large measure attributable to the catalogue of Labour's planning mistakes (Krieger, 1986). Scant wonder that New

Labour has trenchantly distanced itself from all notions of public ownership (Plender, 1998: 33).

Liberalism claims to have the answer: with its motto 'set the people free'. Allow all to use their best talent free of constraint, allow competition to flourish for the enrichment of the community, dismantle the fusty ineffective intrusion that planning entails, and thereby liberate not merely the economy but the entire spectrum of communal life. Free trade rules over protection, *laissez-faire* over interventionism, universalism over nationalism, while collective interests count for less than enterprise. Industrialization rapidly spread throughout the western world, while progress and rationalism seemed destined to continue their forward march without limit. Then came a reaction that few had expected, condemning liberalism into the wilderness for many years. Utilitarian principles had failed to bring about all they had claimed. Recurrent bouts of severe economic depression, huge pockets of poverty and social neglect in the midst of newly made wealth, the 'dark satanic mills' in which millions of workers from infancy up were compelled to labour for inadequate wages, the demoralizing scourge of long-term unemployment, and not least the growing effect of working-class mobilization were swaying established opinion towards policies of compromise – and as it turned out, co-optation into the capitalist system. Bismarck in Germany, Disraeli in England together with many like-minded conservative leaders elsewhere reset their sights in the direction of emancipation and welfare for the working class. No one has equalled the vivid manner of Dangerfield's account of *The Strange Death of Liberal England*. As he illustrates, ideological hubris, the legacy of the ravages of untrammelled free enterprise, the crises of market conditions plus the imminence of 'the workers' rebellion' all interacted to consign liberalism to the back seat for a long period (Dangerfield, 1996). However, during the twentieth century's final quarter, a reaction occurred that is only now showing signs of petering out.

Neo-liberalism – in fact more a new form of self-identification rather than a new philosophy as such – emerged into prominence. The Reagan/Thatcher revolution, based on Milton Friedman's advocacy of monetarism and supply-side economics, swept away mountains of accumulated restrictive legislation, trade union power, instruments of social engineering plus discredited plans. The watchword that 'the government is the problem and not the solution' gained widespread adherence (Krieger, 1986). The dramatic bloodless fall of the Soviet Empire – claimed by many as a direct effect of the policies of good sense – opened up the entire world to the free market with even China demanding entry into the World Trade Organization (WTO). Not until recently have the first cracks begun to appear. The rapid contagion of economic 'Asian "flu"', the destabilizing effect of speculative capital, global protest from environmental and other NGOs disrupting the world's major cities, the growing internal and global gap between rich and poor, together with a return of structural unemployment even in affluent western societies have lent socialism some renewed credibility (Ansell, 1998; Cowling and Sugden, 1994). In the following section, a brief appraisal will be offered of the differing modes of left-wing analysis.

## 2. Socialism

The left-wing option has four major variants. Two, namely anarchism and syndicalism, are of relatively minor account. The other two – socialism and communism – have for the past hundred years appeared as major players in the political field. Inasmuch as anarchism has shaken off its Marxist roots and is customarily denounced by Marxists as guilty of inachievable utopianism, it is the odd man out. Until the recent phenomenon of neo-socialism, the Marx/Engels dogma had been largely unquestioned. In its original concept, Marxism survives in distant outposts such as China, Vietnam and Cuba, but has sunk to obscurity on the western stage. The resurgence of communist parties in Russia and other ex-Soviet states has recently moved in the direction of an ominous red–black alliance, linking extreme ideological opposites committed to a militant anti-western nationalist stance – one further demonstration of Marxism's inherent capacity to adapt its guise to changing conditions. Western intellectuals, in the past prominently in the forefront, have tended to turn to other forms of ideological concern but with a narrower, more sectional focus. Feminism, racism, sexuality, socio-cultural affairs, and above all postmodernism have taken the space vacated by Marxism. The industrial proletariat, the vanguard on which revolutionary change had consistently been concentrated, has virtually disappeared from the western demographic scenario. De-industrialization, privatization and embourgeoisement have eroded the proletarian base to an extent where short of redirected appeals to middle-class values, left-wing parties seemed destined to spend an eternity in the political wilderness. Hence, pragmatism, self-reliance and modernization feature prominently in manifestoes of the New Left.

Though closely alike in their basic philosophy, the four variants have since their inception been prone to embittered fratricidal dissension. At times, most evidently during the final days of the Weimar Republic, internecine conflict peaked at a point where communists even accused social democrats of being 'social fascists'. Yet even then a firm line was drawn against capitalism as a tolerable alternative, it was unquestioned anathema: the final stage of class oppression, more brutalized and beset by internal contradiction than all previous historic stages, but at the same time destined to lead to future liberation and classlessness. Before that occurs however, it had one final historic mission to fulfil. Capitalism's unique capacity for technological progress, innovation and production was capable of bringing advanced society close to the point of finally conquering the immanent condition of material scarcity. Distribution alone – namely the task of ensuring that the full productive flow will not be inhibited by capitalist market constraints, that resources are optimally utilized, and that the lack of demand that inequality enforces will one day be replaced by policies of social justice and redistribution will become paramount. Capitalism's demise is projected to lead directly into the haven of socialism (or communism as traditional followers aver), where conditions are equalized and freedom from material scarcity does away with the competitive urge for accumulation. In an environment of accord and cooperation adequate standards will be universally assured. In societies close to abundance, allocating scare resources will be redundant. Laws of value will have moved from material considerations to criteria of social justice and self-realization (Marx, 1972).

Today, with the denunciatory terminology of the Stalinist rhetoric of 'traitor' and 'mad dogs' notably muted, the ideological gap between the two leading contenders is more clearly defined. Neo-socialism, a distinctly affluent societal preference well accommodated to the market economy, finds itself comfortably at home in the benefits and social habits that capitalism provides. Communism, by contrast, seems unable to free itself from past authoritarianism appearing to be stuck in a time warp. Even when shifting in the direction of market exigencies, countries such as China, North Korea and Cuba give few signs of political liberalization. Confrontation with 'decadent self-seeking democracy' comes equally easy to Russia's communists, now openly deploring the passing of 'the good old days'. Western socialism, in contrast, has edged closer and closer towards the centre until it now occupies a position where, abjuring its Marxist past, it is claimed essentially to resemble the last century's liberal stance (Marr, 1998). Were it ever to resurface, it seems increasingly likely that a radical left-wing resurgence would lie at the point of the 'weakest link'. Namely, that point of the developing world's capitalist chain where enfeebled defences can resist neither internal pressure nor external competitive force.

Anarchism and syndicalism, which in the inter-war years were of real account in some western societies, have virtually faded from the contemporary scene. The former has lost much of its credibility having been co-opted by libertarians of an extreme right-wing inclination. While syndicalism, essentially founded on the concept of the industrial proletariat's spontaneous fraternal cohesion, has been deprived of its natural constituency. Post-industrialism has for ever dissolved the unionized, solidaristic militant armies of the working class.

Anarchism's philosophy rests on three fundamental assumptions:

- State institutions are by the very virtue of their assigned tasks inevitable sources of social evil. Both the nation state as well as the institutions of central control need to be abolished for freedom to reign.
- Freed from repressive political machinery, people will spontaneously regain their natural capacity for amicable cooperation. Within authentically democratic loosely aligned small communities, conditions of peaceful coexistence and free exchange will make coercive apparatuses a thing of the past.
- Unless all organs of state power are permanently removed, the threat of tyranny becoming reimposed by workers in power acting as turncoats will always prevail. Even equality cannot be imposed. It needs to be nurtured by free social intercourse where the evils of the past will have faded away (Joll, 1964; McLellan, 1979).

Marx's challenge as to why and how there could have come about an evil state in the first place if people were fundamentally comradely and good, remains valid today. In the interim, the tenuous life-span of actual cooperative and communal experiments, casts deep doubts on the persuasiveness of the anarchist cause.

Syndicalism rests its case on the natural fraternal affinity of producers, to which capitalism with its impulse towards concentration serves as the ideal finishing school. United in their common destiny of wage oppression and exploitation, the grim reality of factory life generates a wave of 'consciousness of itself' that spurs solidaristic action towards positive change. This turns the previously inert mass of the working class into a force that capitalism cannot resist. As Rosa Luxemburg persuasively argued, when it comes to the confrontation of the general strike or militant protest, capitalists whose lifeblood of profits is seeping away are faced with either humiliating surrender or the option of overt repression. Once the military joins to make common cause, even that option proves futile. Workers' committees will form to administer decentralized factory production, while democratically established local municipalities will federate within a political structure of grass-roots self-government (Geras, 1996; Castoriadis, 1998).

During the inter-war years, syndicalism flourished in several parts of the West. The German Spartakist movement, Italian followers of Gramsci's analysis, and especially armed militias during the Spanish Civil War, made committed efforts to translate syndicalist theory into reality. For good or ill, their efforts proved short-lived. Internal disunities, disregard of the complexities of large-scale organization, and especially working-class susceptibility to the Fascist and Nazi seduction, virtually wiped out the cause. Curiously there are distinct syndicalist traces in some literature of the Third Way movement, where they advocate workers' direct participation or workers' cooperatives. The charge of 'collective capitalism' where insiders are empowered to conspire against the public interest, must serve as a warning sign of what, not infrequently, occurred in the past (Roemer, 1991).

Theoretically, socialism and communism are ideologically directly aligned. Marxist analysis considers socialism to be the necessary transitory step towards communism, when contradictions of scarcity and class conflict have at last ceased to prevail. For possibly as long as the passing of the first generation, old habits will most likely persist. The deep ravages of capitalism, notably the survival of the cash nexus paradigm, will not disappear overnight. The socialist praxis of gradualism and limited differential reward based on principles of 'to each according to contribution' will be allowed to operate while it lasts. Come communism, inequalities will be removed once and for all. The principle of 'from each according to ability, and to each according to need' ensures full equality where all will freely develop their talents to their own best capacities for the benefit of the community. And with repressive apparatuses now obsolete, even the state will perceptively 'wither away' (Sassoon, 1996).

Even in his own day, in the wake of the 1848 national uprisings and later in the heady days of the Paris Commune, Karl Marx had boldly pronounced that capitalism was in its last throes. Since then, the imminent 'final crisis' has been a recurrent theme. The crisis-ridden days of the turn of the century, the battle horrors of the 1914–18 World War, and the transcendental triumph of the 1917 Revolution. Later the inter-war miseries of the long-lasting World Depression, then in the Nazi era, capitalism's alleged 'true ugly face', and finally the 'assured mutual nuclear destruction' confrontation of the Cold War, were all taken as evidence of the system's final days. Instead, the Bolshevik state has collapsed, while capitalism, alive and well, has emphatically prospered in the course of the past decade. Its triumph, however, has done little to stifle optimistic prognostication from the opposition. Upbeat texts such as *Beyond Capitalism* (Cowling and Sugden, 1994), *The Future of Socialism* (Tabb, 1990), *Socialism after Communism* (Pierson, 1995) or *Alternatives to Capitalism* (Elster and Moene, 1989) address themselves to audiences well beyond the converted. While capitalism is depicted as static and stale, the left-wing's modified agenda prompts vision of a better future.

Socialism and communism are, if anything, even further apart today than before. Socialism has, at all times, favoured gradualism and moderation. However, according to Sassoon, the post-1945 reformism of the new Labour government was based not on their own distinctive goals and agendas, but rather adopted what he calls 'social capitalism' – a mixture of improvisation, borrowings from bourgeois refomers (for example, Keynes and Beveridge in the United Kingdom, Myrdal in Sweden), and the aspirations of their own members. There followed an expansion of welfarism and a new concept of social citizenship, with Keynesian full employment policies through state coordination of the economy including nationalization, as central objectives (Sassoon, 1996). Thus confident that capitalism, for the sake of self-preservation alone, needs to award the working class through enfranchisement and emancipation determinate power, the armed struggle became unnecessary throughout the West. Constituting a substantial majority, the ballot box will deliver political power to the working class. The precious quality of pluralism will thus be preserved, while measures such as the common ownership of the means of production, radical redistribution, together with comprehensive social reform and rational planning on behalf of the entire community will one day transcend the capitalist interlude with socialism forever firmly entrenched.

Communists dismiss the presumption of capitalism willingly signing its own death warrant as fundamentally flawed and naïve. The apparatus of covert control has been refined to an extent where ruling-class command over common resources is more total than ever before. When all else has failed, as the Nazi era is taken to demonstrate, the iron fist soon takes the place of the velvet glove. Liberty is worth fighting for and has never been gained by mere wishful thinking. Communism is bold enough to look facts in the face. As happened in Russia, China, Cuba and Vietnam even victory in the armed struggle will not be the end. Sabotage, denunciation, conspiracy and foreign intrigue will ruthlessly be resorted to in order to deny the working class their well deserved victory. Only constant vigilance, with wrongdoers and miscreants given a dose of their own medicine, will make the triumph secure. With fraternal cooperation taking the place of strife and cupidity, and scarcity thanks to the rational management of common resources out of the way, the pathway to free universalization lies open to all (Kolakowski, 1978).

Socialism has always attracted stronger allegiance in western democracies, much fortified in recent years when the true face of communism in power was revealed (Pipes, 1994; Conquest, 1990). Even then, it has been forced into trimming its sails, in abjuring centralization and demands for common ownership. Market hegemony, making strides even in communist states, is now taken for granted. Neo-socialism is an altogether different animal from the pattern of old, with its appeal clearly directed to the broad band of the new middle class, overwhelmingly content with the status quo, comfortably off if not affluent, individualized and putting the good life well above common cause. Where equality and redistribution stood as first principles, modernization and pragmatism have taken their place. The class prism, once defining all, has yielded to a sense of social fluidity where life chances depend more on acquired skills and qualifications than on destinies ruled by ascription.

How to reconcile the vision of a better society characterized by values of equal fellowship with the realities of a market mechanism where, more often than not, 'the winner takes all' is hugely problematic. Especially when coupled with the question of whether a movement that has come to terms with the latter effects can still rightfully lay claim to the title of 'socialism' are contentious matters. The Third Way launched by New Labour and now gaining adherents elsewhere, claims to be a possible way out of the conundrum. Whether and how this will materialize will be the principal focus of this book. We will expand on some of these issues in the next chapter on social democracy, before examining the prospects of the Third Way.

## References

Ansell, A.E. and K.O. Moene (eds) *Unraveling the Right* (Boulder, CO: Westview Press,1998).

Castoriadis, C., *Political and Social Writings*, ed. by David Ames Curtis (Minnesota: Minnesota University Press, 1998).

Conquest, R., *The Great Terror: a reassessment* (New York, NY: Oxford University Press, 1990).
Cowling, K. and R. Sugden, *Beyond Capitalism: towards a New Economic Order* (New York: St. Martin's Press, 1994).
Dangerfield, G., *The Strange Death of Liberal England* (London: Cox & Wyman, 1935)
Elster, J. and K.O. Moene (eds) *Alternatives to Capitalism* (New York: Cambridge University Press, 1989).
Friedman, D., *The Machinery of Freedom* (New York, NY: Arlington House, 1978).
Friedman, M., *Capitalism and Freedom* (Chicago, IL: University of Chicago Press, 1962).
Fukuyama, F., *The End of History and the Last Man* (London: Macmillan, 1992).
Gamble, A., *An Introduction to Modern Social Political Thought* (London: Macmillan, 1982).
Geras, N., *The Legacy of Rosa Luxemburg* (London: New Left Books, 1976).
Greene, D.G., *The New Right* (Brighton: Wheatsheaf Books, 1987).
Hayek, F.A., *The Constitution of Liberty* (London: Routledge and Kegan Paul, 1960).
Joll, J., *The Anarchists* (London, Penguin Books, 1964).
Kolakowski, L., *Main Currents of Marxism.* Vol. 1. The Founders (Oxford: Clarendon Press, 1978).
Krieger, J., *Reagan, Thatcher and the Politics of Decline* (Oxford: Blackwood, 1986).
McLellan, D., *Marxism after Marx* (London: Macmillan, 1979).
Marr, A., 'Blair's Big Secret: He's a Liberal', *The Observer* (London: 26 July, 1998).
Marx, K., *Capital*, Vol. 3 (London: Lawrence and Wishart, 1972).
Moore, B. Jr., *Social Origins of Dictatorship and Democracy* (Boston, MA: Beacon Press, 1966).
Nettle, P., *Rosa Luxemburg* (Oxford: Oxford University Press, 1969).
Nozick, R., *Anarchy, State and Utopia* (London: Blackwell, 1974).
Pierson, C., *Socialism after Communism: the New Market Socialism* (Pennsylvania, PA: The State University Press, 1995).
Pipes, R., *Communism, the Vanquished Specter* (Cambridge, MA: Scandinavian University Press, 1994).
Plender, J., 'A New Third Way', *Prospect* (London: February 1998), 33–7.
Rand, A., *The Virtue of Selfishness* (New York, NY: Signet, 1964).
Roemer, J.E., 'Market Socialism: a blueprint', *Dissent* (New York: Fall 1991), 562–9.
Rothbard, M., *For a New Liberty: the Libertarian Manifesto* (London: Collier-Macmillan, 1978).
Sassoon, D., *One Hundred Years of Socialism* (London: Fontana, 1996).
Schumpeter, J.A., *Capitalism, Socialism and Democracy* (London: Unwin University Books, 1943).
Seldon, A., *Capitalism* (Oxford: Basil Blackwell, 1990).
Smith, A., *The Wealth of Nations* (London: Dent, 1776).
Tabb, W.K., (ed.) *The Future of Socialism: Perspectives from the Left* (New York: Monthly Review Press, 1990).
Wallerstein, I., *Utopistics* (New York, NY: Free Press, 1998).

# 2
# Social Democracy

## The varied traditions of socialism

The socialist tradition that developed in the latter half of the nineteenth century consisted of three main pathways. First, were the followers of Marx. They accepted his revolutionary prognosis, that capitalism was ultimately incapable of meaningful reform, and so its rejection, through revolutionary means by the active agency of a self-conscious working class, was vital. Secondly, came the democratic socialists who largely retained Marx's analysis of capitalism, of class domination and exploitation, but who nevertheless saw that the system could be democratically reformed from within, so recourse to revolutionary means was unnecessary. Their task on winning power would be to socialize the means of production. Finally, there existed social democracy. As Paterson and Thomas note: 'It was essentially a way of distinguishing between the minority of democrats who were also socialists and the majority of democrats who were not ...' (Paterson and Thomas, 1986: 1). Social democrats rejected the Marxist analysis as deficient in its methodology, conceptualization and predictive qualities, arguing that capitalism was adaptable and could be democratically reformed through the ballot box. Their goal was greater material and social equality through redistributing the surplus generated by capital by means of progressive taxation. The economy consisting of both a private and public sector would remain capitalistic, as the outright social ownership of production was deemed unnecessary. However, the democratic state would exercise control over property relations, including, where necessary, outright public ownership, as the state did not conceal class relations and class rule, but was the means for the realization of a socialist society.

The origins of social democracy can be traced to the internal disputes which accompanied the foundation of Germany's Social Democratic Party in the 1860s. Tension existed between orthodox Marxists who naturally followed the teachings of Marx and his analysis of capitalist society, including his critique of the new party's policy (the Gotha programme of 1875), and those who wanted a more conciliatory and reformist stance towards capitalism. The First International addressed by Marx in 1864 later split in a row with the anarchists. Its successor, launched in Paris mainly by German Marxists in 1889, became known as the Socialist International. Reformers argued that the adoption of a universal franchise would lead to them winning state power, and mobilizing legitimate power, through legislation and administration, would achieve many working-class goals without recourse to revolution. The state could be an agency of liberation and social justice, following Hegel's lead, and not necessarily one of class rule and oppression.

By the turn of the century, the leading proponent of what came to be known as German revisionism or social democracy was Eduard Bernstein, who had been influenced by English Fabian reformism following a period of exile. Revisionism is a confusing term that in reality offers a rejection of Marx's key ideas. Bernstein argued that Marx's predictions grounded within a positivistic 'scientific socialist' methodology, forecasting the ultimate demise of capitalism due to widening class differentiation, conflict and immiseration, were actually false. To the contrary, German society was becoming more prosperous with wealth more widely distributed than ever before. New forms of employment for a vastly expanded middle class now dominated the state bureaucracy, suggesting that Marx's analysis of social structure and power needed revising, as society harmoniously evolved. The transcendence of capitalism, if it were to occur, would come through cumulative and gradual piecemeal reform based on working-class economic and political organization and struggle. The tendency of German capital to forge monopoly concentration and cartelization would, if anything, force its eventual socialization as a consequence of working-class demands. Socialism had become a moral necessity, an ethical imperative built not on dialectical laws, but embedded within a movement which men of good will could follow and eventually realize. Capitalism was malleable and the sum total of reform would express the revolution, despite the lack of a definitive aim (Bernstein, 1898 and 1961).

The First World War was to make a decisive break in the solidarity of the socialist movement, especially internationally, as the alternative values of nationalism and 'defence of the motherland' assumed centre stage. This schism was aggravated by the Bolshevik revolution in 1917, which not only widened the gulf between revolutionaries and reformers within nations, but projected contrasting visions of the future ahead. On the one hand, was the revolutionary model of Lenin and the Comintern (later the Communist International), and on the other, the representatives who followed the Second International committed to peaceful means of social advancement within capitalism. The situation, as it developed during the inter-war years, was characterized by escalating tension between the two groups and their supporters as they confronted the menace of Fascism and Nazism. By refusing to collaborate in a broadly based anti-fascist alliance in Germany in the early 1930s, they inadvertently assisted the accession to power of Hitler in January 1933. The Social Democratic Party (SDP), committed to the democratic process that underpinned the Weimar Republic, were accused of propping up a discredited monopolistic capitalist system that, according to objective Marxist scientific prediction, would soon be doomed to extinction. Such is the force of tragedy, dogma and its unintended consequences. Too late the adoption of the 'popular front' strategy offered a mere postponement before the full brunt of Nazism was unleashed on all of Europe.

Britain, the birthplace of the Industrial Revolution, saw parallel developments at the end of the nineteenth century echoing those of Germany. Socialists of various persuasions, including those deriving their radicalism from Christianity and other ethical sources, were politically active. Liberalism had dominated much of the century, but the deficiencies of the market system were ever more apparent and the need for radical reform imperative. The new emerging social liberalism, associated with Hobhouse, promoted a more positive view of individual freedom. The state, acting in a regulatory role, would balance individual needs with those of the collective, thereby representing (perhaps somewhat idealistically) the common good. These ideas were given credence with the Asquith–Lloyd George reforms of 1908–11, introducing an embryonic welfare state and reform of the Tory-dominated House of Lords. The emergence of an independent Labour Party in 1900 was based on trade union sponsorship, and their support for these reforms extended to an electoral pact with the Liberals. The Fabian Society became an important middle-class intellectual pressure group within Labour. Initially it had not seen any great need to establish an independent party as such, seeking instead to influence liberalism along more progressive lines by emphasizing meritocracy, gradualism, planning, expertise and democratic participation.

The Labour Representation Committee which became the Labour Party in 1906, followed a broadly reformist agenda of furthering working-class interests, but largely eschewed Marxist analysis. The Party was predominately organized within the trade union movement, with the support of various socialist societies and cooperative groups, including the Independent Labour Party of Keir Hardie, founded earlier in 1893. Power ascended from the bottom up (at least theoretically), with the annual conference playing a pivotal role allowing the various affiliated organizations and constituencies a voice in decision-making, including elections to the ruling National Executive Committee. The aim was to maximize working-class political representation in parliament, with the parliamentary wing answerable to the democratic will of the conference. Their political programme was the pursuit of greater opportunity for all with an expanded welfare state operating within the contours of a mixed economy.

Ironically, the adoption of a revised and more radical party constitution in 1918 followed Labour's successful first experience of government (albeit within the wartime coalition), which had given them the confidence to strike out on their own. The commitment to nationalize the means of production, distribution and exchange (clause 4), brought the Party much closer to Marxism than before, although the subsequent reality of Labour in office belied such a policy. As in Germany, theory remained divorced from practice, while Labour in principle could perhaps be better described as a democratic socialist party as it saw the elimination of capitalism as necessary to achieve its goal of 'common ownership'. Post-1918 witnessed that division within the progressive tradition of British political life, with the Liberals marginalized and their electoral base narrowing in subsequent elections thereafter. The Conservative Party were to be the beneficiaries of this split for much of the rest of the century, as Labour and the Liberals effectively neutralized each other's vote in many closely contested constituency elections based on the principle of 'first past the post' (Gould, 1998; Beer, 1998). It is not for nothing that some call for the breach to be healed.

Another variant on this model was to develop in Sweden and in other Scandinavian social democratic movements. Swedish social democracy developed at the same time as liberalism in the late nineteenth century, and both were prepared to cooperate during those crucial stages of early industrialization and franchise reform. This cooperation by left-of-centre progressive forces led eventually to the much envied and renowned consensual political culture. Unlike much of Europe, the conservative right and its allies were sidelined during the twentieth century. In the 1930s, Sweden was considered to have pioneered the 'Third Way', a term coined by the American, Marquis W. Childs in 1936, who observed that the settlement being developed would be neither capitalist nor socialist. This came about following a series of severe and increasingly bitter labour disputes that led to the 'Adalen Valley massacre' of 1931, when five workers were killed by state troops.

Following the electoral victory of the Social Democrats in 1932 (who remained in office though allied at different times with the Agrarians and Liberals till 1976), a public works programme was instituted that was funded by tax increases, which also included unemployment insurance, pension increases and schemes to help young married couples to obtain housing in Per Halbin Hansson's visionary 'People's Home' of 1937. Equally important was the 'Saltsjobaden Accord' between trade unions and the employers' federation in 1938, which saw the tacit acceptance by trade unions of the 'managerial prerogative' and industrial peace in return for promises of welfare state expansion and higher wages. This agreement provided a framework for collective bargaining, with protection for workers from arbitrary dismissal and employers from irresponsible strikes, thus stabilizing the economic environment by institutionalizing industrial conflict. A commitment to full employment and wide 'socialized consumption' through developing welfare institutions, but predicated on an acceptance of the legitimacy of private property, with virtually no large industrial concern under public ownership, became the norm. A new and extended form of social citizenship was born.

This 'historic compromise' and its subsequent refinement into developing the world's most extensive welfare state was based on new forms of corporatist decision-making. It represented an early departure from the tenets of classic socialism that existed elsewhere in Europe in the 1930s and later. In the post-war era Sweden quickly assumed the mantle of social democracy's utopia as it combined large-scale production and full employment with extensive social welfare.

The variety of experiences subsumed under the rubric of socialism and social democracy varied according to national context and the particular stage reached in the development of industrial capitalism. The Depression of the 1930s was to disfigure all with unprecedented levels of unemployment and a systemic crisis without parallel. Unemployment was finally conquered by placing most of the industrial West on a wartime footing, and in the aftermath of war, by adopting the general economic principles associated with Keynes and his ideas of demand management and deficit financing. What is clear is that the inability of the left to unite for long, with the notable exception of Sweden, has been instrumental in procuring the ascendancy of the right. Division spelt defeat, and the calamitous policies of the 1930s were a grim reminder of the high social costs associated with failure.

## 2. The post-war consensus and the triumph of social democracy

The fears that a post-war return to market conditions would herald a return to mass unemployment proved unfounded. The need to build anew was based on the shared belief across Europe that a better world would include extensive support for new citizenship rights. In his influential history, Sassoon argues that socialist parties faced with power improvised successfully, borrowed ideas from bourgeois parties, even at times adopting populism, but they lacked a clear vision of an alternative socialist future and the means by which this could be achieved (Sassoon, 1996). In Britain, Attlee's Labour government reconstituted the welfare state on universalistic principles, largely paid for out of social insurance, a principle they had inherited from the Liberals. A comprehensive National Health Service, free at the point of delivery and available to all was another landmark achievement and this in a country nearly bankrupt and dependent on US Marshall Aid. The need to nationalize some of the leading sectors of industry such as coal, steel and the railways was as much through pragmatism (there was little private capital available for investment) as from ideological conviction. The question of public ownership carried enormous emotional freight for many within the Labour movement, but was not necessarily shared by the leadership, who recognized early on the practical difficulties of extending this commitment further while in government. However, the central idea of planning was never really adopted in a consistent way, as war-time controls were gradually abolished. Paterson and Thomas express it well when they write:

> The social democratic paradigm of commitment to political liberalism, the welfare state, the mixed economy managed on Keynesian principles, and the gradual transformation of society in an egalitarian direction seemed more likely than its rivals to provide the basis for a widely shared consensus (op. cit.: v–vi, 1986).

Throughout Europe conflict, such as it was, became externalized in the Cold War confrontation. The unprecedented economic expansion until the mid-1970s satisfied most critics, including those on the left who were never quite reconciled to America's leading role. The fortunes of the increasingly sclerotic and bureaucratic communist parties were in secular decline, and attempts to revive them along more consumer-friendly lines failed to increase their support. The western Eurocommunist movement, led by the innovative Enrico Berlinguer of a still extensive Italian Communist Party, had committed itself to democratic change through the ballot box along with power sharing – the ill-fated 'historic compromise' with the ruling Christian Democrats collapsed acrimoniously in 1979. They also unceremoniously dumped much of the negative Marxist language of class conflict and proletarian dictatorship, including adherence to the Moscow line. This strategy proved ultimately unavailing, not just in Italy but across Europe, as communist parties became marginalised in electoral contests. The flag of protest, such as it was, was carried by student activists inflamed by the American example of campus opposition to the war in Vietnam and US militarism in general. This also extended into a sense of disgust and Sartrean 'bad faith' with the newer forms of successful managerial capitalism and developed consumerism from which they benefited, but which they felt had been gained at the expense of the 'Third World'. One significant outcome was the emergence of a radical and critical 'new left' which rejected all current political models available, and gave breathing space to newer forms of single issue protest which were developing.

Much of the economic success of the post-war era, at least until the early 1970s, has been attributed to the adoption of Keynesian demand management, by a majority of industrial states. Keynes rejected the Marxist analysis of class contradiction and international rivalry in arguing that capitalism was efficient and protected individual liberty, but the anarchy of an unregulated market could not be a guarantee of full employment nor social justice. An activist state exercising greater control over investment and saving decisions, through stimulating public works programmes, or lowering interest rates, would promote stability, boost demand through deficit spending and increase employment. In Britain, Keynesian ideas during the late 1930s quickly found new adherents including such former Marxists as John Strachey.

In Germany, the Social Democrats, naturally expected to be the victors in the post-war elections, found themselves in an opposition role to the ruling Christian Democrats. They co-opted Keynesian ideas but were averse to economic planning, developing instead the idea of a 'social market'. The state ensures fair conditions for market competition, but offers generous compensation for those negatively affected by market operations, with ample social security provision and housing subsidies. Successive defeats forced on the SDP a revised agenda at the famous conference held in Bad Godesberg in 1959, when Marxist theory was formally jettisoned for social democracy. Rising prosperity and full employment had diminished class conflict, and with it a supportive analysis which by now seemed redundant. The SPD endorsed the free market and rejected public ownership. And in government (in coalition with the moderating influence of the Free Democrats) extended the principle of codetermination between workforce and corporations by making the latter more accountable, with a strong emphasis on job security, including a degree of economic planning. The problem everywhere was that this successful conjunction of events might not last for ever, although most on the left operated on the assumption of a benign capitalism, amenable to state-led reform.

In Britain, a similar debate was held within the Labour Party between 'revisionists' and 'fundamentalists'. The latter subscribed to what Tudor Jones calls the 'socialist myth', a doctrinal and emotional attachment to the idea of public ownership (Jones, 1996). Attempts to revise and demythologize Clause 4, and promote the virtues of a more market-oriented mixed economy, were attempted under the leadership of Hugh Gaitskell. He had been influenced by Tony Crosland's *The Future of Socialism* (1956), which had emulated Bernstein, in advocating a socialism based on values of which social equality was foremost. Essentially, Crosland accepted the changed nature of modern capitalism, based now on a new managerial elite, and of growing shareholder wealth rendering obsolete traditional ownership functions. Powerful trade unions were equally capable of defending their members' interests (albeit of the full-time *male* breadwinner) as indicated by falling poverty and full employment. Public ownership should not be a defining objective of Labour, but simply another means (along with others such as comprehensive education) to further extending social equality. Generating economic growth would provide the state with fiscal benefits for socially desirable objectives, in a general levelling up, to improve the lot of those worst off. The adoption of this differing prescription was however doomed to failure in the acrimonious internecine party struggles of 1958–59, which left an ambiguous legacy for the future direction of policy.

Of course, it was deeply frustrating for Labour that the Party, when in government, implicitly accepted the tenets of social democracy, as advocated by theorists like Crosland and Douglas Jay. Policies promoting growth and stimulating a 'new technological revolution' could be relied upon, if successful, to generate the taxes necessary to pay for desirable social objectives. Throughout the 1960s and 1970s, Labour governments were pragmatic in approach, despite left-wing rhetoric of 'selling out', embarking upon extensive ways of regulating both sides of industry in new but relatively weak corporatist forms of decision-making (Newman, 1981). After the oil shock of 1973, new controls embodying a new Social Contract over prices and wages were introduced and policed by the major producer groups themselves, in a desperate attempt to reign in runaway inflation. The problem was compounded by sluggish growth and rising unemployment, inducing electoral resistance to raising taxation to pay for state indebtedness, and promoting industrial militancy to protect ever eroding living standards, including those dependent on state welfare. Left-wing critics argued that state corporatism was simply a new form of class subordination and co-option, rather than a new form of monopolistic interest group mediation with the agencies of the state (Panitch, 1977).

Whatever explanation is advanced, the reality is that state corporatism failed to work for long, with big business and the unions increasingly frustrated by their inability to freely negotiate with each other. Many parliamentarians felt they had been sidelined by this new administrative forum for decision-making which by-passed their traditional scrutiny. Furthermore, the state's role in facilitating capital accumulation was criticized as ineffective, and government 'overloaded' by irreconcilable demands (Brittan, 1975; King, 1975) and provided ammunition later for Margaret Thatcher's renunciation of what remained of the post-war consensus. This consensus once extended to all of the parties – a preference for a mixed economy with support for welfarism – and within the Conservative Party was embedded in their inclusive 'one nation' tradition. By the latter half of the 1970s, Labour was forced into accepting humiliating IMF-inspired 'reforms', an early adoption of monetarism, including the abandonment of full employment, and a pact with the Liberal Party to sustain them in office.

Across Europe similar trends were evident. The goals of low-inflationary growth, full employment and extensive welfarism were viewed, at least initially, as being only temporarily unattainable and accountable to the one-off external shock of the five-fold oil price increase. Critics argued that the problems were both deeper and more systemic in nature (Offe, 1984; Brittan, 1983). In general, the dismantling of the social democratic heritage went much further in post-Fordist Britain than in the more disciplined labour movements across Europe, where trade union involvement with capital and management had deeper historical roots. However, social democrats did experience reversals. Most graphically in Mitterrand's first term of office in France after 1981, and in the post-Fordist crisis in Sweden in the early 1990s, when employer demands for 'flexibility' reached a crescendo as the powerful regulatory role, exercised by the increasingly autonomous international financial markets, on independent state action, became evident.

## 3. Social democracy in retreat

As noted earlier in Chapter 1, after 1979 there emerged in Britain a more radical form of conservatism invoking *laissez-faire*, deregulation, privatization, reform of trade unionism and the welfare state. A flexible workforce with an emphasis on supply-side reforms and monetarism effectively ended the social democratic interlude. Henceforth, the state was not viewed primarily as an agency of redistribution, or employer of last resort, as the costs paid in rising taxation on individuals and companies were excessive and acted as a disincentive to initiative, self-reliance and innovation. Anti-statist rhetoric paid electoral dividends despite the severity of the economic recession in the early 1980s. Selectivity, and the means testing of a range of benefits became normative, although the overall level of state expenditure continued to rise following in the footsteps of rising unemployment as old industrial practices were 'shaken out'. The individual was to be freed from the mountains of red tape and bureaucratic inefficiency attributed to state regulation and control. Britain's relative economic decline was politically challenged by reinstating the values of a more unfettered free market with appropriate rewards for effort. Public interest theory was in its heyday as post-war shibboleths and 'received wisdom' were disputed. A new right-wing intellectual ascendancy was born on both sides of the Atlantic. This perhaps more than anything freed Labour from its historic commitment to public ownership, as the cost of re-nationalizing so much of what was now in private ownership would have been prohibitive. The weakening power of the trade union movement, graphically epitomized by the failure of the year-long miners' strike in 1985, gave symbolic recognition to trade union disarray as government reform formally brought the unions within the rule of law.

The issue of public ownership and other traditional icons of Labour's ideological baggage were only finally resolved by Tony Blair in 1995, when he announced a pro-market, pro-business outlook for New

Labour, in his defeat of the 'traditionalist' wing of the party against the values of the 'modernizers'. This followed the experience of disastrous electoral losses, most notably in 1983, when Labour lurched sharply to the left on a platform of state economic planning and social ownership, which in reaffirming its socialist purity proved to be an electoral albatross. The internal discord within the Party after the 1979 defeat was severe, with Tony Benn leading populist calls for greater involvement of the constituency parties in matters of candidate and leadership selection. This prompted a breakaway group of parliamentarians to form the Social Democratic Party in 1981, who quickly reaffirmed their support for the mixed economy. Neil Kinnock, Labour's new leader following Michael Foot's electoral defeat, steered the party towards a more centrist position, and in the process expelled the militants, who had used some local constituency organizations as a vehicle for their more esoteric views. His successor continued in a similar vein, with John Smith remodelling the internal party democratic procedures by abolishing the trade union block vote in the selection of party candidates and leadership (in 1993).

The Labour leadership were aware of their declining 'traditional' working-class electoral base of support and partisan loyalty to the party (the manual working class actually dropped from around 60 per cent to 40 per cent of the electorate between 1964 and 1997). 'Class de-alignment' from the late 1970s meant they needed to recruit far more of the rapidly expanding white-collar sectors of British society. However, it took four consecutive electoral defeats by the Conservatives to force on Labour concerted reform, not just of its traditional organization, but also its ideological platform. Today, support for Labour is drawn widely from across all social strata, with tribalism long gone, and perceived leadership skills and economic managerial competence in government counting for everything.

Within Europe, there was a less dramatic downward trajectory in the political fortunes of the left than in Britain. In Spain, Felipe Gonzalez became a notably successful socialist prime minister for 13 years – with such achievements as entry into the EU and NATO and the securing of democratic rule after Franco – until he lost power to the centre-right Popular Party in 1996. In Italy the PSI (the Socialist Party) under Craxi formed the first minority-headed government with the majoritarian Christian Democrats in the mid-1980s. As leader he had earlier 'modernized' the Party's ideology, as Prime Minister after 1983 he made the first cut in the *scala mobile*, the system automatically linking workers' wage increases to inflation, and which proved so ruinously expensive to public finances. However, like many other politicians in Italy, Craxi and the PSI were caught out in the anti-corruption investigations of the early 1990s, revealing the extent of kickbacks for public sector contracts, and a web of bribery for personal gain and party financing, right across the political establishment.

The German SDP were out of office from 1982 until 1998, although admittedly the Christian Democrat–Free Democratic coalition steadily built on the earlier consensual decision-making approach, with welfare provision still remaining amongst the most extensive in Europe. Indeed, the social costs on business were charged with making German labour increasingly uncompetitive in global markets in the late 1990s, although the rising volume of exports and marked improvements in productivity would seem to belie the critics. On being returned to office the SDP is still equivocating on how far it can commit itself to maintaining existing welfare provision set against relatively high unemployment. However, the gravest crisis of advanced social democracy was witnessed in Sweden and it is to this example that we must now turn.

Swedish neutrality during the Second World War had been to the benefit of her economy, extending into the post-war era as others lay prostrate and in need of economic assistance. The policy innovation post-1945 was the adoption of the so-called Rehn–Meidner model. This was based on an expansion of the economy and of full employment with a 'solidaristic wage' policy (based on narrow differentials between various skill levels) across different sectors of the economy, but with an eye kept on the incipient tendency to inflation that occurs with a tight labour market. Better paid workers in fast growing firms were to adopt wage restraint, while those in declining sectors would be allowed to fail as the state would not prop up ailing industries. Workers made redundant, would benefit from an active labour market policy devoted to retraining so as to facilitate their easy access and re-entry into profitable and growing sectors. Higher wages would be boosted by productivity increases and thus price stability would be maintained.

By the 1960s, productivity growth, and economic restructuring did not necessarily translate into further employment, with much of the slack offset by the rapid build-up of state-directed employment, typically in the expanded welfare bureaucracies. Furthermore, a complicated system of societal corporatism, with the power to make decisions delegated down to the entrenched pressure groups – especially the trade unions led by the LO and the employers federation (SAF) – along with a recognized role for public administration, defined the process for many years. Royal or state commissions regularly consult widely before making recommendations to parliament. The result: a rapid expansion until the mid-1970s, plus an extensive and well-funded welfare state, reliant on high levels of personal taxation, and based on similar agreements being negotiated with white-collar professional workers and their employers.

Sweden's large, capital-intensive and highly profitable export industries faced not just the oil crisis in 1973, but hostility from the LO (including wildcat strikes in 1970) concerned at what they felt to be excessive profits. The LO pushed for new labour laws, which established union representation on company boards, and negotiation rights over corporate policy affecting workers. This was further supplemented by the so-called 'wage-earner funds' which were essentially a workers' share-ownership scheme. This would convert about 20 per cent of a company's annual 'excess' profit into a share scheme owned by the workers. In a relatively short time (about 25 years) the workers would be in the driving seat, as they would enjoy *de facto* ownership functions themselves. In the event, a watered-down scheme was adopted but eventually sidelined, as the Social Democrats were to suffer their first electoral defeat in 44 years in 1976. The pact between the unions and Social Democrats became weakened and the business community radicalized. The corporatist bargaining system was challenged and later suspended, despite the fact that 90 per cent of Swedes were members of unions. Furthermore, big business started to relocate overseas (to escape high taxes and labour costs), along with a massive flight of capital into the European Union during the latter half of the 1980s, especially after 1989 when financial and exchange controls were liberalized.

Domestically, the early 1990s were years of economic crisis in Sweden. Inflation was growing, productivity falling and budgetary deficits rising along with unemployment. This was attributed to the 'legacies from developments and policies in the 1980s, ... steep wage inflation and an increasingly overvalued exchange rate, the fall in "blown-up" asset prices and the collapse of the overheated building boom' (Lindbeck, 1997: 67). To cap it all, in 1991, a new right-wing coalition government in winning the election had reduced the Social Democrat's core base of support to 32 per cent only. Business pressures to cut taxes and introduce more flexible work patterns, along with a slimmed down welfare bureaucracy and social spending, were met positively by the new government.

The return of a Social Democrat government in 1994 has not changed the basic commitment to engaging in market reforms and reducing government spending, so many commentators view 1991 as denoting

'... an epitaph to Swedish social democracy' (Wilks, 1996: 93). A version of the 'Third Way' survives today despite the critics (Pontusson, 1987), but under somewhat straitened circumstances. However, as 65 per cent of the electorate receive most of their income from the state either in the form of employment or living off transfer payments, this could herald, as Lindbeck notes, 'a point of no return?' (op. cit.: 89), with the distinctiveness of the Swedish model proving to be no more than a brief historical interlude as it returns to 'normality' within the EU. The high level of female participation in the labour market – 'wage earner feminism' – coupled with excellent child care, are still without peer in Europe. There is still a basic social democratic consensus, as witnessed by the renewed electoral success of the Social Democrats in 1994. Electoral success was reconfirmed again in September 1998, but this time they suffered a sharp fall in their support (to just over 36 per cent), thereby making them dependent on the radical Left Party whose share of the vote doubled to 12 per cent and are committed to defending the welfare state and oppose EMU. But the really hard question, posed so graphically by Swedish capital – so concentrated and mobile – is whether a form of national 'Keynesianism' can survive the momentum of globalization, and whether the lack of any net job creation over the last 25 years is sustainable?

## 4. Social democracy: the challenge of the new

The 1980s, saw the general retreat of social democracy across Europe as it faced new challenges. For Sassoon, the decline of the nation state and of social democracy are interlinked, as the former lost control of its own economic destiny with the emergence of a global capitalist market, rendering it incapable of protecting its inheritance. National policy becomes impotent without Euro-wide supranational structures prepared to regulate this global market (Sassoon, 1996). A further challenge is posed by the new political and cultural environment, in which the traditional 'catch all' party strategy, based on what was essentially a class-based politics, has become redundant. Now, social democratic parties have to succeed with a more sophisticated and complex electorate where women (whose participation in the labour market rises annually), cultural and racial minorities, and a growing professional white-collar class need to be more effectively targeted. And all this at a time when the traditional blue-collar worker represents at most only 25 per cent of the labour force, and is itself becoming more differentiated by income and job security. Achievement is made difficult within more pluralistic cultures, which lay stress on individual choice and civil liberties, environmentalism, more devolved government and civic participation, and widespread consumption as a major leisure activity. This has limited the options of parties once overtly centralized, bureaucratic and oligarchic (as so aptly depicted by Robert Michels and his 'Iron Law of Oligarchy'), and reliant on sustaining a mass working-class membership.

Parties of the left face much internal resistance in adapting to this new environment, as it means abandoning or watering down their traditional social concerns in order to accommodate a changing electorate. A simplistic recourse to nationalism would not work, nor be desirable, and would in any case be outflanked by parties of the right flirting with a politics of xenophobia and exclusion. In addition, the old certainties – solidarities – once associated with relatively fixed class moorings, including class discourse, have been replaced by a world of divided loyalties in the workplace and elsewhere, where questions of education, gender, skill and occupational role establish new identities, commitments and political constituencies. Joel Krieger, bleakly observes:

> Expressed both in the post-Fordist decollectivization of 'male manufacturing' and the fragmentation of labor experiences of women and ethnic minorities, the 'unmaking' of the English working class effectively nullifies social democracy. (Krieger, 1999: 156–7).

New Labour in the 1990s, has been at pains to re-create a new political constituency by moving into the centre, with some advocating a formal link up with the Liberal Democrats thereby uniting the progressive left. By ditching much of the party's contentious socialist content it has attracted a wider middle-class spectrum of support, thereby truly becoming a 'broad church' party, although this strategy admittedly runs the risk of alienating dwindling 'traditional' support. In the USA, Clinton has adopted a similar strategy through triangulation – avoiding 'tax and spend' liberalism, and defining his position against more right-wing Republicanism. Both hope to become natural governing parties in the new millennium.

Though much of the above analysis has clear implications for the future of the social democratic left, the declinist argument can be exaggerated, as it suffers from a form of sociological and psephological determinism in extrapolating trends from only the immediate past. After all, until the late 1970s the political picture was painted bright red, despite the Conservatives consistently polling half their vote from the working class. Although the British Labour Party suffered more than most, electoral support elsewhere has held up much better (Mair,

1997). Furthermore, job insecurity and 'downsizing' impact as equally on the middle class as they once did on the industrial worker – formerly employed in such vast numbers in the now depleted steelyards, coalfields and textile factories across Europe. All of this suggests that the possibilities of new cross-class alliances are evident, centred around the sustainability of the existing welfare state. Parties, and their leaders, have to be responsive and adaptable, as the competitive inter-party struggle intensifies. This will involve new initiatives and a reappraisal of ideology with an ability to construct new coalitions. Kitschelt expresses the dilemma well when he writes:

> If social democratic parties wish to remain 'progressive' in advanced Keynesian welfare states, they cannot confine themselves to the pursuit of equality ... Instead, they must also consider the liberating potential of market transactions that free citizens from collective dependency relations and allow them to develop a measure of personal accountability and control. ... Social democrats must rethink the role of libertarian community that surfaces in citizens' quest for social autonomy from markets and state bureaucracies (Kitschelt, 1994: 292).

Today, social democracy needs to focus more on civil society – that complex pluralism of associations, unions, churches, mutual aid societies – with the universal state defending their particularistic autonomy against the remit of a near hegemonic market ruled by profit and the cash nexus. This includes support for increasing numbers of the excluded and those in the insecure, contingent labour market now comprising one-third of society. Walzer lists three crucial variables: the freedom to be socially mobile through wide educational opportunity; the defence of 'complex equality' based on an avoidance of social tyranny so that no one group can usurp too much; and finally the creation of a cooperative commonwealth through localized, bottom-up, mutual aid fellowship available to all. He writes: 'The state regulates civil society, but it is itself constituted as a democratic state by the civil society that it regulates' (Walzer, 1998: 53).

## 5. Social democracy – future prospects: employment and politics

Much of the debate surrounding social democracy, in the vastly changed circumstances of today, rests on the analysis of sociologists, such as Anthony Giddens in Britain or Pierre Bourdieu in France

(Giddens, 1994 and 1998; Bourdieu, 1990). The former emphasizes community fracture and the decomposition of the traditional class structure, and an increasing global cosmopolitanism associated with post-industrial societies where detraditionalization has become the norm. Allied to this is the narrowing of choices that the nation state pursues within the constraints of globalization, where export-led growth widens trading opportunities and increases the economic interdependence of nations, and 'manufactured risk' based on new forms of knowledge poses unique challenges. In addition, the emergence of a more self-conscious, reflexive and *observed* citizenry – learning new responses, whilst adapting to the uncertainties of employment in an unstable market system, based on a winner-takes-all culture, takes centre stage (Hutton, 1997: 26–36). This altered social framework is theoretically viewed as being both post-industrial and postmodern, making the construction of a winning electoral coalition difficult, as ideological beliefs no longer 'fit' class expectations closely. For Giddens, politics is beyond left and right. Employment however, remains central to the debate as it impacts on all social strata equally.

The new work culture increasingly lacks stable expectations, is constantly undermined by innovation and the speed of informational flows, and demands a constant upgrading of skills. The new team work mentality where responsibility remains opaque has resulted in what Sennett calls a 'corrosion of character' (Sennett, 1998). The gradual feminization of work in the expanding service economy exposes young men in particular to the threat of failure, as their traditional occupations disappear. If left unattended, social marginality becomes a possibility, as the universalistic assumptions once underpinning the welfare consensus have fractured along with community support. There is widespread political concern across Europe with the growth of an underclass: composed of the young, often racial minorities, mostly unskilled and increasingly embittered, accompanied by growing community fragmentation – a complex set of circumstances that national governments find it exceedingly difficult to resolve. This has led to a renewal of the idea of civic society – the exercise of local control through non-hierarchical organizations – with new ways of targeting and funding solutions.

Social democracy needs to reinvent itself within these new sociological contours. Socialism in the past became sidelined by its insistence on public ownership, despite the coherence this gave to its underlying philosophy. For many users of state services their perception and actual experience were negative. Service delivery was bureaucratic and inadequate, and frankly less than the public had a right to expect. This opprobrium extended to the trade unions, which suffered a severe decline in their membership, with a consequential increase in decentralized wage bargaining and its uncertainties. Both found few defenders in the face of the neo-liberal critique. Social democracy has to reaffirm the autonomy of civic society and pluralism against the cash nexus, and advance an agenda for those economically excluded, whilst at the same time, holding on to its erstwhile allies within the middle class. Social inclusion, it hardly needs saying, is not the same as the former engagement with equality.

Social democracy, if it wishes to regain its former pre-eminence, will need to renew its commitment to full employment and job growth. The task will be far from easy, as the means are so indeterminate and contested. However, at the Labour Party conference in September 1999, Gordon Brown announced that the goal of full employment was again 'within reach', providing that investment by employers and pay restraint by employees was exercised, coupled with the government's determination to limit public borrowing to sustain the fight against inflation. Government will engineer macro-economic stability, but not actively create employment. That task is to be fulfilled by the market if conditions are right. Unemployment currently remains relatively low, as compared to much of the EU, in a deregulated, flexible labour market with low minimum entry wages. Free-market reform has become institutionalized but at a cost, noted earlier, of greater insecurity and less stable patterns of employment, where union intervention has been curtailed and where social security safeguards have been significantly pared down. This observation extends even to Labour's adoption of the European Social Charter which co-opted the measures at a minimum level and introduced flexibility into their application. Whether such an approach, owing much to the American example, will be sufficient in the United Kingdom, lacking as it does the capital resources and productivity of its powerful mentor, is an even bet. Even if it succeeds, inequalities of wealth and income, coupled with economic insecurity, show few signs of abating, and it is well to remember that there seems to be little conclusive evidence linking high levels of welfare spending with a negative economic performance amongst the rich nations of the world (Atkinson, 1999). A progressive politics that inadequately addresses this central concern will discourage its core supporters.

The new Schröder-led red–green coalition government in Germany, elected in September 1998 offered 'modernization with social justice', but suffered public displeasure as unemployment remained stubbornly high. Serious tensions emerged between the 'new centre' programme of the Chancellor and his radical Finance Minister (Oscar Lafontaine, who resigned in March 1999), over a more active state-driven policy towards job creation by boosting demand, embracing tax harmonization and demanding greater European Central Bank (ECB) flexibility over monetary policy. This prompted criticism from the German business community, fearful of the spectre of further corporate tax increases, higher wage and social costs, and threatening to relocate elsewhere. Responding to their call for tax reform has compounded Schröder's internal party problems, with hemorrhaging support in *land* and local elections potentially threatening the SDP heartland of North Rhine-Westphalia. Core supporters felt betrayed by his proposal, announced in the Summer of 1999, to cut the budget and reign in social security spending by linking pension increases to inflation, rather than wage rises, as a first step in dealing with the rising demands of an ageing population. Local electoral defeat, through supporters staying at home, has lost him control of the upper house, the Bundesrat, to the Christian Democrats thereby undermining his continuing resolve to embrace a modernizing Third Way agenda. However, the slush fund scandal, embroiling Kohl and other leaders within the CDU, came to his political rescue, as did the fall in value of the euro which has boosted exports (and jobs) so unemployment is falling. Schröder seems prepared to capitulate to trade union demands on early retirement rights, but has cut income and corporation taxes. Unlike Blair, Schröder never had the luxury of reforming his party in his own image prior to his electoral success.

Across the EU, a similar story can be told of high structural unemployment, helping the return to office of left-of-centre governments, but all of them limited by a 'system of institutional governance for EMU that is rooted in neo-liberal values of "sound money" and public finances' (Dyson, 1999: 196). Dyson argues that they will have to work with the grain of the global markets with a more politicized ECB acting as a 'policy entrepreneur' especially in the event of a financial crisis. However, at the time of writing (July 2000) the OECD predicts growth within Euroland at 3.5 per cent leading to a fall below 10 per cent in the unemployment rate, stimulated in part, by adopting more flexible labour standards so that part-time or temporary work accounts for much of recent job creation. At present there is no consensus on which direction EU governments will pursue. Generous pension arrangements in Europe (unlike the United Kingdom), based on a declining proportion of workers (retiring earlier and living longer) may fuel higher taxation (or the politically difficult task of cutting provision), thereby discouraging wealth and job creation (with only a 4 per cent net increase in jobs over the last 25 years). Polling data suggest that people are loath to give up such supports. Indeed evidence affirms the counter-intuitive position that employment protection does not cost jobs as secure workers are more productive. Across the EU over the past twenty years 'rising inequality and rising unemployment are positively correlated', as high-wage economies encourage a more diverse employment structure and those at the bottom are sustained through public bureaucracies and subsidies. Thus an expansionist monetary policy operated by the Federal Reserve Board plus extensive use of the earned income tax credit, are credited with the American success story in reducing unemployment in the 1990s. Europe too could develop a single labour market to encourage those seeking work, or establish transfer payments and employment subsidy schemes – such as operate successfully in the USA. The alternative is to continue in the same (failed) way as before (Elliott, 1999).

However, it is not even enough to reassert the goal of full employment, as this needs supplementing by a qualitative insistence on personalizing employment opportunities. For instance, there seems little point in finding poorly paid employment for mothers of young children as they lose many of the advantages of work – as a source of independent income and workplace community – if not offset by supportive, easily affordable and reliable child-care facilities. Frank Vandenbroucke writes: 'Employment is the core issue for the future of the welfare state, both for fundamental reasons of social cohesion and individual self-esteem and for reasons of economic sustainability' but he qualifies this by arguing '... the core social democratic ambitions ... (are) egalitarian employment policies' (Vandenbroucke, 1998: 4–5). Egalitarian employment pays attention to the following: rewarding jobs based on notions of 'unacceptable inequality' in order to eliminate working age poverty; more widespread job distribution; reconciliation of work and family responsibilities; and finally, support for those unemployable. He wants clearly defined escape routes out of poverty for men and women, based on a reciprocity of responsibilities with more personalized targeting on the problems of the low skilled. Additional help for those entering work from not being penalized by high marginal tax rates (the problem of the poverty trap) is vital. The 'intelligent welfare state' would balance social spending with social investment (for example in education and training), and at the macroeconomic level engage in regional coordination across the EU (op. cit.: 60–62).

Politically, social democracy faces stark choices. Critics are already convinced that its political agenda is irrelevant, and incapable of being sustained, in an era of rapidly developing global capital markets dominated by predatory transnationals and technological diffusion. Governments concede and share responsibilities with external regulatory bodies which limit their freedom of action. Domestic electoral constraints on state intervention, if this necessitates major tax increases, and governing within a more consumerist self-reflexive culture, cripples the agenda still further. One indicator of the future lies in attitudinal surveys of the young in Britain, which points to their greater tolerance of sexual and racial diversity, yet are cautious of state encroachments on their liberty, making any easy definition of their political outlooks hazardous. The young seem beyond the simple divisions of left and right.

In Sweden, 'Keynesianism in one country' suffered a dire fate in the early 1990s, with a severe loss of business confidence. However, since 1994 the Social Democrats have slowly started to rebuild, not just domestically but by influencing employment policy across the EU with new innovative thinking. *The Economist* argues that Sweden's 'third way has turned out to be a cul-de-sac'. With growth at a limited 2 per cent over the last three years, an ageing population and company relocation and capital still fleeing overseas, they suggest that current welfare commitments are insupportable in the long term. Yet despite their opprobrium, their conclusion seems positive: 'Sweden is still a remarkably comfortable, steady, decent, peaceful and egalitarian sort of country' (23 January 1999: 10). Indeed, eighteen months later, Sweden's growth rate had accelerated to 4 per cent.

Germany may offer a future role model, as the internal struggle within the SPD becomes resolved and the claims of 'stakeholding' are more fairly reappraised. It still involves more taxation, and correspondingly higher levels of social welfare support, more regulation of industry, co-determination of decision-making and long-termism than anything currently available in Britain (Hutton, 1999). Whether the social market can withstand the challenge of banking mergers and hostile foreign take-overs, indicative of a more adversarial and shareholder-driven capitalism, is exposing uncertainty and doubt as to its long-term viability. The British government, currently pirouetting on the 'third way' is in need of a core philosophy if it is to escape a mere shifting pragmatism. The current market-led approach, emphasizing a reduction in labour costs through flexibility, with welfare-to-work cutting unemployment especially amongst the young, assisted by judicious boosts to spending on education and health, has sustained the early tests of electoral popularity. Where this will finally come to rest, is still undecided. The choice may lie in a more communitarian-based liberalism, coupled with further political and constitutional modernization, or alternatively but far less likely, embracing and linking up with European-based parties on the left. These parties are prepared to advance new structural forms of Keynesianism – including green issues and a defence of social spending, in what would constitute a revival of the fortunes of social democracy within the 'global-regional' economy of the EU. Central to this agenda is a boost to employment.

The Jospin-led coalition (Socialist–Green–Communist) in France has already introduced the 35-hr working week to encourage job growth. Though deeply opposed by employers as an act of class warfare, it has in fact greatly improved labour flexibility, as ossified contracts were soon renegotiated. Jospin remains adamant that capitalism needs regulation 'according to our values' and favours new Euro-wide infrastructure projects and a more growth-oriented policy, including moves to democratize the European Central Bank itself. This would be difficult as the ECB, like the Bank of England, is overtly monetarist, operating within a remit to target and control inflation. But the really big question concerns improving productivity and business competitiveness in the face of global forces, as indicated by the Lisbon summit of EU leaders in March 2000, when a 'Blairite' agenda spelling out the advantages of the 'new economy' was readily endorsed. The Blair government has already conceded which way the future points, and that lies across the Atlantic and not the English Channel.

## 6. The challenge to social democracy

Tony Blair is committed to modernizing social democracy, but rejects Keynesianism as incapable of dealing with incipient inflation. The ends for New Labour remain the traditional ones, but are realizable through different means and underpinned by strong ethical commitments (Blair, 1998). The approach is all-inclusive, emphasizing 'community' and linking rights to responsibilities, but within a neo-liberal market paradigm. This motivates Will Hutton to deride the Third Way 'as pointing in two directions at the same time', as it lacks a coherent political economy, with no new forms of ownership or corporate governance advanced, while giving inadequate recognition to the need for long-term sustainable investment. Hutton urges the adoption of the 'stakeholder' model (to be explored in Chapter 7) and is critical of public/private finance initiatives. Rather the stultifying British disease of seeking immediate profit based on 'short-term' thinking dominates (Hutton, 1998, 1999). Jospin, the French Premier, has insisted that he will have no truck with the Third Way if it splits the difference between Thatcherite neo-liberalism and social democracy.

A more radical reform agenda for Britain, proposed by Krieger, argues for a re-collectivization of labour to prevent further disaggregation, and a 'real world' social policy approximating to the best in Europe, especially with regard to child care. The political and civic culture needs reconfiguring to accommodate new 'modular communal identities' and the context-dependent claims of ethnicity and race within an evolving national identity, complicated now by devolution (and the emergent claims of nationalism) in Scotland, Wales and potentially Northern Ireland. Labour needs to reconnect to 'interests grounded in lived experiences', not to a middle-down aggregation of voters, and to mobilizing 'a grounded interest based collective coalition' in more decentralized workplaces and beyond. The fragmentation and individuation of industrial, cultural and political life; the challenges posed by post-Fordism; constitutional reform and EMU, all cry out for resolution (op. cit.: 158–73). Implicit in much of Krieger's analysis is concern with the decline of civic society and the possibilities for collective action.

Looking beyond Britain does the future lie in a more Americanized Europe, swallowed into a neo-liberal vortex, which steadily assumes a hegemonic role as the new common sense of society? Will Europe abandon its social democratic heritage on the altar of twenty-first century globalization by adopting a more libertarian outlook – a mix of economic and fiscal conservatism coupled with more socially liberal attitudes expressive of individual freedom and autonomy – but based on a residual 'safety net' welfare state? Alternatively, will it continue with the tried and tested *dirigiste* model embodying a defence of collective organization, social equality, extensive citizenship rights, a universalistic welfare state and notions of a wider public interest, but also updating and redefining its contours? Certainly its values and legacy are stoutly defended in a majority of centre-left parties in Europe, and the secular changes of social and occupational structure underpinning most sociological re-evaluation may not be too negative either (Callaghan and Tunney, 2000).

Can social democracy reinvent itself at a transnational European-wide level, based on sustainable growth, the protection of key areas of welfare plus community spending, with full employment once again becoming the norm, despite the competitive pressures exerted by globalization? The emphatic answer adopted by the Socialist International held in Paris in November 1999 was to reaffirm the political language of solidarity, freedom and equality. Social democrats argued for change, not merely consensus, and a 'critical relationship with capitalism' in which the optimization of profit must not be at the expense of public services, while an 'active modernized state' sustains enterprise through cooperation while maintaining the social market. As one critic remarks: 'Blair looks increasingly like an offshore islander, isolated from the mainstream of European democratic left politics' (Taylor, 1999). With so many deeply suspicious of the American model, will the Third Way challenger find its lodestar in developing a more coherent sense of direction, based on a new electoral compact, thereby gaining wider influence? Already *The Economist* notes the adoption across Europe of what it calls 'liberalization by stealth' with the gradual acceptance of what in effect are many Third Way objectives (12 February 2000: 19). As a 'progressive' third way politics advances along with its erstwhile allies in the Dutch and Nordic countries and the Democratic Party of the USA, can the more mature Socialist International fight off the new challenger, and reinstate the fortunes of the older more critical social democratic project? The jury is still out, but maybe not for long.

## References

Atkinson, A.B., *The Economic Consequences of Rolling Back the Welfare State* (MIT Press: 1999).

Beer, S., 'The Roots of New Labour: Liberalism Rediscovered', *The Economist* (London, 7 Feb. 1998).

Bernstein, E., *Evolutionary Socialism* (New York: Schocken Books, 1961).

Blair, T., *The Third Way, New Politics for the New Century* (London: Fabian Society, 1998).

Bourdieu, P., *In Other Words* (Cambridge: Polity Press, 1990).

Brittan, S., 'The Economic Contradictions of Democracy', *British Journal of Political Science*, No. 5 (April 1975), 129–59.

——, *The Role and Limits of Government* (London: Temple Smith, 1983)

Callaghan, J. and S. Tunney, 'Prospects for Social Democracy: a critical review of the arguments and evidence', *Contemporary Politics*, Vol. 6 No. 1 (March 2000), 55–75.

Crosland, C.A.R., *The Future of Socialism* (London: Cape, 1956).

Dyson, K., 'Benign or Malevolent Leviathan? Social Democratic Governments in a Neo-Liberal Euro Area', *Political Quarterly*, Vol. 70, No. 2 (April–June 1999), 195–209.

*Economist*, 'The Nordic Countries Survey: Happy Family?' (London, 23 January 1999), 3–16.
Elliott, L., 'Learning a Lesson from America', *The Guardian* (4 October 1999), 23.
Giddens, A., *Beyond Left and Right: the Future of Radical Politics* (Cambridge: Polity Press, 1994).
——, *The Third Way: the Renewal of Social Democracy* (Cambridge: Polity Press, 1998).
Gould, P., *The Unfinished Revolution* (London: Little Brown, 1998).
Hutton, W., *The State to Come* (London: Vintage, 1997).
——, *The Stakeholding Society: Writings on Politics and Economics*, ed. D. Goldblatt (Cambridge: Polity Press, 1999).
——, *The Observer* (20 September 1998), 30.
Jones, T., *Remaking the Labour Party: from Gaitskell to Blair* (London: Routledge, 1996).
King, A., 'Overload: Problems of Government in the 1970s', *Political Studies*, No. 23 (June–September, 1975), 290–5.
Kitschelt, H., *The Transformation of European Social Democracy* (Cambridge: Cambridge University Press, 1994).
Krieger, J., *British Politics in the Global Age: Can Social Democracy Survive?* (Cambridge: Polity Press, 1999).
Lindbeck, A., *The Swedish Experiment* (Stockholm: SNS Forlag, 1997).
Mair, P., *Party System Change* (Oxford: Clarendon Press, 1997).
Newman, O., *The Challenge of Corporatism* (Macmillan: London, 1981)
Offe, C., *Contradictions of the Welfare State* (London: Hutchinson, 1984)
Panitch, L., 'The Development of Corporatism in Liberal Democracies', *Comparative Political Studies*, No. 10 (1977), 61–90.
Paterson, W. and A.H. Thomas (eds), *The Future of Social Democracy; Problems and Prospects of Social Democratic Parties in Western Europe* (Oxford: Clarendon Press, 1986).
Pontusson, J., 'Radicalisation and Retreat in Swedish Social Democracy', *New Left Review*, No. 165 (1987)
Sassoon, D., *One Hundred Years of Socialism, the West European Left in the Twentieth Century* (London: Fontana, 1996).
Sennett, R., *The Corrosion of Character: the Personal Consequences of Work in the New Capitalism* (New York: W.W. Norton, 1998).
Taylor, R., 'The Social Democrats Come Roaring Back', *New Statesman* (London, 20 December 1999), 25–7.
Vandenbroucke, F., *Globalisation, Inequality and Social Democracy* (London, Institute for Public Policy Research, 1998).
Walzer, M., 'Pluralism and Social Democracy', *Dissent* (London, Winter 1998), 47–53.
Wilks, S., 'Class Compromise and the International Economy: the Rise and Fall of Swedish Social Democracy', *Capital and Class*, No. 58 (February 1996).

# 3

# The End of Socialism?

*The ex-communist world is in some ways a caricature of the vicious capitalism the old communist propagandists warned the masses about. Money, for many, is the new master.*

'Europe after Communism', *The Economist*, 6 November 1999, p. 26.

## 1. Introduction

The end of socialism, including the age-old distinction between left and right, has been widely proclaimed by scholars and pundits of all political hues (Dahrendorf, 1990; Boggs, 1995; Bobbio, 1997). On the face of it this is somewhat premature, as socialist traces survive not only in nominally communist states (such as China, Cuba, North Korea and Vietnam), but also in other parts of the world including Europe, where in what was once part of the Soviet empire ex-communists of varying hues have made a startling comeback since the heady days of 1989.

Notably, the People's Republic of China survives in a somewhat mutated form since the days of Mao, offering an alternative model of development based on the gradual extension of economic freedom, including entry into the World Trade Organization(WTO) and its discipline, coupled with political centralization. Under the leadership of Deng Xiaoping, 'open door freedoms' – a general relaxation of social life with the introduction of western ideas – were mixed with a more pragmatic commitment to free-market initiatives, highlighted by the dismantling of collective agriculture in the 1980s. The *China Daily* attributes the success of the policy to 'relatively cautious steps in reform, establishment of a legal framework, decentralization moves and rapid development of the rural industry'. The next great challenge is reform of the state sector currently comprising 47 per cent of national economic activity (Weiling, 1999). The Communist Party, however, retains its centralized political control, carefully guiding the pace of economic reform with, for example, special economic zones along the coast providing a magnet for foreign investment and western style development. Yet this creates a revolution of rising expectations which will be profoundly difficult for the party leadership to sustain, and contain, in the decades ahead. With a population of 1.23 billion, nearly one-fifth of the world's total, and a regime deriving its legitimacy from Marxism, it is likely that, despite profound domestic upheaval, what emerges will still be in marked contrast to more conventional western capitalist development. Whether this can be subsumed under the rubric of socialism is contestable, but equally capitalism is hardly monolithic and will evolve in new directions too. Meanwhile, that other bastion of socialist idealism, Cuba, struggles to maintain its distinctive identity despite the recent adoption of a dual economy, where dollar transactions in the expanding tourist industry are welcomed in a desperate effort to sustain its faltering economy against an intransigent USA.

The 'end of socialism' mostly refers to regime failure, that of the state socialist or communist variety that collapsed between 1989–91 in Europe, and with it a particular form of political economy based on central planning and single party direction. Whether the *idea* of socialism and its espousal of collectivist values such as equality, fraternity and human progress have also become redundant in a more individualistic age is highly debatable, although clearly some of the *means* (such as forced industrialization and collectivization) once deployed in the past to achieve this end can be consigned to historical oblivion. Complicating the picture further, the advent of a majority of left-of-centre governments within the EU hardly allays the suspicion of many on the Left, who simply refuse to subscribe to their revamped 'market-friendly' social democratic platforms and continue to yearn for more radical solutions. Interestingly, many social democratic governments are currently reliant on the new post-communist left to sustain them in office: the Greens in Germany; the Left and Green parties in Sweden; while ex-communists are in Jospin's coalition in France, and an ex-communist was recently prime minister of Italy.

At its most simplistic, nothing ever seems finally to depart the stage of politics. Even that most reviled of ideologies, Fascism/Nazism still claims its contemporary adherents despite the historical record of crimes committed in its name against humanity. For socialists, the unenviable parallel lies with Stalin, and his creation of gulags, political purges and the horrors of forced collectivization, ensuring the deaths of millions of innocent people in the inter-war years. The totalitarian model describing Stalin's regime (and other dictatorships of the inter-war years), was gradually to lose its more overtly repressive features after his death in 1953. Its demise was hastened by Khrushchev's denunciation, at the Twentieth Party Congress in 1956, of Stalin's crimes and the 'cult of the personality' which he had fostered. As western Kremlinologists reported a general relaxation of the 'police state'-like characteristics of the regime, so it was understood more as a form of autocracy very much in the mould of previous Tsarist regimes, but one equipped with nuclear weapons. The Cold War reinforced the mostly justifiable stereotypes of Soviet-type regimes, with membership of fellow western communist parties suffering a secular decline in terms of numbers and commitment. Repressive state action against protesters in East Germany (1953), Hungary (1956) and perhaps most vividly of all in Czechoslovakia (1968), created a revolving door membership where finally only the most die-hard of members could offer much comfort to Moscow. As noted earlier (in Chapter 2), western communist parties split between the orthodox and the reformers wishing to pursue a more 'user-friendly' line. But despite their ideological relaxation, decline continued, and was perhaps hastened, as the scale of the political and economic problems experienced within the USSR and other state socialist systems became more widely understood. In fact few socialists in the West, even of the Marxist variety, defended the Soviet system and its satellites, and many felt relief when it finally expired, as it meant that they could no longer be equated with its failures.

There is a large corpus of literature on the nature of past and current socialism. Some commentators deny the socialist designation to totalitarian regimes which violated the principles on which its values were based (Callinicos, 1991). Postmodernists reject socialism's basic positivist teleology of universal reason and modernity, together with the vision of the good society realized immanently through the agency of the mobilized working class – in their analysis typically serving as a cover for vested power (Schwarzmantel, 1998). Post-Stalinist divisions between 'Westernizers' and 'Russophiles', evident particularly within the parties and intelligentsia, were responsible for additional levels of embittered schism (Brown, 1997: 21). While charges of inevitable descent into patrimonial bureaucracy dependent on almighty leaders (Stalin), were later revised to include the *nomenklatura*, as the ultimate monopoly power base, thereby highlighting further contradictory trends (Waller, 1993: 61). Trotsky's indictment, in a similar vein, portrayed the USSR as representing a half-way house neither socialist nor capitalist. Stalin had so disfigured social ownership and planning that it resulted in the formation of a parasitic, bureaucratic party elite controlling and personally benefiting from the economic surplus generated. Subsequently, Trotsky's followers developed his critique into that of 'degenerate state capitalism', thus opening up additional dimensions of adverse critique. Ultimately, and more seriously still, the events of the '89 Velvet revolution can be interpreted to demonstrate a groundswell of public rejection of the very tenets of socialist concern – public ownership and state control – in favour of a restoration of markets, private property and liberal democracy.

It would be misleading, however, to suggest that the events of 1989 produced any unanimity of opinion as to what happened, and whether the reforms so far introduced in the former communist bloc should be unequivocally welcomed. Opinion across the political spectrum is divided, with the left, in particular, now in the process of actively regrouping – either by being absorbed into mainstream social democracy, or for those on the political left of what remains of the communist parties seeking new critical formulations which can either preserve the best of the Marxist heritage, or define new areas of opposition to rampant global capital. In the postcommunist era now unfolding, new opportunities arise for political renewal. As Richard Sakwa notes: 'The collapse of communism removed the traditional fear of the left and opened its way to power in Italy and elsewhere' (Sakwa, 1999: 109). In examining the idea of socialism and its potential demise, discussion will focus largely on the failures of the Soviet and East European model before finally turning to explore recent developments within the Left in western Europe.

## 2. Looking eastwards: the Soviet Union

Gorbachev's task at the time of his becoming General Secretary of the Communist Party of the Soviet Union (CPSU) in 1985 was daunting. His predecessors had bequeathed a visibly failing economy, and one moreover indebted to the West for economic loans, high technology transfers and most humiliating of all, basic foodstuffs. Gorbachev, unlike previous octogenarian general secretaries, was relatively young and well-educated, and had not been marked by any direct experience of fighting in the Great War. He was oriented to the future, and though initially a committed communist was aware of the failings of the system and prepared to institute reforms. He saw his task as 'perfecting socialism' rather than its completion, and argued that rigorous reform through economic restructuring (perestroika), rebuilding an independent civil society by promoting openness and genuine critical debate (glasnost) and democratization, would be enough to restore the fortunes of an ailing system. Until the early 1970s, the economy had grown rapidly and with it also living standards, with surpluses traded with the Eastern European satellites and Third World. However, towards the end of the long Brezhnev era, though stability and continuity had characterized his regime, his inherent caution and aversion to risk-taking meant that structural problems were left unresolved, leaving the system to 'slow decline rather than terminal crisis' (Brown, 1997; 309).

From the mid-1970s, the Soviet Union gradually realized that in the race with the West they were stagnating. Though outproducing western manufacturers in terms of basic raw materials, such as cement and oil, the West meanwhile, had evolved beyond the dictates of the Fordist mass production and mass consumption, by developing new information technologies able to customize consumption. Flexibility had replaced predictability. The Soviet system based on central planning was becoming cruelly exposed. Its production, organized on fulfilling the plan's five-year targets, rather than responding to changing consumer preferences (which remained largely unknown and unresearched), resulted in poorly designed goods limited in both quality and supply. This was aggravated by a dearth of competition between producers, by a lack of incentives to improve or reward effort, with much concealed behind an edifice of bureaucratic complexity (and illusory statistics) that acted to stifle innovation and risk-taking. Without a functioning price mechanism (since prices were determined by fiat from Moscow), luxury imported goods (and some necessities) could be bought through the illicit black market, but at prices reflecting the laws of supply and demand. Consequently, they were destined for the elite, who turned a blind eye to their provenance, and those privileged members of the *nomenklatura* who had access to special hard currency stores.

Productivity levels were woefully inadequate by western standards with massive wastage, duplication and recurring bottlenecks in production forcing cancellations and idleness. The economy in effect was beginning to approximate a Third World pattern of exporting raw materials in exchange for western technology. The only exception lay in the sophisticated and ring-fenced industrial-defence sector which absorbed vast amounts of the state budget (up to a third), in the ruinously expensive arms-race with the West, denying the Soviet people the opportunity to purchase much-needed consumer goods.

### Economic reform and failure

Gorbachev was determined to shake up this stagnant and inefficient system, but faced a paradox he could never fully resolve. In order to restructure the economy he needed the co-operation of the Party bureaucracy, the 'new class' depicted by Djilas, who would lose their privileges if the reforms were successful. The command structure had ossified over the years. A job commanded loyalty to one's superior all the way through the hierarchy, but when challenged the bureaucracy mostly remained obdurate and effectively stifled new initiatives. Gorbachev underestimated the 'human factor', the deeply felt need for security with reward accredited not simply for merit, but also for loyalty. Entry into the CPSU was a hard-won privilege not readily jeopardized, and as Brown notes, in the mid-1980s the membership constituted about 6 per cent of the total population or about 10 per cent of adults (Brown, 1997: 21).

At first Gorbachev envisaged the idea of developing a 'third way' between old-style communism and capitalism and, as Timothy Garton Ash notes, actively encouraged reform communists in Eastern Europe to experiment and revive the spirit of 'socialism with a human face' (Garton Ash, 1999). In the event, the economic reforms were a failure and the third way an illusion. Radical monetarist 'free marketeers' by the late 1980s, saw perestroika as being 'too little, too late' in their demands for budgetary cuts, privatization and the elimination of subsidies, while the conservative opposition and vested interests within the KGB, the military-industrial complex and economic ministries, criticized his partial dismantling of the economy, so that by 1988 it lay prostrate. The vertical chain of command had been fractured but no new horizontal exchange mechanisms had appeared among producers, distributors and the consumer to replace the old. It was neither a proper market nor a command economy, while mounting state deficits fuelled inflation. A few examples will illustrate the problems.

At first, Gorbachev believed the system was failing, not because it was unworkable as such, but because many people were not pulling their weight. An early objective was *uskorenie*, the qualitative acceleration of growth, now viewed as the responsibility of each worker. In 1985, he tackled alcohol abuse, a particular problem within the work situation, by closing many distilleries (a state monopoly), but this lost the state much-needed revenue (indeed more than was raised from income tax) and was deeply unpopular. New quality controls on production also proved ineffective. These traditional top-down approaches seemed inappropriate in the new glasnost atmosphere and were soon abandoned. Later a new attempt to breathe life into the economy with moves to liberalize controls on factory managers, decentralize decision-making, adopt new forms of self-financing, reduce compulsory output targets, and let managers seek their own outlets and markets, in order to cut costs and introduce quasi-market situations were effected. The bureaucrats had other ideas, sabotaging this endeavour by ensuring that state orders dominated the output of enterprises, rather than the enterprises seeking new consumer markets with new products. Some enterprises and cooperatives chose to produce scarcer and more profitable goods, inadvertently causing shortages in such basics as soap and salt. To cap it all, for those that failed, the state would still continue to provide subsidies (otherwise unemployment would rise), thereby discouraging those incipient entrepreneurs who attempted something new.

New laws granted rights to form small industrial and service co-operatives, including the leasing of farmland on a 50-year basis. However, the state and collective farm managers resented this development, and complied with the letter rather than the spirit of the law by offering only the poorest parcels of land for private leasing. Reform meant tension and uncertainty, exposed the inexperienced and non-entrepreneurial, and led to mounting opposition from the apparatchiks to what they suspiciously viewed as introducing the private profit motive. In fact, the economic situation worsened as inflation became a problem fuelled by the growth of money incomes, as the new laws could not operate properly without a general price liberalization and de-monopolization. Whether this constituted Gorbachev's vision of a 'third way' – a mixed economy based on European standards of market regulation, but socialist in ownership terms – proved illusory. He would not countenance the market as the sole economic regulator, as the state and party were still needed for 'guidance' in matters of economic development, although there was some evidence of a successfully emerging private sector led by the co-operatives (White, 1993: 117).

The adoption of half-way measures was premised on a refusal to accept land privatization, or indeed the revival of private property. Unfortunately, the unsatisfied desire for consumption engendered new types of criminal activity, prompted in part, by the state refusing to sanction what would have been considered 'normal' elsewhere – creating associations or making profits. Added to the already endemic corruption necessary to make life palatable, this simply fuelled an explosive growth in criminal cartels and violence (Lloyd, 1998).The growing economic chaos by the late 1980s saw food shortages, a falling gross domestic product, rising trade deficits, a declining rouble and a deteriorating environment (Ellmann and Kontorovich, 1992). In late 1989, following a serious coal-miners strike in the summer, Gorbachev admitted the need for more radical measures. The adoption of the '500 days programme' would have ended state socialism, but he soon rescinded his support and 'turned to the right', away from reformers like Shatalin and Yavlinsky. His careful balancing act between reformers and the old guard would soon be resolved in favour of the former again, but the dénouement would no longer be under his control, as Yeltsin would command centre stage.

## Political reform

Political reform was preceded by the advent of glasnost, which both domestically and internationally, culturally transformed the prevailing perception of the USSR. Values long taken for granted within western societies were given a real substantive meaning – freedom of speech, of the press, of religious observance, and of assembly – and so strengthened the emergence of an independent civil society outside the remit of the party-state. The changes came fast and furious. Bukharin, an old Bolshevik who had been publicly humiliated at his show trial in the 1930s, prior to his execution by Stalin, was rehabilitated. Sakharov, the leading nuclear physicist and dissident, returned from internal exile to his home in Moscow. *Dr. Zhivago* was published at last; the Katyn Forest massacres were acknowledged. Critics argued that this exposed and talked up the problems too much, while others simply luxuriated in their new-found freedom to read and criticize. This later extended into the unprecedented experience of watching live, the unedited televised proceedings of the newly created Congress of Peoples' Deputies.

Internationally, the emergent Polish opposition movement *Solidarity*, had gestated from a trade union into a fully fledged nationalist movement opposed to communist rule. Following limited but contested elections in 1989, the first power-sharing executive with the ruling communists had been formed. Gorbachev, both here and elsewhere, accepted the will of the people and their desire for change which might (the situation was still indeterminate in the Summer of 1989) involve independence from Soviet control. Brown argues that Gorbachev from being a reformer evolved into a 'systemic transformer' which ultimately led to the dismantling of 'the pillars of communism' (Brown, 1997: 309). Nothing demonstrated his resolve more in pushing forward the reform agenda (not in terms of some broad ideological programme but pragmatically), than his decision in 1988 to create the Congress of Peoples' Deputies, a proper legislative body with real powers based on contested elections. Indeed, Brown argues, that by the time of its first meeting in June 1989, the communist system was as good as finished, well before Yeltsin formally abolished the Party in Russia following the failure of the putsch in August 1991. Brown lists the following criteria to support his contention: the leading role of the Party in the Soviet Union was ended; opposition parties were rapidly developing and were free to do so; democratic centralism within the CPSU was giving way to open discussion; limited but legal service sector cooperatives were active elements in the emergence of a new mixed economy; the abandonment of Marxism-Leninism by Gorbachev and his growing acceptance of socialism along social democratic principles; and finally the acceptance of the East European communist states' right to develop on their own, without Soviet military intervention (the Sinatra doctrine), plus the acceptance of the international order.

Once the decision had been made to accept the principle of contested elections, the Soviet Union began to unravel. The hegemony of the CPSU was broken, as former dissidents who had won seats in the new Congress openly offered alternatives and criticized the ruling executive. Gorbachev had believed that elections would shake up a moribund party. In reality, it exposed the divisions between the differing cliques, none of whom seemed able to influence in a consistent way the actions of the leadership. Recognizing the declining legitimacy of the Party, he reconfirmed his own position by transferring his power base from that of the Party to becoming President of the USSR. However, Gorbachev unwisely did not seek the validation of the whole people through holding a presidential election. The advent of further elections at local, regional, and republican level in the Spring of 1990, brought further outsiders into the various local assemblies. By the Summer of 1990, with fully fledged opposition nationalist movements active in all of the 15 republics, the possibility that the USSR would disintegrate became apparent. This was confirmed when Yeltsin, the leading critic of Gorbachev, was elected President of the most populous and wealthiest republic of them all, the Russian Federation a year later. Gorbachev's negotiations conceding a new liberal union treaty which would offer real independence to the republics from Moscow control, prompted the coup in August 1991. Led by hard-liners from within his own government, they were desperate to forestall what they correctly discerned as the imminent unravelling of the USSR. Their failure aptly symbolized how far reform had already penetrated a civil society slowly emerging from its embryo. Possessing neither legitimacy nor legality, the leaders of the putsch were quickly apprehended, thanks in part to their own folly and the support of key military units loyal to Yeltsin.

**Post-communism: reform and nation building.**

The failure of the August coup ended communist party rule, and so limited opposition initially to Yeltsin's reform proposals in the Duma of the Russian Federation. He moved quickly in the following year, with the advice of the Harvard economist Jeffrey Sachs, to promote a 'shock therapy' to kick-start the creation of a market economy with a package of measures involving price liberalization, government spending controls (including defence and subsidy cuts), and the privatization of half of the small and medium-sized enterprises, in addition to the unprofitable state and collective farms (Jeffries, 1993: 90–1). The results were immediate with permanent price rises in the cost of basic goods, accompanied by a precipitous decline in industrial production; prices were rising three times as fast as the agricultural sector. Living standards for 80 per cent of Russians fell dramatically by the end of 1992, with little done to preserve what was best in the old system, such as a commitment to welfare and jobs (Daniels, 1993). Above all, the leadership – the 'Gaidar gang' schooled in Chicago-style monetarism – felt it necessary to reject caution, having witnessed Gorbachev's earlier fumbling attempts, but were equally unable to stabilize the economy. Many firms now operating in the uncharted waters of profit and loss accounting, reduced their output due to rising prices and a desperate shortage of cash. The rouble was made convertible and given some limited support by the IMF and World Bank as trade barriers came down to encourage foreign imports, and it was hoped, foreign investment. Neither in the event was immediately forthcoming.

One casualty of the transition was the belief in the efficacy of the free market. The old elite still remained powerful within the Duma, while the continuing deterioration of the economy with runaway inflation and a bungled privatization of state assets, further undermined the liberal cause. Privatization had secured some initial popularity but had failed to create the hoped-for 'popular capitalism'. The early rapid privatization of a quarter of enterprises (mostly shops and workshops), utilizing some of the capital from illegal activities, was succeeded by more ambitious plans in 1993. The government issued vouchers to the public exchangeable for shares, but many citizens remained confused and simply exchanged them for petty services or alcohol. Often, the workforce and their managers took a majority stake in their enterprises realizing that this was a way to sustain jobs, keep their independence, and maintain continuity with the past. This avoided the painful reality of seeking new markets and new sources of capital including foreign outlets, as old contacts could be relied upon as well as the state itself. Much of the old plant associated with the once dominant military-industrial complex survives, when in reality it should have faced bankruptcy, and produces little of value which is tradable. A form of oligarchic crony capitalism has resulted, as the dominant state enterprises were transformed into the private sector more or less intact, aided by the lack of a proper legal and commercial framework (Lloyd, 1998). Now over 80 per cent of output is within the privatized sector, with much of that under the control of the Mafia.

To add to the problems, those who had benefited under communism by operating within the black economy had acquired money, entrepreneurial skills and contacts amongst the ex-party officialdom, typically becoming a new industrial bourgeoisie. Forming 'clans' within the major sectors of the economy – in energy, media, military-industrial, banking and finance – and supporting rival factions and parties operating at the heart of government, they have corrupted the process itself. For example, the failure to free up energy prices has created a situation where oil and gas can be sold at world market levels based on contracts of production at controlled prices, thereby guaranteeing instant profits to the owners without their bothering to reform anything. A form of 'robber capitalism' characterizes the growing anarchy with criminal cartels operating protection rackets and siphoning off a lion's share of the profits. The state is unable to raise needed revenue as the law is openly flouted, not least by some of the regional governors. Because of the excessively tight monetary squeeze adopted since 1994, monetary transactions have given way to bartering between enterprises, supported by the local authorities, who often provide rudimentary welfare to their workforce in lieu of actual wages. Thus in 1998, some 70 per cent of industry's net proceeds were obtained in 'non-monetary form' through bartering and other means. This hugely exacerbated the tax-raising functions of central government which was forced into compliance by accepting more and more non-cash payments (Woodruff, 1999). Tax avoidance has become an art form producing a sort of virtual or fictitious economy, but parallelled by a real one, offering valuable raw materials for export paid for in hard currency and controlled by an elite (Malia, 1999).

Today the situation is becoming worse, lurching from crisis to crisis. An international debt default by the government in the Summer of 1998 plundered the savings of the people yet further, as the rouble crashed once again and foreign investors took flight. Russia in fact is broke, with non-monetary exchanges maintaining a form of subsidy, insulating much of the state and former state sector from the rigours of the market and a true price system. Much of industry still acts to destroy value (Thompson, 1999). Yeltsin's recurrent changes of prime minister, and endemic conflict with the Duma, all indicated a lack of a coherent strategy, and a sense that the country was becoming ungovernable. The need for effective laws, publicly accountable institutions and a rebuilding of 'social capital' and trust, so squandered under communism, is imperative yet is still a distant possibility. Critics in the West now blame the mad rush to privatize without first securing the necessary institutional/legal reforms as the gravest mistake of all (Lloyd, 1999).

There is understandably little support now for market liberalization which has left so many ordinary Russians destitute and passive. Nor is there much faith in foreign experts, who promised nirvana if only reforms were speedily implemented, but neglected to modify their prescriptions to the circumstances in which Russia found itself. Stephen Cohen denounces the attempt to implement western concepts of modernization as being 'almost Orwellian in its detachment from reality', leading instead to the progressive de-modernization of the country (Cohen, 1999). Central to the problem is the sheer length of time that communism lasted, thereby making subsequent reform so difficult. As Nowotny observes: 'Reform now has a pejorative connotation, and Russia is drifting away from the other countries of Europe' (Nowotny, 1999: 26). Stability remains unlikely without an enforceable legal order. The corruption has even infected the West's lending agencies as they belatedly reacted to the depth of the economic crisis. After 1995 they started to pump money into the reform process partly to assist Yeltsin's hold on power, only to see much of it squandered and squirrelled away into foreign off-shore accounts.

The politically powerful role of the president – a role designed by and for Yeltsin himself – means that so much power in the hands of one person constitutes a veritable 'presidential pyramid' and makes his eventual successor a matter of great importance. As Lilia Shevtsova has remarked 'Russia dreads him, but it dreads the alternatives even more' (1999; 271). Since the elections of December 1993 sanctioned a new constitution and gave Yeltsin his presidential mandate, the constitution remains unbalanced, rendering the Duma supine on most key issues involving appointments to the government and legislative responsibility. The bankers, led by the former privatization minister Chubais, funded Yeltsin's successful re-election in 1996, following on from the loans-for-shares scandal in 1995. This had transferred the commanding heights of the state economy – energy, nickel, telecommunications – into the hands of the bankers and their acolytes at give-away prices as the state was short of revenue. If the communists had won in 1996 their investment might have been imperilled. Yeltsin, who appeared to have only a forlorn hope of winning in early 1996, thus gained his majority vote, as his financial backers controlled the mass media. This final stage of privatization cemented the oligarchical rivalry around Yeltsin and other power seekers, as they control so much of real value within Russia.

Seven prime ministers have come and gone under Yeltsin's capricious rule. This took on an added poignancy because the Communist Party of the Russian Federation, led by Zyuganov, was until the December 1999 Duma elections by far the largest parliamentary group and rejected much of Yeltsin's programme. Zyuganov with some justification felt cheated out of the 1996 presidential election as he lacked access to the media. He was further aggrieved that in the 1999 parliamentary election the ultra-nationalist propaganda surrounding the war in Chechnya gave an undue advantage to the recently formed pro-government Unity 'Bear' party supportive of the Prime Minister Vladimir Putin. Since Yeltsin's unexpected resignation on New Year's eve, Putin was being groomed 'as an alternative both to a Communist restoration and the incompetence of the "democrats"' (the group associated with Yeltsin), and his phoenix-like rise owes everything to the bitter war against the Chechens (Kovalev, 2000). In the event, this former ex-KGB officer easily won the presidential election in March 2000, on the single-issue campaign of victory in Chechnya. This was secured without recourse to a second ballot, although Zyuganov's 29 per cent polling was possibly higher than pundits had forecast. The communists remain the largest party, but have lost their dominance and ability to obstruct. The deteriorating situation, obscured by the temporary popularity of a government fighting a war, is not simply one of irresolution resulting from the clash of reformers versus reactionaries in terms of market reform, but the deeper and more serious issue of building reliable state institutions which can actually deliver an agreed policy with professionalism and competence under the rule of law (ibid., Woodruff). The new President quickly acted to curb the autonomous tax-raising powers of the regional and provincial governors, as he desperately needs to centralize taxation, and has warned the oligarchs about their continuing tax avoidance and money laundering abroad.

A further festering sore is the nationalities question, still unresolved within the Russian Federation and home to over one hundred recognized nationalities, with the Chechnya conflict a stark reminder of internal dangers. The loss of the old 'imperial territories' left many Russians stranded in former parts of the empire which are now independent countries. They feel that they are discriminated against and are in effect second-class citizens. Opposition deputies who formed a clear majority until the December 1999 election, the so-called red–brown alliance within the Duma, can easily exploit populist tension arising from disaffected nationals living within what was once a part of the motherland. This, coupled with a loss of international status, humiliating dependency on support from the IMF, a more assertive Nato including new member states now abutting Russia's borders, a collapsing rouble, and anger at those pilfering former state assets and exporting capital abroad, could yet herald a return to a more illiberal form of ultra-nationalist rule, destabilizing further what remains of the transition to capitalism.

*The Economist*'s *The World in 2000*, indicates that Russia's GDP in US dollar terms will be some 205 billion, a figure roughly the size of Turkey's, and far removed from the expansionist USA. The situation remains grim with fears of a form of Caesarism emerging. John Lloyd suggests that unless corruption and criminality are controlled, Russia could become 'a candidate for the world's first significant Mafia capitalist state' (Lloyd, 1998: 35). Whereas Daniels, noting that Yeltsin's reference points were located in 'the semi-constitutional czarism of 1905–1917 and the *laissez-faire* utopianism of Western theory', admits of the possibility, following repeated failure, that Russia might head back one day towards some form of social democratic government (Daniels, 1999: 39). Whatever speculation is advanced, freedom has come at a heavy price. Social solidarity has been fractured, chronic insecurity has become the norm, along with unprecedented levels of destitution, while a few prosper mightily.

## 3. Eastern Europe

The events within the USSR were closely monitored within the Warsaw Pact countries of Eastern Europe, the 'buffer zones' established against the West by Stalin after 1945. The realization, unlike with Brezhnev earlier, that Gorbachev meant what he said, and would not intervene in their own attempts at reform, proved conclusive. The initial experience of communism across Eastern Europe had been very mixed. For countries like Czechoslovakia, the establishment of communism enjoyed some electoral legitimacy immediately after 1945, as the Red Army had liberated the country from Nazism. In Poland, it was neither wanted nor ever popular, and was literally forced on the people from above. The experience of reform also differed. *Solidarity* founded in Gdansk in Poland in 1980, had evolved from a trade union movement into a multifaceted nationalist struggle by the late 1980s, whereas in Hungary the impetus for change came from above, from within the more progressive elements of the existing communist leadership under leaders like Pozsgay. However, in the 'round-table discussions' held in Hungary between the communists and the new political forces, pressure for a power-sharing model (as initially adopted in Poland), was rejected for a truly 'competition-based system' with full media privatization following free elections held in 1990 (Orban, 1999). One general observation is that the more peaceful the transition, the more stable has been the form of democratic governance and 'success' in adapting to a market system. Equally intriguing has been the variation in subsequent analysis. Was it to be understood as a classic liberal revolution in 1989, or a 'catching-up revolution', perhaps a restoration, or what Garton Ash has termed a 'refolution' – a mixture of reform and revolution, but without the benefit of any new ideas? (Ash, op. cit., 1999). *The Economist* noted wryly on the tenth anniversary of the fall of the Berlin Wall that 'it will be sad, if the slogan of the 1989 revolution amounts to no more than "Dialectical materialism is dead. Long live materialism"' (6 November 1999: 17). Though there is no unanimity of explanation a few general features can be isolated.

The heritage bequeathed by communism varied. Narrow income differentials, but widespread, though often poor quality health and welfare benefits, produced at least a degree of solidarity. Over time, following Brandt's *ostpolitik* and the 1975 Helsinki agreements, a better educated population were only too keenly aware through television and growing contacts with westerners, of how the West was rapidly moving ahead, sustaining a quality of life they could only dream of. As Timothy Garton Ash noted, they had 'lost the battle of ideas' and in technologically falling behind suffered declining living standards, and more onerously, a civic society lacking independent pluralistic associations. They lived what a leading Czech dissident of *Charter 77*, Jan

Orban, described as '*absurdistan*' – leading a dual existence within a public realm, demanding conformity under strictly controlled censorship, but whose official utterances were believed by no one, and yet where one transgression in one's private/social life could prove fatal if reported (Prins, 1990). The alternative for Vaclav Havel and other dissidents was a commitment to 'living in truth' and a refusal to be co-opted. In Eastern Germany, that most repressive of states, control was reinforced by the secret police with the Stasi 'employing' one in sixteen of the population as informers. Usually the state, as the sole employer, was enough to enforce compliance, and the manipulation of privileges for select groups of workers outside the Party would also ensure continuity. Few dared entertain the role of dissident, as in Kundera's *The Unbearable Lightness of Being*. Thus opposition demands for the recognition of a truly independent civil society were based on new forms of self-organization, outside the remit of the state, in which non-violence and forms of 'anti-politics' were adopted as a means of rejecting official state lies.

Leslie Holmes in *The End of Communist Power*, argues that over time the internal dynamic of communism saw regime power relying less on coercion, and more on legitimacy, and so invoked mass public and bureaucratic support. The goal of achieving the classless society thus assumed great significance. The 1980s however, were a 'contradictory transition', creating an identity crisis for regime legitimacy – as by now it rested on the more prosaic goals of effectiveness and satisfying the material needs of the people – what Holmes terms 'social eudaemonic' legitimacy. In attempting to rival capitalism on its own terms it met its nemesis. It contradicted its own ideology, and with it the support of its functionaries, as unemployment and other social ills grew, but without any of the compensatory benefits of individual freedom being obtainable. Thus in seeking to outperform the West it ended up nowhere, a hybrid of Weberian contradictions. Attempts at re-legitimation through adopting new forms and experiments in market socialism (Hungary); redefining a new official nationalism by invoking a heroic national leadership (Ceauşescu in Romania); relocating reform in terms of past successes such as Gorbachev's links to Lenin's NEP; or even instituting anti-corruption campaigns were all ultimately of little avail (Holmes, 1993).

## Making the transition

Once the communist elite had been effectively challenged – either through negotiation and popular protest, such as Czechoslovakia's

Civic Forum in the 'Velvet revolution', or occasionally through sustained mass violence (as in Romania) – the need to rebuild, and the scale of the task confronting the new leaderships was overwhelming. Power-sharing arrangements now needed to give way to elected government. The political unity, and moral absolutism forged by nationalist opposition to communism, quickly became dissipated in the messy electoral contests to re-establish democratic legitimacy, which also acted as a referendum on securing popular approval. New electoral rules (not always too well formulated) and novel opportunities gave birth to fresh parties, or helped revive parties formed earlier with old historical, religious and national associations. The reformulated ex-communist parties now suitably chastened also entered the new democratic arenas.

Poland's *Solidarity* movement represented a peculiar hybrid of differing groups from across the political spectrum, backed by the Roman Catholic church. In Romania, the situation saw a return to traditional national values with 'progress', such as it was, strictly limited. In general, a bewildering variety of inexperienced politicians and parties confronted electorates who were as divided in their attitudes, beliefs and hopes as the leading political figures themselves. Many of these new states had only a limited earlier historical experience of democratic governance and political pluralism, if indeed at all, and old authoritarian ways of acting are not so quickly discarded. The need to reconstitute the state and its institutional framework of power, and also redefine the electoral rules to guarantee more stability, would soon become closely contested (Henderson and Robinson, 1997).

It was not just in political reform that new initiatives were needed, as the transition to democracy would have to be parallelled by the creation of a market system. In East Germany, the fall of the Berlin Wall, which ended the *de facto* division of the country, was quickly followed by the USSR agreeing to unification. Only then, did the true scale of the economic and social problems that the German government faced become apparent. Much of the industrial system was distorted and misdirected, often as not through the sheer size of the now unwanted defence sector, or though the perverse way in which state subsidies operated. The GDR was, after all, one of the model communist states with the highest standard of living and an 'efficient' industrial structure which on closer inspection proved illusory. The psychological unity forged by Kohl's insistence on establishing a parity between the two currencies of east and west, exposed the east to levels of competition which ensured it could not successfully trade. The resulting closure of factories and accelerating levels of unemployment, despite lower wage levels, led to a residue of bitterness on both sides of the once historic divide. West Germans felt indignant about paying higher taxes to fund the vast fiscal transfers eastwards to rebuild its moribund economy, while easterners resent their supplicant status and implied sense of inferiority.

In other East European states a similar story can be told, although one lacking the munificence set by the example of the German government. The loss of once familiar markets with the collapse of Comecon in 1991 (the Eastern trading bloc), plus the need to pay market rates for once formerly subsidized energy imports from the Soviet Union has caused severe hardship. Bulgaria, for example, lost 80 per cent of its export of manufactures with the collapse of the USSR (Turnock, 1997: 225). The loss of markets, and need to redirect trade with the West, also required a concomitant western response in providing capital and expertise to replace much that was obsolete. Instilling confidence meant the existing legal system needed drastic revision, so as to secure full rights to private property and new contract law, whereby a private market sector could once again freely operate. Unlike Marshall Aid after the Second World War which offered mostly non-repayable grants, in the early 1990s: 'Western aid commitments to Eastern Europe were niggardly' taking the form of trade credits, loans or guarantees from western firms (Bideleux and Jeffries, 1998: 608). Some debt relief did follow, but in general the lack of capital resources and entrepreneurial skills has hindered the transition to the market, made more difficult by the lack of a coherent political and policy consensus underpinning the reforms.

Poland's introduction of 'shock therapy' in January 1990, was facilitated by the large agricultural sector being mostly private prior to the power-sharing agreement of 1989. The liberalization of prices produced the anticipated inflation, of which the main casualties were those on relatively fixed incomes such as pensioners. The exposure to market conditions with the removal of state subsidies to loss-making factories, accelerated unemployment, led to falling wages and a collapsing GDP. Privatization has meant that the majority of Poles now work in the private sector, but the problem of dealing with the huge state-owned heavy industry factories has become acute. Rising poverty and crime, and declining standards of health care are persistent problems. On the positive side, however, the zloty is convertible, consumer goods are widely available, though expensive, and fast economic growth (Poland is now designated as one of Europe's 'tiger' economies) since 1995, is feeding through into improved living standards. Membership of the OECD in July 1996 and the promise of eventual fast-track entry into the European Union, suggest that Poland has turned the corner. The Polish example is nevertheless a rare exception.

Politically within Poland, the complexities of a political system, based on proportional representation, has fragmented electoral choice, producing recurrent turmoil with a change of government every year. Thus, the Olszewski government in 1991 attempted to slow down the pace of reform worried by its negative economic and social consequences. September 1993 saw the electoral victory of former ex-communists in alliance with other left parties, and the new government, promising to reduce the pace of reform, including privatization, as the painful effects of market capitalism took their toll. By then the support of the Catholic church to what remained of *Solidarity* appeared divisive, as many saw it compromising the integrity of the new civic society by compromising newly won individual rights. In December 1995, President Walesa lost the presidential election to an ex-communist but pragmatic modernizer, Kwasniewski, dubbed the 'polished Pole' by no less than *The Economist*. His demise signified 'the symbolic end to the politics of anti-communism' leading to the 'reemergence of normal politics, defined by representation of the left as part of the Polish political spectrum' (Holmes, 1997: 182). Kwasniewski has welcomed Nato and OECD membership and hopes to join the EU soon. In the parliamentary elections of 1997, a *Solidarity*-led coalition (of some forty parties) was once again returned to office but now in political cohabitation with the President. One central problem is the difficult task of trimming the budget, reforming the state industrial sector and agriculture, at a time when unemployment remains in double figures and strike activity is on the increase. Further hard decisions will need to be taken prior to Poland becoming a member of the EU, as it remains relatively poor and non-competitive compared to its rich western neighbours, but fast growth continues.

Hungary has benefited from significant foreign investment as market reforms were already in place prior to the collapse of its centrally planned economy in 1990, but it has taken a decade to restore the levels to those of 1989. The Czech Republic has secured some inward investment, particularly from its neighbour Germany, all aggressively touted for by the monetarist-led government of Vaclav Klaus, leader of the Civic Democratic Party which collapsed in 1997. Despite the surface prosperity of Prague, GDP per head is just above the level of a decade ago. Many industries are near bankrupt and plagued by corruption, while political life has been tainted by xenophobia, despite the moral leadership of President Havel.

Elsewhere the picture is more depressing. Anthony Browne (drawing on the European Bank for Reconstruction and Development's 'Transition Report') notes:

> While the total economy of eastern and central Europe and the former Soviet Union has shrunk by over a quarter over the past decade, all the countries in Western Europe have enjoyed economic growth.

The EBRD blames the lack of progress on the failure of adequate reform and argues that those which took the courageous path, such as Poland, are now reaping the benefits (Browne, 1998). Clearly, there is much that is less than desirable in what has occurred. In Romania, privatization has been discouraged, prompting the liberal economist Ilie Serbanescu to note that 'Romania's leaders don't want privatization – they want the assets for themselves so they can supply their parties with money' (*The Economist*, 27 June 1998: 46). Elsewhere the suspicion remains that the prime beneficiaries have been the corrupted leaders of the former system, making gains through their contacts, education and access to capital resources denied to ordinary citizens. The rapid changes in the fortunes of the political parties across the whole region reflect public disquiet over growing poverty and inequality, now at unprecedented levels in some countries, so that emphasis is placed on the need to secure adequate social security provision despite growing state deficits.

As in Russia, Eastern Central Europe presents a confusing picture now that the homogenizing effects of communism are giving way to cultural and regional diversity, including the revival of an authoritarian populist Right. There are some achievements, but at the cost of much uncertainty, pain and misgiving. The democratization of state and society is proceeding, although not fully consolidated everywhere, with some constitutional ambiguity over who does what exactly, needing further clarification in some nations. The emergence of a civic form of nationhood is taking root, despite the ever-present dangers of nationalism, especially ethno-nationalism filling the ideological void left by the departure of state socialism (Spencer and Wollman, 1997). The current events in Kosovo and the conflict within the Balkans are witness to a scenario which could engulf other newly emerged nations, especially in the former republics of the USSR where living standards have been in catastrophic fall. However, the return to power of ex-communists through the ballot box heralds the return of a 'normal' politics, and their subsequently varying fortune mirrors the economic state of the nations they govern.

The marketization of the economy has so far produced only a few national winners, while internally greatly enriching a small minority at the expense of the rest. Western support, though evident in words and rhetoric, has not yet been matched by extensive investment (with Germany an honourable exception), although the promise one day of accession to the European Union is dangled tantalizingly before all. The social experiments conducted since 1989 offer a sobering lesson to ideological combatants, keen to allocate blame and reward virtue. Capitalism, though rampant in its pristine Anglo-Saxon version, is too narrowly based and chaotic with socially damaging consequences. In Russia, a more gradualist, state-directed and co-operative model, extending perhaps into a form of corporatism, may have been preferable. In Central and Eastern Europe, the cultural inheritance from the past, including an earlier experience of democracy and respect for the law, has often proved critical to the successful modernization of both economy and state. State socialism however, while promising an ideal destroyed idealism and the utopian project, building instead a closed, inward-looking society. As Schopflin once remarked it became a 'power without purpose': corruptive of innovation and responsibility, needlessly cruel and intolerant, and in the end lacking all justification. Its replacement has mostly eroded social solidarity in the name of individual freedom and choice. The social costs of transformation have been excessive, but despite that, few would turn the clock back, grimly holding on to the prospect of better times ahead. Nato and the EU have replaced the Warsaw Pact and Comecon. Europe has once again become a diverse mosaic of peoples, cultures and histories seeking, however imperfectly, to perfect an idea of democracy and civil society.

## 4. The end of socialism?: western developments

The ending of the Cold War, the 'demonstration effect' of the collapse of the Soviet bloc, together with the profound changes wrought to the social and economic structures of the West, heralded by the emergence of new technologies and the global market, have seriously questioned the relevance of socialism both as theory and practice. The range of academic commentary is extensive. Even if socialism is eclipsed as a doctrine, the objectives it fought for still command public support. The labels of 'Left' and 'Right' still focus political perceptions, and act as reference points even when the content has altered. Implicit in much of the Left's discourse is the argument that if unfettered capitalism becomes more destructive, it will need the reforms of socialism (or other progressive elements) to save it from itself, as Roosevelt once duly obliged with his New Deal in the 1930s. Indeed, the point is often reiterated, that capitalism survives in such rude health precisely because its worst excesses have been largely tamed by social reformism, from whatever source. The welfare state's regulatory frameworks provided the necessary means for its continuance, as can equally be said of liberal democracy which 'in substantial part, (is) a product of socialist (social democratic) forces' (Pierson, 1995: 71). But the collapse of communism has reawakened the fears of many that the hard-won gains of the last half century could be jeopardized.

Carl Boggs remains convinced that socialism and other equally statist leftist projects are dead, unable to cope with the objective reality of changed circumstances, especially globalization which renders the ideal of universal class struggle redundant. His condemnation extends to social democracy, no longer viewed as an agency of liberation, and entangled in the distorted logic of economic rationality and capital accumulation. Though capable of piecemeal improvement, providing the imperative of economic growth is sustained, this 'productivist vision of change' is now obsolete. Instead, he welcomes the emergence of 'post-materialist' protest movements, which reject the untenable life-styles associated with mass consumerism, and instead focus on ecological and feminist issues that have universal significance in the struggle against inequality and domination. Boggs remains sceptical as to whether the necessary coordination of aims, leverage and widespread grass-roots support, capable of affecting the current disposition of power beyond the merely localized, are realizable (Boggs, 1995).

Clearly, the social structure which produced a mass working-class electorate has now altered beyond recognition, and with it the aspirations heaped upon the working class as the historical universalizing agency of transformation have become redundant. Other competing claims now command attention in the more diverse and richly textured national cultures of the EU (and USA), fed by mass immigration in the post-war years. Class has become de-centred, with a new 'identity politics' resting on gender, ethnicity, culture, homosexuality and even the consumer asserting a political claim for recognition and a share of the spoils. As Schwarzmantel observes, a situation was created which 'made people's individual acts of consumption more salient than their propensity for collective struggle and group (class) identity' (Schwarzmantel, 1998: 108). In Britain, numerous surveys mark the positive attitudinal shifts to wealth and business creation, as share-owning becomes more widespread, personal aspiration is rewarded, inequality more tolerated and where even the TUC now welcomes employee share-ownership (Smith and Grimston, 1999). The women's movement gave expression to 'the personal is the political', suggesting that all social relations including that of the household could be viewed as both individual and collective in character, and dependent on the exercise of traditional *patriarchal* state power. The nation state itself is conceding elements of its historic sovereignty to supranational and multilateral agencies, and acceding or sharing powers downwards to a more enriched and revitalized civic society based on NGOs and other voluntary agencies. If the nation state can function adequately only in alliance with others, then 'socialism in one country' is rendered inoperative. These changes, when allied to the transformed workplace and de-industrialization of the last few years, mean that the 'taken for granted' assumptions underpinning socialism, and the complicit role of the working class in furthering that objective has ended, unless it can remodel its traditional agenda to win mass support again.

To offset the above, there have been various proposals asserting the viability of 'market socialism', implying social ownership within markets. One influential study, Alec Nove's '*The Economics of Feasible Socialism*' (1983), drawing on the evidence of the failure of central planning in the USSR, offers the model of a dual economy. The state sector representing the interests of the national community, deals with all the macroeconomic questions such as investment, planning, regulation, inflation, and the oversight of natural monopolies; with a parallel private-based market sector offering widespread choice through cooperatives and profit-oriented small firms, which are also collectively represented, within a democratized workplace. This attempt, along with a number of others, of trying to square the circle of allying markets with socialism, has proven difficult. Pierson in his extensive review of the alternatives draws the negative conclusion that 'in trying to bridge the gap between socialism and markets, market socialism ends up embracing the worst, rather than the best, of both worlds (op. cit.: 135). He argues: 'that which makes market socialism seem feasible is its attachment to the market, but that which makes it socialist is the very thing that renders it infeasible' (op. cit.: 211). In a nutshell, socialists unlike neo-liberals, cannot easily remain neutral to the prospect of market failure or indeed market outcomes, which could necessitate state intervention and further regulation. Given the evident difficulties, discussion now concentrates on more prosaic matters, such as extending workplace democracy, or promoting self-managing enterprises, with the idea of stakeholding offering future possibilities (explored in Chapter 5). However, all is predicated on giving a leading role to the political realm and not to the socialization of production.

A final word should perhaps be given to Ralph Miliband, a long-time leading crusader for a socialist alternative to capitalism, and one who passionately argued for a renewal of the faith. He rejected all the limited and fragmented meta-sagas associated with postmodernist analysis; reasserted the need for a qualified 'totalizing' socialist perspective; he took on board elements once scornfully rejected as merely bourgeois, such as the necessary limits to popular power and recognition of individual freedom. Furthermore, Miliband accepted the need for state cooperation with the private sector, which in any case competes with it, but argued for the centrality of public ownership, as the only corrective to private corporate power, especially that exercised by an oligarchic controlled mass media which had so successfully demobilized the Left. Miliband remained confident that the nation state retains relevance as an agency promoting meaningful reform, and hence its electoral capture is vital. However, the means are currently inadequate, as social democratic parties have gone too far down the path of abandoning their cherished beliefs on the altar of modernization (Miliband, 1994).

For many on the Left, the renewed emphasis on the primacy of the political is in marked contrast to earlier Marxist analysis. The focus is on reviving ideas of citizenship, reforming state (and EU-wide) institutions to make them more accessible and 'transparent', devolving power downwards to encourage citizen/community initiatives, while recognizing that the diversity of civil society assumes pride of place. Within the EU, the ruling social democratic governments equivocate on defining the means to dealing with central problems, with their hands tied by the tightly drawn Maastricht criteria. But a recognition that they may soon need to mobilize their collectively pooled resources, to offset the power exercised by the global financial markets, which severely limit independent state activity, is gaining ground. The achievements gained since 1945 in terms of higher living standards and adequate welfare provision appear threatened, as further integration into the competitive global market develops. The high transitional costs in moving to a market system in Eastern Europe and Russia, are a salutary reminder that one day soon these new and potentially low-cost producers may exert further downward pressure on EU living standards as well.

On a positive note, the 'Europeanism' of the Left, has achieved that rare quality – unity, on both the need for further EU integration and devolving power. Yet in accepting capitalism, social democrats are still:

> bereft of plans for social reorganization which would live up to the aspirations of their followers. Their aims are defensive: to protect the achievements of the past, to continue to improve social life under capitalism, to promote an ethos of co-operation and to enhance social and civil rights (Sassoon, 1997: 16).

In moving further to the political centre some traditional support has filtered away, tempted by the more radical platforms of ecological or democratic socialist groupings, or attracted by the focus of single-issue politics.

## 5. Conclusion

With neo-liberalism in partial retreat during the last decade in the West, the irony of the free market experiment being conducted in its name within Russia's borders, and resulting in so much destitution, will not have escaped the attention of the intelligentsia or wider public. Uniform property rights still remain inadequate and discourage lawful entrepreneurship, while denying equal opportunity to many of Russia's citizens. Many of the countries comprising the Commonwealth of Independent States are similarly facing economic ruin, while the Balkans have been devastated by internal feuding and ethnic cleansing once Tito-style communism collapsed. Opinion as to the future direction of policy is as polarized in the West, as within Russia itself. One real lasting benefit that all can agree on is that freedom of association and expression are more firmly entrenched, as civic society re-establishes itself within the vacuum created by a weakened central state. Some 200,000 voluntary organizations have now sprouted 'dealing with anything from disability rights to ice fishing' (De Waal, 2000: 40). Furthermore, as Robert Conquest, one of communism's fiercest critics acknowledges, Russia was bequeathed the durable legacy of a well-educated population. With some qualifications democracy has been re-established. Putin needed to win a popular electoral mandate in order to govern, ably assisted it must be admitted, by the state-run newspapers and television stations, which some fear is a prelude to the exercise of greater central control again one day. However, press criticism of the handling of the *Kursk* submarine disaster against old-style *raison d'état* secrecy, indicates the rapid emergence of a revitalized civil society along with its increasingly westernized press.

In Eastern and Central Europe, the economic results are a little more promising, but again marked by wide variations, though democratic foundations have been more successfully established. In Poland and Hungary, a form of social democracy is firmly secured, albeit one lacking the welfare resources of the West. Elsewhere the continuing strength of the post-communist parties from the mid-1990s, after their initial reversal of fortune, registers a strong protest vote at continuing falling living standards. Class voting has once again been resurrected. In most countries a small but growing property-owning middle class, is emerging which sees its future more closely integrated in Europe and perhaps one day Nato too.

In western Europe, the conjunction of a retreat of socialism in its many manifestations, along with that of neo-liberalism, created the ideological vacuum which the Third Way is trying to fill. The Third Way in recognizing how the world has changed rests on a credible foundation, but in rejecting so much of the earlier socialist paradigm, lacks strong convictions of its own. That socialism has been marginalized is incontestable, despite some early signs of renewal. Necessity has bred new alliances, such as the Spanish Socialist Party linking up with the communists to fight the conservative administration of Aznar, but to no avail, against the more centrist 'third wayism' of the ruling People's Party. Whether the former conditions heralding socialism's birth have totally disappeared in the far wealthier societies of today is debatable. The search for a new Jerusalem continues. But a form of European exceptionalism rivalling that of the USA still appears unlikely.

## References


Bideleux, R. and I. Jeffries, *A History of Eastern Europe: Crisis and Change* (London: Routledge, 1998).

Bobbio, N., *Left and Right: the Significance of a Political Distinction* (Cambridge: Polity Press, 1997).

Boggs, C., *The Socialist Tradition: from Crisis to Decline* (London: Routledge, 1995).

Brown, A., *The Gorbachev Factor* (Oxford: Oxford University Press Paperback, 1997).

Browne, A., 'East Fails to Live up to Early Promise, *Observer* (London: 6 December 1998).

Callinicos, A., *The Revenge of History: Marxism and the East European Revolutions* (Cambridge: Polity Press, 1991).

Cohen, S.F., 'Transition Is a Notion Rooted in U.S. Ego', *New York Times* (27 March 1999).

Dahrendorf, R., *Reflections on the Revolution in Europe* (London: Chatto, 1990).

Daniels, R.V., 'The End of the Yeltsin Era', *Dissent* (New York: Winter 1999), 34–9.

——, *The End of the Communist Revolution* (London, Routledge, 1993).

De Waal, T., 'Russia's Swamp', *Prospect* (London, April 2000), 37–42.

Ellmann, M. and V. Kontorovich, *The Disintegration of the Soviet Economic System* (London: Routledge, 1992).

Garton Ash, T., 'Ten Years After', *New York Review* (NY: 18 November 1999), 16–19.

Henderson, K. and N. Robinson, *Post Communist Politics: an Introduction* (Hemel Hempstead: Prentice Hall, 1997).

Holmes, L., *The End of Communist Power* (Cambridge: Polity Press, 1993).

——, *Post Communism: an Introduction* (Cambridge: Polity Press, 1997).

Jeffries, I., *Socialist Economies and the Transition to the Market: a guide* (London: Routledge, 1993).

Kovalev, S., 'Putin's War', *NY Review* (10 February 2000), 4–8.

Lloyd, J., *Rebirth of a Nation: an Anatomy of Russia* (London: Michael Joseph, 1998).

——, 'The New Class', *Prospect* (London: January 1998), 34–9.

——, 'The Russian Devolution', *New York Times* (NY: 15 August 1999).

Malia, M., 'Communist Legacy Foreclosed Choices', *New York Times* (27 March 1999).

Miliband, R., *Socialism for a Sceptical Age* (Cambridge: Polity Press, 1994).

Nove, A., *The Economics of Feasible Socialism* (London: Allen & Unwin, 1983).

Nowotny, T., 'The Russian Crisis', *Dissent* (New York: Spring 1999), 21–6.

Orban, V., 'When Did Communism End?', *The Independent*, The Thursday Review (London: 5 August 1999), 4.

Pierson, C., *Socialism after Communism: the New Market Socialism* (Pennsylvania: The Pennsylvania State University Press, 1995).

Prins, G. (ed.) *Spring in Winter, the 1989 Revolutions* (Manchester: MUP, 1990).

Sakwa, R., *Postcommunism* (Buckingham: Open University Press, 1999).

Sassoon, D. (ed.) *Looking Left: European Socialism after the Cold War* (London and New York: I.B. Tauris Publishers, 1997).

Schwarzmantel, J., *The Age of Ideology: Political Ideologies from the American Revolution to Post Modern Times* (London: Macmillan, 1998).

Shevtsova, L., 'Yeltsin's Russia: Myths and Reality', Carnegie Endowment for International Peace (Washington, DC, 1999).

Smith, D. and J. Grimston, 'Smashing the Politics of Envy', Focus: *The Sunday Times* (London: 23 May 1999), 16.

Spencer, P. and H. Wollman, 'Nationalism and Democracy in the Transition from Communism in Eastern Europe', *Contemporary Politics*, Vol. 3, No. 2 (London: Carfax, June 1997), 171–88.

Thompson, W., 'The Price of Everything and the Value of Nothing? Unravelling the Workings of Russia's "Virtual Economy"', *Economy and Society*, Vol. 28, No. 2 (London, Routledge, May 1999), 256–80.
Turnock, D., *The East European Economy in Context: Communism and Transition* (London, Routledge, 1997).
Waller, M., *The End of the Communist Power Monopoly* (Manchester: MUP, 1993).
Weiling, L., 'Country Model for Economy Transforming', *The China Daily* (Beijing: 24 July 1999).
White, S., *After Gorbachev* (Cambridge: Cambridge University Press, 1993).
Woodruff, D.M., *Money Unmade: Barter and the Fate of Russian Capitalism* (Cornell: Cornell University Press, 1999).

# Part II
# The Post-Cold War Era

# 4
# The Triumph of the Market Economy

## 1. The New Right

For Britain the decisive turn-around came in 1979 with the election of Margaret Thatcher as Prime Minister. Unceremoniously the 'Iron Lady', as she soon came to be known, disposed of the social consensus that had existed since the end of the Second World War. Keynesianism became public anathema. Wholesale privatization, ranging from giant public utilities to millions of publicly owned homes, was put into motion. The powers of the trade unions were drastically curbed. Her own cabinet was uniformly tailored to present a common front. Public largesse in the dispensing of funds to all manner of organized working-class interests plus 'needy recipients' was drastically stopped. And monetarist policies designed to trim the money supply to levels where inflation no longer threatened stability were proclaimed as the panacea that would make Britain great once again (Kavanagh, 1987; King, 1987).

Ronald Reagan's presidential election – the second formal leg of the 'Reagan/Thatcher revolution' – was to follow in 1980. However, his long-standing governorship in California, the most populous state of the union, had earlier served as a proven test-bed for the New Right reforms that were soon to be adopted nationwide. Inclining to seek a remedy for the 'years of dissipation and neglect' by means of the Chicago school money-supply measures – that is, abjuring government action, cutting taxation, and in all economic matters 'setting the people free' (Schupparra, 1998) – the means then employed by his administration during the years in the White House, were somewhat divergent from Thatcherite policies. Nevertheless, however subtly different the means, the ends were the same. The 'Reagan–Thatcher revolution', spreading from the two dominant Anglo-Saxon nations to virtually all parts of the world, represented an enduring shot in the arm for western capitalism while restoring the hegemony of the market economy to the primacy it has held for the past two decades. It is the strongest empirical affirmation as yet of Joseph Schumpeter's analysis derived during the dark years of the Second World War. For all its apparent weaknesses plus contradiction, Schumpeter held that capitalism possesses the unique in-built capacity to renew itself in advance of crises serious enough to threaten its dominance. It has done so repeatedly since establishing itself with the coming of the Industrial Revolution, and would do so again even in the face of inherent divisiveness, the emergence of working-class collective consciousness, its chronic economic instability, and no less the horrendous destruction of two major world wars (Schumpeter, 1943). Many believed in the days of the 1970s depression that the 'final crisis of capitalism' was imminent. The Reagan–Thatcher revolution not only gave it a new lease of life – by the time it had run its course, socialism, its main antagonist, appeared to be in a state of terminal decline while market capitalism seemed, once and for all, to have conquered the world.

Britain's problems at the time Mrs Thatcher entered office were acute. Not without cause, it was designated 'the sick man of Europe'. Its world power status had been badly eroded in the aftermath of the Second World War. For a while Churchill's inspired war-time 'standing alone' refrain, followed later by the inspiration of the Labour administration's progressive reforms had helped to maintain a respectable place at the top table. Yet even then the cracks in the edifice were becoming apparent. By the time Mrs Thatcher assumed office, a succession of failures and tribulations, had led to a state of affairs where even well-wishers perceived the record as 'Britain against Itself' (Beer, 1982). Beer speaks of a recurrent 'wage-price explosion' that combined with an incessant 'benefits scramble', impoverished the exchequer, devalued the currency and led to leap-frogging, militant union demands, wage demands and catastrophic inflation. 'Hubristic Keynesianism', he adds, was feeding a spending explosion; chronic 'U-turns' in putative long-term policies, destabilized government; minimal effort and low productivity debased living standards; 'stagflation' – a condition categorically denied by economic theory where endemic stagnation coexists with currency devaluation had impelled the country to turn cap in hand to the IMF for a rescue package. More seriously still, morale had sunk to a point where 'ungovernability' had virtually become normalized. The 1978–79 'Winter of Discontent' saw industrial disruption on an unprecedented level with hospital emergency services shut down, corpses lying unburied, rubbish spilling out into the streets, and power cutbacks causing blackouts. This proved to be the final straw as millions who for years had loyally voted Labour, welcomed Mrs Thatcher's change of course with open arms.

Reagan's task – in dealing with a demoralized country reeling from the ignominy of the post-Watergate scandal and defeat in Vietnam, rising unemployment and inflation, an increasingly embittered contest between 'moral majority' concerns and sub-cultural permissiveness, plus widespread opposition to some of the Civil Rights actions – seemed only slightly less onerous. Yet, he stepped into the presidential office determined to restore American respect abroad and to make the White House a centre of power again, and one, moreover, where appeals to unite against the 'Evil Empire' rallied overwhelming support. Thus, throughout, his role was that of the senior partner – though as records now show, the Iron Lady was never reluctant to 'box above her weight'.

Achievements were many, and setbacks – such as a mounting budgetary deficit, but a few. The agenda of monetarism, supply-side economics, deregulation, privatization and minimal government proved a startling political success. As inflation levels were drastically brought down and unemployment was gradually reduced, productivity rose and with less onerous taxes, material well-being extended to groups in society previously left out in the cold. There may indeed be more than a grain of truth in the assertion that the spectacular triumph of the revitalized market economy directly led to the downfall of the Soviet system and with it the end to the Cold War. The fact is that socialism, in all its various guises, is widely regarded as locked in terminal decline and in consequence the methods of collectivism, statism or the command economy are considered infamous, and should never be allowed to return. Significantly, progressive leaders – not long past referred to as 'men of the Left' – in their public utterances ritually disavow any desire to interfere with any part of the market economy. Blair's Third Way agenda, ties its putatively superior virtues of modification guardedly short of the advocacy of structural change. Mrs Thatcher's vehemently proclaimed 'there is no alternative' ('TINA') mantra disavows its ideological context to an extent that it calls for critical consideration. We will turn our attention to it in the section below.

## 2. 'TINA'

Curiously, many in the past chiding Marxism for its deterministic dogmatic stance, will readily aver that there is 'no alternative' to ongoing policies. Thus, in place of the materialist imperative that Marx proclaimed, we are presented with a technological imperative in matters of the market economy, the rise of transnationals, speculative money flows, globalization or the decline of the nation state. The option is solely to sink or swim – there is no alternative, no middle ground, just one right course of action, all else is counter-productive or merest chimera. Peremptorily this divides the wheat from the chaff. On the one hand, the circle of initiates who possess the full mantra, embody the cause, know right from wrong, carry no hidden agenda, while readily showing the way to doubters. While, on the other hand, the benighted will dissemble and flounder, will innocently or otherwise attempt to mislead, will undermine collective resolve, and if proving impervious will be bound to inhibit progress, if not inciting open revolt. Thus debate becomes stifled, and dissent deplored or even outlawed.

Mrs Thatcher famously employed the 'Tina' dogma in matters such as privatization, monetarism, 'union bashing', or in foreign affairs with respect to the European Union or Falklands war. Effective as it might have been in enhanced efficiency or bypassing delay – even in her own cabinet 'wet' colleagues were given short shrift – in the longer term, the absence of deliberation or of alternative views both narrows the vision and alienates many who are able to help.

There are two mutually reinforcing prongs to the Tina calculus: one is technological and the other focused on growth. The former holds to the view that what exists is there because it is wanted, and whatever is actual can never be uninvented. The latter contends that the desire for material well-being is the one universal dominant trait, that economic betterment advances well-being and the more that is produced, the more that is available to be consumed. As such, the logic is strongly compelling. Few would disavow the advances of modern technology such as internal combustion, electricity, antibiotics or pesticides, air-conditioning, let alone innovation in communications. Fewer still would advocate poverty over prosperity or misery over well-being. Stating the issues in such crude terminology, however, does violence to the complexities. These are not yes or no issues, matters without ambiguity, but concerns where even if one view predominates, there are choices present at every step.

Transnationals, for instance, grew up in an environment where their proliferation has been entirely *laissez-faire*, and have since the years of their early growth gestated into formations that few would have foreseen, and even fewer might have desired. As they are now, they are virtually informal mini-states – not untypically with budgets well in excess of medium-range nation states – subject to minimum law or regulation, able to roam the world at will, accountable to no one but a small inner group of corporate executives, while sought after to such an extent that, in an effort to woo their physical presence, all kinds of enticements such as subsidies, tax exemptions or trading preferences are made available by competing national governments. Hot money similarly is given a free ride in current conditions. Again, it is an argument typically put forward allowing no alternative option. One must not give offence to those willing and able to invest in one's country, otherwise funds will be channelled elsewhere. Hence, 'there is no alternative' to a state of affairs where huge flows of speculative capital seven days a week and 24 hours a day circle the globe in their quest of 'a quick buck' – except, of course, the sums involved typically run into billions.

Globalization itself is such an elastic term that it can virtually be applied to a welter of mutually contradictory interpretations. Some take it to mean the move towards a 'One World' situation where all distinctions of culture, ethnicity or nationhood have been merged into one single form of affiliation. Others perceive a parallel process of United Nations governance to match the unification process in the economic field. While others again, contend that globalization in the economic sphere already has gone well beyond levels of social tolerance (Bauman, 1998; Schrecker, 1997). While finally, a certain number contend that in the final analysis virtually all of the assertion of globalization is a mere empty sham, and in a crisis the same militant xenophobia asserts itself that has fuelled bitter conflicts in the past. The nation state, in such a perspective, is far from suffering the fate of terminal demise. Socio-political identification with supranational bodies such as the League of Nations, the United Nations, Nato or indeed the European Union – as the Spring '99 collective resignation of the entire European Commission in the face of serious charges of internal corruption demonstrates – appears exceedingly feeble. National self-consciousness might well be undergoing a process of change. However, its final outcome is extremely indeterminate, as likely to veer in the direction of exclusive reassertion rather than pointing to the end of the nation state.

The gist of our critique rests on the fact that the determination of major issues is not a simple 'yes/no' affair, but a matter full of complexities that calls for open-ended debate and not for a quick-fix resolution. The 'there is no alternative' presupposition deprives democratic societies of their outstanding advantage over totalitarianism, it fundamentally dichotomizes discourse, while tending to demonize interested parties who, for the purposes of commonality, require inclusion into the debate. The negative effects are not always apparent. The euphoric first-off-the-block climate helps to paper over the cracks, while the downside surfaces only when 'unforeseen contingencies' and 'unintended consequences' start striking home. The 'hot money' crisis of the late 1990s occurred when expectations were rising and economies buoyant yet unexpectedly hit the global community hard, and offers a prime example. One need not endorse the Leninist view that finance capital, of making money out of money, is totally parasitic to desire a curb upon speculative capital. For the global community to stand helplessly by while 'hot money' in its search for quick profits destabilizes the economic structures of advancing nations, as it has done throughout the 1990s, can surely not be the only alternative.

Corrigan ranks the appeal to 'necessity' and 'realism', as leading elements in the Tina campaign. The 'we can only do what we can afford' chorus of stringent necessity, instrumental in switching public expenditure from direct (progressive) to indirect (regressive) taxation, has made the rich vastly richer while penalizing the middle classes and even more so the poor. Measures such as sales taxes and user fees, linked to the policies of contracting-out, outsourcing and privatization are presented as fiscal necessity and have debased the character of social democracy. Concomitantly, 'realism' dictates that government should be cut back to minimal levels, that all institutions are judged by the laws of the market, and that all, regardless of function, must pay their own way. The IMF/World Bank consortium, in such a context, has imperceptibly acquired a predominant influence (Corrigan, 1997). The subtly compelling Tina logic, for all its negative consequences, cannot be lightly dismissed. There is much that has gone awry in the workings of the New World Order, yet at the same time there is a great deal that has been achieved. We will, in the rest of the chapter, firstly examine the principal disadvantages and then the outstanding triumphs of the free market.

## 3. Disadvantages

'Parties in the market should be free to buy and sell at any price at which they can find a partner to the transaction – free to produce, buy and sell anything that can be produced and sold to all' (Hayek, 1944: 37).The above dictum on the part of the neo-Right's principal guru, aptly sums up the essence of 'The New World Order's' philosophy: let markets run free for the 'invisible hand' to generate enterprise and give all their deserved due; let trade flourish to spread the gospel of liberty and democracy; let material wealth accumulate to uplift the quality of life in every direction; and let the minds and efforts of humankind be directed towards mutually beneficial peaceful exchange rather than the bloody, destructive ravages of recurrent war. Dissenting voices, not by any means confined to the Left, have started arguing otherwise. We will summarize the apparent disadvantages under eight separate headings.

**The visible hand**

George Soros's denunciation of 'market fundamentalism' denotes a startling conversion. For years, a leading mover in the hedge fund explosion, widely held accountable for the 1992 British pound's devaluation (netting him a profit of $1 billion), the renowned mastermind behind the Eastern bloc's capitalist transition, and pointedly singled out by the Malaysian Prime Minister as the source of his nation's crisis, he has now dramatically moved to the opposite side. The current fashionably vulgarized version of *laissez-faire* economics, propounds a 'market fundamentalism' policy that appears 'a greater threat to open society than totalitarian governments today' (Soros and Madrick, 1999: 36). The international crisis – that started in July 1997 in Thailand, then spread from Taiwan and Malaysia to Singapore, the Philippines, Indonesia and South Korea, threatening Hong Kong and China, then fundamentally destabilizing Russia and Brazil – is a pointer, if left unchecked, of what might be lying ahead. Markets are essentially amoral, not always stable, and frequently prone to excesses – 'That's why I say that markets, instead of swinging like a pendulum, can sometimes act like a wrecking ball, knocking over economies' (op. cit., 36). The 'legitimate capitalism' he advocates in place of the 'robber capitalism' (now rife within Russia), discourages speculative currency transactions, regulates the volume of bank and hedge funds, while it vests the IMF with wide-ranging global controlling functions. Far-sighted as this may be, it departs radically from the free market version that made him powerful and rich.

Ackerman and Alstott, in their effort to reset capitalism on its optimal course, perceive rescue in The Stakeholder Society where each American citizen on their twenty-first birthday is awarded a stake of $80 000 as of right (Ackerman and Alstott, 1998). Thus, at a stroke, the growing wealth gap that has brought about 'the 80/20 society' with its divergent life chances' path, by allowing each and every adult citizen to develop assets through the stock market, would create a society that is more democratic, more productive and also more free. The fact that, imaginative as the scheme may well be, the stake becomes repayable with interest at death, that public loans are notoriously prone to being uncollectable, and that while some may prosper others might lose everything in the market or dissipate the loan in other ways, impels a measure of scepticism. In passing, it seems worth mentioning that the US model and the versions of stakeholder society put forward in western Europe are fundamentally dissimilar. Whilst the former perceives remedy in the market, the latter typically rests its case on workers' participation and co-determination in decision-making

### Inequality

According to the findings of the 1996 United Nations Human Development Report, in 70 countries average incomes are less than they were in 1980; in 43 of those 70 they are less than they were in 1970. 'In 1960 the richest 20 per cent of the world's population were 30 times better off than the bottom 20 per cent; in 1993 they were 61 times better off ... life expectancy in sub-Saharan Africa is moving rapidly from 62 years to 47 years' (Corrigan, 1997: 249). Within the United States, 97 per cent of the past two decade's income increment has gone to the top 20 per cent of income earners. The median family income – even taking increasing dual employment into account – has fallen by $400 in the past decade. Recent capital concentration is even greater. Whereas in 1970 the top one per cent held 13 per cent of national wealth, they are now holding 38.5 per cent (Beatty, 1999: 105). The discrepancies could be replicated over and over again. The free market nexus, hinged on the maxim of competitive success, drives social structures apart. Within and between nations, the rich become richer, the middle ranges enjoy some of the disbursements of the rising tide (nearly 50 per cent of Americans now own shares), while those who are unsuccessful – be it due to lack of skill, lack of effort or the mere chain of contingency – fall further behind. The fact that, even where once strongly established, union membership has drastically declined, increases the discrepancies even further.

### Flexibility

Widely embraced as the symbol of progress and globalization, flexibility is equally charged with extensive destabilization. It has gathered dramatic momentum since getting underway with the early initiatives of the New Right. Measures of downsizing, privatization, control of restrictive practices, flexi-time, and de-routinization have put an end to the concept of lifetime careers. The motives, in many ways, appeared irreproachable. Yet the dismantling of old, outdated practices that obstructed progress, has led to interminable schisms and internal disputes, promoted stagnation, and made workers of all kinds slaves of machines. After all, even Adam Smith, the arch-apostle of *laissez-faire* capitalism, warned against the dehumanizing effects of endless routine. 'The man whose whole life is spent in performing a few simple operations', he cautioned, '... generally becomes as stupid and ignorant as it is possible for a human creature to become' (Smith, 1937: 109–12). What could be more enlightened than liberating the poor downtrodden wretch, transforming workers of all grades – however low-skilled and humble – into models of the executive and the entrepreneur, dissolving the network of fusty fixation on outdated practices, institutionalizing permanent innovation, while equipping each and everyone for potential top-flight success.

The reality, critics contend, looks very different. The Anglo-American model of free-market flexibility, demonization of government, nominally low unemployment and widening inequality, as Robert Reich, President Clinton's ex-Labour Secretary contends, serves up 'a two-tiered society composed of a few winners and a larger group left behind'. Sennett, who categorizes the process as 'leanness and meanness', takes a critical look at what 'flexibility' implies in terms of today's work. In the USA – with Britain not far behind – as much as one-third of the labour force are now in 'contingent' work. An amalgam of part-time, casual and seasonal work and above all, so-called 'contractor' status, where secure careers no longer exist, income is intermittent, benefits eliminated, and all too frequently two or more jobs are needed to earn an adequate wage. His original combination of micro- and macro research, critically evaluates the impact of 'leanness and meanness' upon the workplace. The vaunted 'empowerment' that flexible work practices have produced at the workplace, he regards as a myth. The long years of downsizing and decentralization instead have concentrated power in a new way. No one knows where the axe will strike next. All, from the bottom right up to the very top, are permanently fearful of being the next in line. The invisible hand of change determines all fates. Team leaders, 'democratized' as 'facilitators', repudiate authority and responsibility. Self-preservation dictates toadying and prevarication. And with everyone cast in the 'victim role', profits and worker productivity have been reaching new lows (Sennett, 1998: 50).

### 'Keynes for the rich' (Baker, 1999: 78)

In March 1999 news leaked out that Rupert Murdoch, the global news magnate, had on seven years' British-based earnings of £1.4 billion paid nothing in taxes. 'True to his anti-statist philosophy', observed *The Economist*, 'Mr Murdoch hands very little of his profits to the government.' His powerful News Corporation – 'a company that seems not to have any employees, nor any obvious source of income from outside Mr Murdoch's companies' (*Economist*, 1999: 63), thanks to a skilful recourse to tax havens, creative accounting and taking fullest advantage of tax breaks, had got off with impunity in regard to tax obligations. The £350 million that, according to laws applying to lesser mortals, should have been paid would have been sufficient to 'build seven new hospitals, 50 secondary schools or 300 primary schools' (Ibid: 63). Two American researchers, estimate that the total value of benefits handed out to corporations and wealthy individuals in their country amounts to $448 billion a year – a figure well in excess of the much vaunted Reagan budget deficit that inspired deep fears of decline in the United States (Zepezauer and Naiman, 1996). Understandably, by their very nature, these figures are problematic. There is no consensus as to what kind of benefits constitute corporate welfare, and how much is transacted on the borderlines of legality, so accounts are contentious. However, even accepting the *Boston Globe's* figure of $110 billion annually – the above authors' publishing house is held to be 'left wing' – the amount is double the sum that the Republican's 'Contract with America' in 1994 was designed to shave off the welfare bill over six years.

Not all of this, whatever one's political philosophy, is there to be saved. Research and Development subsidization is essential, and workers' training should equally qualify for support (Chait, 1996) . The critical point is the balance between redistributive as against regressive taxation, since the Reagan/Thatcher era decisively tilted in the latter's direction. Reductions in graduated taxation and capital gains tax, the heavy incidence of indirect taxes (especially VAT), and the consequent boom in the stock markets, property vales and offshore trading – all in the name of market freedom – have greatly disadvantaged the less well-off sections, while massively favouring the rich.

### Externalities

This refers to damage done by business organizations for which the community is required to pay. McMurty, (1997: 182) lists these as 'increased poverty, pollution, unemployment, illiteracy, ill-health, environmental degradation and destruction of natural resources. The free-market nexus empowers business organizations, and even more so transnationals, to set up and close operations wherever they choose, abandon unwanted sites and redundant labour without notice or recompense. Corporations widely cut costs by dumping their waste and causing air plus water pollution, disregard hazards to health and the well-being of the wider community.

Exposure is not quite the same for advanced economies as against countries of the developing world. The latter will be more prone to the infliction of increased poverty, ill-health and illiteracy; while the former will suffer more severely from pollution, environmental degradation and destruction of natural resources, and especially from unemployment when millions of jobs are exported to low-wage economies. The European Union's seemingly iron ring of near 10 per cent unemployment (much of it long-term) – which the UK and USA have succeeded in bypassing thanks to the creation of the contingent labour force – is in many ways due to job emigration to countries where workers will be only too eager to perform the same task for a fraction of western pay levels. For instance, according to 1994 data, American garment workers earning $7.53 an hour found themselves in competition with Bangladeshi workers making 25 cents an hour, while steelworkers paid $13 an hour were confronting Brazilian workers making $1.28 (Beatty, 1999: 105–6). Underemployment then turns into one added developing nations' externality, when rural masses stream into the towns in search of new work. Urban squalor, overcrowding and huge festering barrio settlements intensify the ill-effects, leading, in turn, to widespread alienation and lawlessness. The western process of deindustrialization, which has been underway for a number of years, has produced zones of social exclusion parallelling this vicious circle. The inner city ghettos have given rise to an underclass that categorically can be traced back to the repercussion of 'supra-capitalism's' externalities. Whilst it would clearly be churlish to lay the entire network of these disbenefits at the door of the free market, the chain of interlocking and mutually reinforcing ill-effects are hard to refute. The parallel expansion of unfettered transnationals on the one hand, and the above-cited disadvantages appear more than coincidental.

### Shock treatment

Since Britain in its former days as 'the sick man of Europe' after much heart-searching made its appeal for financial aid, IMF supplication has become commonplace. Most of the Asian developing nations, Mexico,

Brazil and several others in South America, and Russia are all regular supplicants, knocking at its bounteous doors. The formula is unvarying: responsible government. This means stringent deflation, a shift to regressive taxation, minimal government, cutbacks in public expenditure, a reduction in real incomes and a tightening of the labour market, with rising joblessness and unions set for decline. Bankers do not ask questions as to supplicants' inconveniences. Whether the shoe fits or not, is not the banker's business. What counts is collateral (if available), the level of risk, capacity for contractual repayment, and then economic stability to ensure that the debtor will not come back. Inevitably the medicine hurts, but generally it does less harm than good. Yet, whatever the direct consequences, the pill is a hard one to swallow. Loss of faith in the government, social unrest, numerous bankruptcies, and swelling numbers of newly dependents at a time when the budget has shrunk. This is coupled with a gradual run-down in services and infrastructural maintenance, and with all that, the almost indelible mark of Cain: within a market-dominated global economy, the brand of insolvency, undermining credit status for a long time ahead.

Survival in the tough international free marketplace is not always forgone due to irresponsible management. There are all kinds of forces at work that can shipwreck economies: natural disasters or climatic change; loss of markets due to changing demand or product substitution; internal unrest promoted by rising ethnic consciousness or dissident militant action, such as occurred in the Kosovo confrontation with a sudden huge influx of uprooted refugees. Often such circumstances are still more disruptive than national mismanagement. Shock treatment, frequently a panacea, has been known to kill patients.

## Democracy

Prevailing wisdom maintains that free trade will lead to universal democracy. Even the most despotic regimes, it is held, will yield in the face of material benefits, free exchange and globalization (McMurty, 1997). Prosperity will give rise to the growth of a western type middle class imbued with the values of rationality, tolerance and respect for the law; an activist civic society will undermine oppressive control; communication, travel and interchange will generate the culture of an open society; while rulers, steeped in autocracy, if not recognizing the errors of their old ways, will be displaced by others with a respect for democratic tradition. Amartya Sen points out that no major famine has ever occurred in a democracy with a relatively free press and other self-correcting mechanisms (quoted in Ignatieff, 1998). In consequence, under the rules of 'total engagement', no distinctions are made when it comes to free trade. Access to domestic markets is unconditionally awarded to transgressing nations, while under the aegis of export promotion, even classified information comes to be shared. All manner of abuse of human rights, sweatshop working conditions, imports produced by child or by convict labour, or persistent disregard of the codes of fair trade come to be tolerated in the name of free trade and democratization.

By any criteria, after more than a decade of engagement, the movement towards human rights has been negligible. It appears evident that privatization, deregulation and even the installation of market conditions can well coexist with human rights abuse, oppression, or denial of civic rights. Embracing tyrannies and filling their coffers, is more likely to subvert the cause of democratization than advancing the cause of civic society and human rights.

### Monoculture

Critical social scientists have for years been expressing concern at increasing materialist standardization. The new flexible modern economy has been claimed as reversing the trend by providing extended variation and choice. The growing world-wide prosperity, range of products, consumer discrimination plus communication is regarded as vastly expanding individual identity and proliferation of choice. Others perceive the same trends as pointing in the very reverse direction. Miller, in his *Egotopia* specifically refers to the 'dark satanic malls' as symbolic of the tightening net of the 'death of the public man' and mindless standardization (Miller, 1997: 1–25), while Vandana Shiva chides 'market imperialism' as liable for inducing an insidious 'monoculture of the mind', now further vulgarized as a result of the widening impact of informatics and communication (Shiva, 1992). Economies of scale, intensifying competition, and ever growing capacity for mind control and dissimulation have widened the conceptual gap rather than led to the personal empowerment that others have claimed.

In this, no less than some of the above categories, the jury is out as to the balance between disadvantages and achievements of the market economy. We will turn to consideration of the latter below.

## 4. Achievements

Generally the New Right depict their campaign as a struggle for freedom versus tyranny. On the one hand, there is constitutional government, free speech, individual rights and freedom of choice; and on the other, collectivism, state control, suppression of liberties and the abolition of enterprise. While the equation might legitimately reflect the western democracies' contrast to the Soviet system, it is evidently misapplied in regard to the west's leftist regimes. Admittedly, the latter aimed for or instituted nationalization of major national enterprises, constraints upon the power of capital, public planning and progressive taxation. However, denouncing their administration as anything resembling tyranny, appears extreme. Mrs Thatcher's different emphasis once again more aptly reflects the real world. 'Opportunity', she proclaims, 'means nothing unless it includes the right to be unequal, let one's children grow tall and let some of them grow taller than others if they have it in them to do so.' The accent is put on competitive enterprise, unequal outcomes due to natural differences, withdrawal of the state from unwarranted interference in matters of private concern, and equally the promotion of talent, innovation and free market conditions. As John Gray, in turn defines: 'The free market enables the individual to act upon his own good and values, his objectives and his plans of life, without subordination to any other individual or subjection to any collective decision procedure' (Gray, 1992: 19)

Essentially the goals of the neo-Right revolution have been fulfilled. In Britain there came early large-scale de-nationalization, wholesale public utilities' marketing, the sale of council housing to owner occupiers, monetarist policy and taxation reforms to promote capital investment plus a decisive shift in labour relations. Mrs Thatcher in her year-long confrontation with the Scargill-led miners' union, and equally President Reagan in his flight controllers' dispute, soon dramatically succeeded in curtailing trade union power. Corporatism, secondary picketing, the closed shop as well as direct links to leftist political parties perceptibly became a thing of the past. Policies of flexibility, de-industrialization and contingent labour considerably aided the process of privatization. In addition, Mrs Thatcher's symbolic defeat of the 'red bastions', such as the abolition of the powerful Greater London Council plus other municipal councils, clearly defined the revisionist climate of the new times, with her triumph complete. Discredited, disorganized and demoralized, socialism found itself in headlong retreat. The New Right had it all their own way, virtually free of challenge, for two decades. The crumbling of the Berlin Wall, purportedly heralding 'the death of socialism', made the triumph total.

As *The Economist* declares in regard to the neo-Right era: 'The past 17 years have done the British economy a power of good' (*Economist*, 1996: 6). Unemployment has dropped spectacularly, the unions' disruptive power is finally curbed, home and investment ownership has spread to ever-widening circles, exports are booming, while the scale of educational qualification has grown extensively. Moreover, Britain's economic decline has been reversed. Labour productivity – as is equally true of output per worker – is comparable to other advanced societies; and, 'total factor productivity' (measuring how well the economy is using both capital and labour) has advanced quite respectably (ibid: 6–7). In short, from its chronic post-war role as 'the sick man of Europe', Britain is once again restored to confident health. Externally, the trend has been the same. 'For good or ill', *The Economist* announces one year later, 'globalization has become the economic buzz-word of the 1990s ... Consumers are buying more foreign goods, a growing number of firms now operate across national borders, and several are investing more than ever before in far-flung places' (*The Economist*, 1997: 79). As Lester Thurow, a leading American economist has put it: 'For the first time in history, anything can be made anywhere and sold everywhere ... Technologically, transportation and communication costs have fallen dramatically, and the speed with which both can be done has risen exponentially' (Thurow, 1996: 115). As he points out in the same text: 'After correcting for general inflation, natural resource prices have fallen by almost 60 per cent from the mid-1970s to the mid-1990s' (ibid: 67). *New Times* has successfully done away with class warfare, Fordism's drab routinization, the stop–go cycle, and the big-brother state, while simultaneously achieving general prosperity and modernization, surely, a legacy of which the movement can justly feel proud. Luttwak's terse formula to the effect that: Deregulation + Privatization + Globalization = Turbo-Capitalism = Prosperity appears aptly applied (Luttwak, 1998).

Yet, a mere eleven months later, reviewing the 'worrying backlash against the free market', the same journal was posing the question of 'Capitalism in retreat?' (*The Economist*, 1998: 21). Within a context of economic crises, tariff retrenchment, persistent deflation, lack of consumer confidence and social disruption the triumph of the unfettered free market witnessed by the last generation seems less assured. The British Tory party, following their huge electoral defeat, became embroiled in a 'civil war' over the Thatcherite ideological heritage. Though the new direction of acknowledging the limited role of the market in matters of education and health – incautiously let slip by the then deputy leader, Peter Lilley, in a public address – has for the sake of unity been quickly toned down, his departure was swift. The 'kitchen-table' version brought back by William Hague, the leader, from his visit to the United States, implies a qualitative new step (*The Economist*, 1999d: 58). Indeed he has set himself the Herculean task, should he win the next election, of maintaining Labour's spending commitments on health and education while at the same time cutting taxes.

The 'compassionate conservatism' that is dramatically gaining George W. Bush pole position in the presidential candidacy race, shares the orientation to a marked degree. It is being acknowledged that for all its emphatic pre-eminence, the free market needs to accord to government an essential role in making the market work. Partnership between the private and public sector, rather than dichotomy – a signal departure – is to be the policy of the twenty-first century's New Right. Quality of life issues concerned with civil society and social capital, rather than an emphasis on the untrammelled free market (echoes of Clinton and Gore), are accorded pride of place (Milbank, 1999). This is a far cry from the relentlessly individualistic 'Tina' stance, excoriating public intervention as destructive of personality and social cohesion (Olasky, 1992; Frum, 1994), and a clear signal that the ideological gap has greatly narrowed.

Yet for all that, it must not be thought that the shift has all been in one single direction. The Left has yielded at least as much as it has obtained. Yergin points to the way in which 'socialist' European leaders and equally President Clinton too, have helped generate 'a new market consensus to an extent where the New Democrats in the United States and New Labour in Britain … seem no less Thatcherite in their economic policies than Margaret Thatcher herself' (Yergin, 1999). In Germany, the finance minister, Oskar Lafontaine was forced out of office as a result of his social equality emphasis, while Prime Minister Blair's abjuring of contradictions between the market hegemony and his advocacy of the Third Way demonstrates the extent of the left's co-optation.

Overall, discourse has moved in a different direction. Critical texts are projecting 'Regulated Capitalism' (Kuttner, 1997), 'Rule-based International Economic Solution' (McMurty, 1997), the 'Rhine Model' (Alberti, 1993), or 'Redesigning Government' (Coyle, 1998) as the way forward under changing conditions. Market dominance, irrespective of political philosophy, retains its status as a prerequisite yet limited governmental intervention, in one form of another, is built into the equation. Some put greater emphasis on the economic sphere (Kuttner and McMurty), while others focus more on social relations (Albert and Coyle). We will in the present context confine ourselves to briefly reviewing the various perspectives, and will return to them specifically in Chapter 6.

Kuttner considers 'regulated competition' to be more an adjustment rather than a transition. Historically, in the USA, 'until quite recently something like two-thirds of this highly capitalized, privately owned economy was very substantially regulated. Indeed, the most dynamic industries of this century – electric power, telecommunications, aviation, radio and television, information technology, among others – have been subject to regulatory constraints on entry, exit, price, demand, supply, profit and terms of competition' (Kuttner, 1997: 225). Regulating the 'Human Environment', especially conditions of work, is another step in a forward direction. Regulation, often in the past proving the 'mother of invention', is there to enhance technology together with socio-economic efficiency. The collaborative rather than adversarial workplace relationships that countries such as Canada, Sweden, Germany and Austria have managed to sustain even in the face of hyper-technology and globalization, have laid a groundwork of collegiate problem-solving and team-work that advances prosperity while operating on a basis of social peace (Kuttner, 1997: 225–49 and 281–301).

Alberti specifically cites the 'Rhine Model' as a superior political instrument to the Anglo-Saxon *laissez-faire* mode of free trade – superior not only in terms of social relationships, but also more productive at the same time.' ... of all the great industrial nations', he declares, 'Germany can lay claim to both the shortest working week and the highest wages, while at the same time building up an enormous trade surplus with the rest of the world' (Alberti, 1993: 100). German productivity continues to grow by 2–4 per cent yearly, while in 1996 labour productivity rose by 8.5 per cent with relative unit labour costs in manufacturing falling by 10 per cent (*The Economist*, 1999a: 9). Though overt unemployment levels are higher, arguably the Anglo-Saxon model disguises the true impact of joblessness.

McMurty represents a more categorical form of analysis. According to him, we have suffered a subliminal coup d'état on the part of transnational corporations, with owners of capital now accorded 'transnational rights to rule the world's production and distribution, uncontrolled by any standards of human rights or environmental protection' (McMurty, 1997: 188–9), He is particularly concerned with the 'disposable humanity' generated by the ever growing gap between jobs and job seekers, as well as environmental and social destruction. The post-war 'mixed society' model (characterizing Scandinavia, Western Europe, Canada, Australia and New Zealand), where a democratically controlled and accountable public sector ensured multiple benefits over a wide range of social activities – such as public utilities, health and education, cultural centres and libraries, as well as welfare provision – is now sadly forgone. His remedy however is not a return to public ownership, but the imposition of tariffs on corporations' incoming products to compensate for environmental destruction plus socially destructive processes. Given his severe indictment, these measures are not only remarkably mild but, with the increasing proliferation of services, exceedingly hard to enforce.

Coyle's 'weightless world' represents a distinct step in a forward direction. Hollowed-out corporations – the giant transnationals stripped down to minimal direct employees – operating in a dematerialized service-oriented environment have substantively diminished the powers and capacities of the national state. 'Our governments', as she states, 'can't control their national economies, can't remove the extensive new economic uncertainties we face, and do not know any better than the rest of us what is happening in the economy' (Coyle, 1998: 217). Hence, fractional agonizing over whether a modicum of more or less government intervention vitally matters, is a dysfunctional diversion. New times are bringing forward new contingencies, calling for new thinking appropriate to the future ahead. The social sphere, where the 'nanny state' needs replacing by the 'teacher state' is her primary concern. Hub cities – such as London, New York, Frankfurt and Tokyo – now span the world in specialized interconnected networks, giving rise to a new concept of civic society. Already, 'the growing irrelevance of conventional politics has been mirrored in the spread of interest groups and lifestyle politics, especially among young people. A sort of alternative opposition movement has developed, embracing environmentalists, animal rights groups, local activists and human development organisations' (ibid: 221). Three key elements rank for specific consideration. They are: globalism, the changed role of government, and the conquest of scarcity.

Though subtle, the distinction between the terms 'globalism' and 'globalization' is important. The former implies an activist, participatory capacity in preference to the latter's connotation of inevitable predetermination. It allows for multiple options, distinctive varieties, together with informality and experimentation. This enables bodies such as the IMF and WTO to play a positive role in making the cyberspace informatics highway an instrument for global prosperity and democratization.

Making markets work best becomes the task of both globalism as well as the revitalized nation state. The 'weightless infrastructure' concerned with inclusiveness, the educational sphere and the 'people system', has become no less significant than the conventional infrastructure charged with the maintenance of such essentials as bridges, roads, airports, hospitals and schools. Setting out new codes of behaviour, mediating between the global and local, market optimization plus the growth of the social economy integrating the underclass and furthering social regeneration, represent a civic agenda in which all are enabled to share.

There are two opposing views in regard to abundance. One, gloomily equates the advanced age – due to population growth, ecological destruction and resource scarcities – as initiating 'the end of limited abundance' (Miller, 1998). The other subscribes to the opposite view, citing the *Wired* magazine's conclusion that 'Today's leaders scorn the possibility of a golden age in which economics are based on limitless ideas, not limited materials. Since they refuse to see that abundance not scarcity drives the future', Coyle points to what the cybernetic revolution might help to achieve (ibid: 228 *et* passim). The end of 'the job' and 'clock time', reflexive relationships in which information exponentially promotes the accumulation of knowledge, and potentially artificial intelligence at the end of the chain, emphatically point to the conquest of scarcity. According to experts, 'the age of spiritual machines' is no longer distant. 'We will soon have computers', declares Kurzweil, pointing to Deep Blue's triumph against the chess world champion, Gary Kasparov, 'that vastly exceed us in intelligence ... With sheer computational brute force, you can solve any solvable problem' (Searle, 1999: 34).

We will, in the present context, only briefly refer to Jeff Gates's contribution, discussed in greater detail in Part III. In regard to the United States, Gates argues, that the 'disconnected capitalism' that has seen a widening gulf between the haves and the have-nots plus growing alienation, has already been supplanted by 'capitalism with a human face'. This involves measures such as employee stock ownership, coordinated private and public-sector initiatives in 'ownership engineering', together with rapidly growing participation in stocks and bonds which have produced an 'ownership solution' where prospectively all will be stakeholders in a prosperous society and where conflictual material relationships will no longer exist (Gates, 1998).

Notably, and irrespective of ideology, there is an abiding consensus in one major respect: the socialist solution is as good as dead. There is no longer even the vaguest inclination towards national planning and public ownership, nor reference to 'the final crisis of capitalism' or to solutions in which the market will not be predominant. The market, in short, stands triumphant. Prevalent Third Way solutions, the substantive subject of our enquiry, moreover are far from exempt. We will in later chapters, in the light of an analysis of available options, attempt to outline a model potentially able to transcend existing constraints.

## References

Ackerman, B. and A. Alstott, *The Stakeholder Society* (New York: Yale University Press, 1998).
Alberti, M., *Capitalism vs. Capitalism* (New York, NY: Four Walls Eight Windows, 1993).
Armstong, P., A. Glyn and J. Harrison, *Capitalism since World War II* (London: Fontana, 1984).
Baker, D., 'Bull Market Keynesiansim', *The American Prospect* (January–February 1999), 78–81.
Bauman, Z., *Globalisation: the Human Consequences* (London: Polity Press, 1998).
Beatty, J., 'Against Inequality', *The Atlantic Monthly* (April 1999), 105–8.
Beer, S.H., *Britain against Itself: the Political Contradictions of Collectivism* (New York: W.W. Norton, 1982).
Chait, J., 'Welfare Queens', *The New Republic* (16 December 1996), 22–3.
Corrigan, P., 'A Dose of Realism? The Social Grammar of Globalism' in Ted Schrecker, (ed.) *Surviving Globalism: the Social and Environmental Challenges* (London: Macmillan 1997), 239–52.
Cowling, K. and R. Sugden, *Beyond Capitalism: towards a New Economic Order* (New York, NY: St. Martin's Press, 1994).
Coyle, D., *The Weightless World: Strategies for Managing the Digital Economy* (Cambridge, MA: MIT Press, 1998).
*Economist, The*, 'The State We Are Really in', 21 September 1996; Survey: 6–8.
—, 'One World?' (18 October 1997), 79–80.
—, 'On the Edge' (5 September 1998), 19–21.
—, 1999a 'Could Be Worse', Survey of Germany (16 February 1999), 1–17.
—, 1999b 'Rupert Laid Bare' (20 March 1999), 63–4.
—, 1999c 'The Challenge Awaiting Romano Prodi' (3 April), 43–4.
—, 1999d. 'Something for the Kitchen Table' (3 April), 58.
Frum, D., *Dead Right* (New York, NY: Basic Books, 1994).
Gamble, A. 'Thatcher – Make or Break', *Marxism Today* (November 1980), 17.
Gates, J., *The Ownership Solution: toward a Shared Capitalism for the 21st Century* (Reading, MA: Addison-Wesley, 1998).
Gray, J., *The Moral Foundation of Market Institutions* (London: IEA, 1992).
Hayek, F.A., *The Road to Serfdom* (London: Routledge, 1944).
Ignatieff, M., 'Neither to the Left nor the Right', *Independent*: Podium 8 (December 1998).
Kavanagh, D., *Thatcherism and British Politics: the End of Consensus*? (Oxford: Oxford University Press, 1987).

King, D.S., *The New Right: Politics, Markets and Citizenship* (London: Macmillan, 1987).

Kuttner, R., *Everything for Sale: the Virtues and Limits of Markets* (New York, NY: Knopf, 1997).

Luttwak, E.H., *Turbo-Capitalism* (New York: Simon & Schuster, 1998).

McMurty J., 'The Global Market Ideology: Anatomy of a Value System', in Ted Schrecker (ed.), *Surviving Globalism: the Social and Environmental Challenges* (London: Macmillan, 1997).

Milbank, D., 'What "W" Stands For'; *New Republic* (26 April and 3 May 1999), 61–72.

Miller, J., *Egotopia: Narcissism and the New American Landscape* (Tuscaloosa, AL: University of Alabama Press, 1997).

Miller, L.H., *Global Order; Values and Power in International Politics* (Oxford: Westview Press, 1998).

Olasky, M., *The Tragedy of American Compassion* (Washington DC: Regency Gateway, 1992).

Schrecker, T. (ed.), *Surviving Globalism: the Social and Environmental Challenges* (London: Macmillan, 1997).

Schumpeter, J.A., *Capitalism, Socialism and Democracy* (London: Unwin University Books, 1943).

Schuparra, K., *Triumph of the Right: the Rise of the California Conservative Movement 1945–1966* (Armonk, NY: M.E. Sharpe, 1998).

Searle, J.R., 'I Married a Computer', *New York Review* (8 April 1999), 34–8.

Sennett, R., *The Corrosion of Character: the personal consequences of work in the new capitalism* (New York, NY: W.W. Norton, 1998).

Shiva, V., 'Monoculture of the Mind' (University of Guelph, Netherlands. Hopper Inaugural Lecture, 1992).

Smith, A., *The Wealth of Nations* (New York: Modern Library, 1937).

Soros, G. and J. Madrick, 'The International Crisis: an Interview', *New York Review*, 14 January 1999), 36–40.

Thompson, G., 'Rolling back the State? Economic Intervention 1975–1982' in George McLennan, David Held and Stuart Hall, (eds), *State and Society in Contemporary Britain* (Cambridge: Polity Press, 1984), 275–98.

Thurow, L.C., *The Future of Capitalism* (New York, NY: William Morrow, 1996).

Yergin, D., 1999. 'Going to Market'; *New Republic* (26 April and 3 May 1999), 50–1.

Zepezauer, M. and A. Naiman, *Take the Rich Off Welfare* (Tucson, AZ: Odonian Press, 1996.)

# 5
# The Third Way

New Labour and the Third Way appeared on the political scene like Siamese twins. After 18 years in the wilderness, there was need for a new approach. Gone was the cloth cap image of the class war, the hegemony of the big unions, the long contentious Clause Four commitment to the common ownership of the means of production, the central planning imperative, plus the idealistic disdain for the compromises involved in the quotidian compromises of political life. Instead new leadership had moved the party into the middle. The hallowed central ground of modern democracies where partisan ideology has given way to exigency, where opinion consolidates and where elections are lost and won. De-industrialization and affluence have eroded the proletarian base. Marxist dogma has long been taboo, while militant self-consciousness (at all times a precarious presupposition) is decidedly a thing of the past.

It is, on historical evidence, unrealistic to expect capitalism to self-destruct. Since the Soviet downfall the market economy has reigned supreme. Embourgeoisement has deeply eroded the working-class base. Friedman's aphorism to the effect that 'with all respect to revolutionary theorists, the wretched of the earth want to go to Disney World – not the barricades' (Friedman, 1998) may well represent a dismissive oversimplification, but its essence cannot be denied. Middle-class comfort consumerism plus the blandishments that the informatics revolution brings in its wake, have drastically altered the political scene. Pragmatism, moderation, gradualism and compromise have made Labour's traditional agenda strikingly obsolete. New Labour is the optimal vehicle for political power, while the vision of a better future ahead is the province of the Third Way.

These comments are neither meant to disparage New Labour nor to decry the programme of the Third Way. Pragmatic realism has been in markedly short supply in left-wing politics, which have equally been marked by fundamentalist attachment to dogma and its misapplication. Not without cause, after more than two years in office, Prime Minister Blair has increasingly felt impelled to contrast the reactionary conservative mindset with the modernizing aspiration of New Labour and the Third Way.

We will, in this chapter, firstly identify the principal proposals of the Third Way. We will then go on to outline its goals and its record with Labour in office, and will then review the main grounds of critique; firstly, coming from sympathetic quarters and then others ideologically antagonistic to the aims and purposes of the Third Way.

## 1. The programme

The Third Way boasts an impeccable pedigree. The two defining expositions derive from Tony Blair, Prime Minister of Britain, and Anthony Giddens, Director of the LSE – the former, in a brief Fabian pamphlet (Blair, 1998) and the latter in a book exclusively devoted to the thesis of the Third Way (Giddens, 1998). Overwhelmingly the leading figures speak with one voice. Though a recent polemic claims to detect material divergencies, charging that Blair emphasizes the skill factor caused by globalization and technological change in regard to employment, while Giddens considers the end of mass production as the crucial element in ongoing change (Froud *et al.*, 1999), we regard the critique as unjustified. There is no ground to assume that the two approaches cannot be reconciled. In fact, the Blair/Giddens perspective is increasingly echoed by a host of close-knit advisers, mostly youngish social science middle-of-the-road graduates, charged with extending the network, as well as implementing measures connected with the Third Way.

There is primary stress on the fact that the Third Way is not a compromise between capitalism and socialism. The ideological conflict that these represent has become obsolete. Notions of irreconcilable contradiction, the class war, industrial strife or statist control plus public ownership of the means of production, if ever valid, no longer fit the realities of postmodern society. Equally, the ravages of social cleavage, exploitation, alienation, and wastage of human resources ascribed to *laissez-faire* capitalism stand in no danger of being revived. Altogether positivism, determinism and all-embracing philosophies – all guilty of failure and brutal excesses – have given way to 'kinder, gentler' outlooks where reason rather than irrationality, argument rather than force, and reconciliation instead of coercion are allowed to prevail.

This is not to say that all problems are solved or that dissent no longer exists. Divergent viewpoints and interests are part and parcel of social existence, to be faced head-on rather than allowed to fester by being ignored. Yet current dichotomies are much less incisive. The 'Old Left/ New Right' juxtaposition presents a far less intractable phenomenon – not, as before, structurally irreconcilable contradictions, but social phenomena amenable to reconciliation. Despite long-standing battles, Old Left traditionalism still tends to resurface in some core constituencies. Class war clarion calls, workplace militancy plus fond recalls of statist control and nationalization disrupt progressive reform. Similarly, the New Right's supply-side economy's effects of gross inequalities, community breakdown and infrastructural neglect – all hallmarks of the 'two-third societies' – jeopardize prospects of concord and modernization. Yet, being maladjustments rather than crass contradictions, they are amenable to reconciliation. Flexibility plus pragmatism – leading watchwords of the Third Way – help to identify common interests, produce interaction, reduce points of conflict and give rise to 'win-win' outcomes, in turn providing models for subsequent change.

The recent diversion towards pointing the finger in the direction of the forces of 'entrenched conservatism' affecting all parties alike, tend to prove the case rather than the reverse. The Third Way is an infinitely pliable, flexible instrument, free of determinist imperatives, based on rational argument, while capable of taking aboard and resolving troubling issues at the same time. Social democracy, the foundation stone of the Third Way, does not recognize insuperable obstacles towards progress, inclusiveness, empowerment and a vibrant community life.

'Pragmatism', declares Prime Minister Blair, 'should not mean value-free. You can be pragmatic about the means you employ but they have got to be related to the ends you are seeking' (Smith, 1998: 6). The programme turns specifically to welfare reform, the relief from social exclusion, the devolution of political power initially from central to regional and local agencies, and likewise internal change (*The Economist*, 28 March 1998: 16). Unlike Communitarianism and the Stakeholder Economy (both concepts that briefly flourished amongst western societies and discussed in Chapter 7), the Third Way is grounded not in moral exhortation but in policies that envisage a measure of structural change. Charles Leadbeater, a leading figure in the think-tank *Demos*, elaborates on what needs to be done:

> The central ethic of the Third Way is disarmingly simple: co-operative self-help. We believe the Government's job is to help people to help themselves ... We believe passionately in self-help, self-reliance and self-improvement (Leadbeater, 1998: 22).

Individuality ranks above individualism; the state and society must work together to achieve an effective civic society whose purpose is cultural as well as political; while connectivity, where social relationships transcend the egocentric instrumentalism that marks the preceding regime, allows creative collaboration in several forms:

> Mutuals and other forms of co-operative self-help to provide housing, finance and employment; collaboration between different arms of the public sector to promote integrated solutions to crime and educational under-achievement (Ibid.: 22).

Giddens's seven-point programme departs even more markedly from the 'old-left' agenda. The seven points are:

- new coalitions in place of divisions and class war in politics;
- measures such as constitutional reform, greater transparency and local democracy to overcome the 'democratic deficit';
- a state-promoted yet autonomous civic society;
- a 'cosmopolitan nation' embracing 'fuzzy nationalism' and 'multiple sovereignty';
- a 'new mixed economy' with emphasis on competition and regulation rather than ownership;
- a 'social investment' welfare state with human capital and the reduction of environmental toxicity as the principal aims;
- a global order directed towards mutuality in a context of globalization, and free of particularism and the urge to fight wars (*The Economist*, 2 May 1998: 52–3).

Giddens's analysis lends a welcome sociological dimension to the debate. Social democracy, he argues, has no cause to adopt a defensive mien. It is thanks to concerted progressive efforts that we now live in a social environment hospitable to the Third Way. Principal credit for the ending of class conflict, division, social injustice, and inequalities in life chances and the quality of life is owed to their reformist achievements rather than initiatives on the part of conservatism in power. However, now when the final leg of social emancipation (following upon the previous two centuries' emancipation in the political and economic sphere), has been attained, the scenario acquires a different perspective. The formerly mandated striving for collectivist goals, state domination plus 'cradle to grave' welfare provision has become not merely obsolete, but is counter-productive. Time has come to mobilize the same spirit behind the goals of the new era's Third Way: equality of opportunity; protection of the vulnerable; no rights without responsibilities; cosmopolitan pluralism; plus – a somewhat ill-matching afterthought – philosophic conservatism (Giddens,1998: 7 and 66). 'The overall aim of third way politics', Giddens expands, 'should be to help citizens pilot their way through the major revolutions of our time: globalization, transformations in personal life and our relationship to nature' (ibid.: 64). The accent is on personal effort, self-regulation, 'a nuanced view of science and technology, in recognition of their ambiguous consequences for us; a respect for the past and for history; and, in the environmental arena, an adoption of the precautionary principle where feasible' (ibid.: 68). However, as Finlayson reminds us, while the 'new' is important for the Third Way as it repositions itself towards the new 'reflexive' society based on recurring technological and global post-Fordist change, its empirical understanding of what is occurring, including how capitalism should be conceptualized, can easily slip into a technological futurism while reifying the present as natural (Finlayson, 1999).

Moderation, modulation, compromise plus a striving for consensus as the natural precondition for all social change seems a matter of course. Now that gaps have been breached and rifts are healed, the Third Way can appeal to all groups alike. The inclusive society, embodying the principle of the social investment state where entrepreneurial initiatives ensure optimal return in regard to material plus human resources is there for the taking. The renewal of civil society can accommodate both a limited meritocracy commensurate with differential contribution, as well as an active government on all levels – global, national and local, ensuring that justice prevails (ibid.: 104–28). As Blair set out in his 1998 Labour Party Conference address:

> societies based on inclusion not division. Countries that are internationalist not isolationist. This is the Third Way, one way of recon-

> necting people to political idealism in an age where political ideology is distrusted (*The Independent*, 30 September 1998).

The underlying dichotomy between the Left's commitment to equality as against the natural presumption of hierarchy on the part of the Right persists and cannot lightly be set aside. Inequality, both material and social is widespread, and has magnified under the neo-liberal regime of the past eighteen years. The advance of science and technology is a double-edged sword. While benefiting the majority, there are many left on the outside as the spread of the Internet so vividly demonstrates. Giddens finds no difficulty in accommodating overtly dichotomous viewpoints. Thus, while stressing the necessity to keep market excesses in check, he commends the opening up of risk-taking at the same time. Government action is essential both at home and abroad. Domestically there is the obligation of protecting the weaker and ensuring infrastructural maintenance (ibid.: 42). While internationally, as the Asian crisis exemplified, there is evident need to provide against speculative capital being allowed to run wild. Giddens goes to the length of favouring the introduction of a Tobin tax – or alternatively the Chilean system of requiring a year's nil interest deposit on foreign investment – as well as the formal linking of the dollar and Euro currencies, together with a UN Economic Security Council to constrain the ravages wrought by roving capital (ibid.: 150–1) – at this point even well beyond the planning stage.

## 2. Policy

After over three years of a massive Labour majority in office, the jury remains out regarding the progress towards the Third Way. Supporters insist that the maximum has been achieved. Having to make good on the years of Tory neglect while, at the same time forced to deal with serious exigencies – principally the continuing Northern Ireland imbroglio and a leading involvement in the Kosovo crisis, a modicum of delay could not be avoided. Yet, for all that, much has been achieved. The administration points to the pioneer groundwork done in the political-institutional field, laying the basis for a more just and modern society, institutionally equipped to resolve problems in contingent spheres. The Scottish and Welsh devolution, the enhanced power given to local and regional bodies, and not least, after complex pressures and counter-pressures, the path-breaking reform of the House of Lords restoring genuine bicameral government for the first time since early this century – not inappropriately referred to as a 'constitutional revolution' (Marquand, 1999). These are by any measure substantial achievements. Parallel social sphere measures have strengthened democratic governance at the grass roots. The working families' tax credit – the lead element in the war on poverty – together with discount cards for post-compulsory school age attendance, attack the impact of social exclusion. Control over truancy plus parental responsibility for their children's conduct are expected to dramatically cut back the self-perpetuating proliferation of the underclass, while the rigorous scrutiny of failing schools will equalize access to advanced education. Blair's 'New Unionism', identifying trade unions as 'a force for good, an essential part of our democracy, but more than that, as a force for economic success', in a climate where the 'them and us' struggle no longer holds relevance, heralds a new partnership between business and their workers (Clement, 1999). This is projected to further cement the groundwork towards the Third Way.

Sceptics readily concede that this has been an exceptionally busy government, not afraid of action, clearing dead wood in several directions, while exhibiting a spirit of continuing initiative that bodes well for new legislation. But questions are rightly asked whether these initiatives point in the right direction, whether they are relevant to the Third Way, and more critically whether they can be identified as left-centre or even inherently progressive.

The paramount credo that 'the class war is over', in a sense predetermines everything else. It follows that now we are truly 'one nation' interests are bound to converge, that, 'a low-paid job is better than no job', and that it is absurd to suggest that 'supporting business means you don't support employment, employees or trade unions' alike (*The Independent*, 14 September 1999). The cornerstones of Community, Responsibility, Accountability and Opportunity (reminiscent of the apparently defunct Communitarian movement), logically follow in train (Freeden, 1999).

The locus of social control is now within the community and involves neighbourhood renewal. The aim is to establish alternative sources of power away from the national state, political parties and corporate associations. First and foremost comes the family where socialization takes place and normative conduct is learned. Next the school, peer groups, churches, voluntary associations plus places of regular gathering such as social or interest groups and, not least, local pubs. Their role beyond social intercourse, is no less directed at muting individual assertiveness, self-seeking or moral neglect in a hoped-for revival of civic society.

Responsibility probably ranks as the most determinate Third Way precept. Collective solidarity and consciousness have given way to the revised presumption that 'the aim of socialism is to give greater freedom to the individual' (Freeden, 1999: 43). The Marxist definition of autonomy as analogous to universalization within a social context where divergencies have ceased to exist, is redefined as implying self-regulation, self-advancement plus an ethos of individual success. Giddens's warm praise of risk-taking as a positive element in social advance – seemingly oblivious of the fact that within unequal societies the scales are unevenly weighed – might almost be taken as legitimation of the 'winner takes all' culture, clearly antithetical to the declared aims of the Third Way.

The final two items are manifestly less problematic. Accountability, if taken to apply not merely to local and national communities but directed at corporations alike, appears non-controversial. If taken to mean transparency in the sense of open conduct of public and private establishments rather than added bureaucracy as well as surveillance, is likely to attract universal support. It must not moreover stop short of government itself where, as Tony Benn asserts, the combined effects of the erosion of collective decision-making in Cabinet, the growth of patronage, the growing centralization of power and the tendency to bypass the Commons, is giving the Blair administration the semblance of a 'presidential system of government', with Parliament turned into a quango and public cynicism increasingly rife (*The Times*, 11 November 1999).

Opportunity provides the most double-edged category. On the one hand, establishing the 'duty to work' workfare imperative as a primary norm invalidates much of the welfare state ethos and does away with the egalitarian principle of social justice by awarding the market nexus undisputed first place. At the same time, the Third Way's emphatic highlighting of education as the vehicle for achieving a dynamic 'wealth owning democracy' opens up prospects of balancing other deficiencies. Whilst primarily perceived instrumentally within a production-oriented concept of 'human resources', educational reform could make opportunity the decisive make or break factor both for New Labour as well as the Third Way. Prime Minister Blair emphatically perceives education as lying 'at the very heart of the problems of British society' and the 'glue of a stable community', reminding us of the divisive consequences of unequal access. While, citing one illuminating statistic, two-thirds of parents with degrees, manage university attendance for their own offspring, a mere one in twenty-five of the unskilled succeed in achieving the same (*The Independent*, 14 September 1999). With graduate status increasingly the determinate factor in lifestyle as well as careers (and similar to the great dividing line in the USA), a breakthrough towards equalization could do much to advance the agenda of the Third Way.

## 3. Implementation

Blair's tangling with the teacher unions and Local Education Authorities (LEAs) is not a propitious start. His tendency to reserve the pejorative 'forces of conservatism' epithet for the ranks of the lower paid will not endear him to Labour's traditional voters. Linking teachers' pay to pupils' performance while putting bonus awards under heads' control – an innovation found wanting even in the more entrepreneurially inclined United States, though in accord with the Third Way's meritocratic emphasis – is seen by *The Economist* as 'caning the teachers' (23 October 1999: 63). This could well be construed as an exploratory attack on a numerous but industrially ill-positioned part of the workforce. Reinforcing hierarchy, applying untested subjective criteria to merit awards, further distancing the unions, while potentially returning education into learning by rote, has *ab initio* mobilized opposition in quarters from which in the past support was always guaranteed. The plan to compel the LEAs to hand to head-teachers a part of their regular budget is similarly seen as an authoritarian move away from the grassroots. That there clearly is wastefulness and major divergence – while Kensington and Chelsea, in London, spend £167 per pupil on administration, Oxfordshire spends just £17 – cannot be denied. However the fact that the proposals foreshadow 'battles between the Prime Minister and members of his own party' (ibid.: 64) cannot be regarded as a promising sign. In a similar manner the implementation of welfare reform has not been without controversy.

This shift may of course be less fortuitous than a strategic move of the point of contact towards the more elevated ranks of the middle class – or, differently put, conceivably a widening split between the interests of New Labour and the aims of the Third Way. The former is devising its policy with an eye to the next election, while the latter is adhering to residues of its socialist ways. The crunch issue is, and will ever be, redistribution, Blair and the Chancellor, Gordon Brown, pinning their faith in the free market, and the dissenters, guided by Mandelson and Giddens, increasingly giving voice to the interventionist imperative for equality ceasing to be 'pie in the sky' and instead turning to reality.

The manifest legislative concentration on constitutional reform gives little clue as to the final direction. Measures such as the setting up of a Scottish parliament together with assemblies in Wales and Northern Ireland; the top-to-bottom shake-up of the House of Lords; the proportional representation experiment in the European parliament and mayoral elections; and not least the autonomy given to the Bank of England to set monetary policy – making a formal euro link-up within the lifetime of the present parliament a distinct possibility – indicate dramatic change. Though all are not high-ranking items of public concern, nor likely to become apparent in their full repercussions for as long as perhaps a decade, their long-term significance ought not to be underestimated. They might well pave the way for a meaningful devolution of power towards the grass roots, a revival of civic involvement, a closing of the two nations divide, and not least, a British-inspired formation of a centre-left EU alliance actively striving to make effective the aspirations of the Third Way. 'Stealth politics', as Ken Livingstone dismissively terms it, may in the final analysis prove a superior strategy to confrontation. One would not wish to ascribe motives unclaimed by protagonists, but seen in a wider context, reforms already underway could greatly expand the entire *modus operandi* of the Third Way.

## The European connection

According to Timothy Ash, the Third Way originated with Michael Gorbachev. His glasnost and perestroika initiatives to reform the Soviet communist government, closely resembled the political philosophy of the Blairite Third Way. 'It was the illusions of Gorbachev and his team', he declares, 'about the possibilities of a "Third Way" between old-style communism and capitalism that made the revolution in Central Europe possible' (Ash, 1999: 16). The fact that both the ex-Soviet heartland as well as the former satellites went to the length of installing market economies, especially in respect of financial flows and union exclusion, with even lesser constraints than the West is tangential. What matters is that it eventually led to an assembly of world leaders of the vaguely centre-left – including the American President

Bill Clinton, the British Prime Minister Tony Blair, the German Chancellor Gerhard Schröder, and the Italian Prime Minister Massimo d'Alema (a former professed communist) – coming together in 1999 at a meeting in Washington to celebrate the new ideology of 'The Third Way'. In essence, a socially minded version of reformed capitalism, abjuring the previously held commitment to the 'transformation of society into a fairer world' (Theuret, 1999: 34), unreservedly subscribing to the market hegemony while purposefully moving away from linkages with the 'Old Left'.

How far this initiative has penetrated into the European Continent is a moot point. That the French are implacably antagonistic, there can be no doubt. Historically the entente cordiale has been an exceedingly fragile instrument on both sides of the Channel incessantly prone to suspicion, recrimination and underhand deals. At least, as long as the Franco-German feud lasted, strategic self-interest provided a bond. Once the Common Market started getting underway for the express purpose of healing the rift, the marriage of convenience soon drifted apart. Now, denouncing the Third Way as a capitalist sell-out and a betrayal of the left cause, the Trojan horse allegation, first raised by de Gaulle to block British EU membership, is once again being revived. The current emphasis in Britain lies less on Commonwealth ties, than on a reformulation of the Atlantic special relationship. The Blairite Third Way, with its infinite capacity for triangulation, is perceived by the French as an instrument for bringing American hegemony directly into the heartland of the European Union's domain. Active British participation through their own backdoor has introduced the whole insidious package of naked materialism, deculturation, homogenization, mindless consumerism, plus the destruction of old and valued ways. For the French, the market needs to be regulated to moderate corporate abuse, to offer protection to the exploited and weak, preserving the mixed economy and the welfare state, while keeping American imperialism safely at bay. Cultural safeguards, given scant attention in the Third Way agenda, are of no lesser account. The historic European values of community, civil society and social accord, must be protected as well as preserved.

Philosophically, Vaclav Havel, President of the Czech republic, reflecting on the issues at stake, puts the case well:

> The dictatorship of money, of profit, of constant economic growth, and the necessity, flowing from all that, of plundering the earth without regard for what will be left in a few decades, along with

> everything else related to the materialistic obsessions of this world, from the flourishing of selfishness to the need to evade personal responsibility by becoming part of the herd, and the general inability of human conscience to keep pace with the inventions of reason, right up to the alienation created by the sheer size of modern institutions – all of these are phenomena that cannot be effectively confronted except through a new moral effort, that is, through a transformation of the spirit and the human relationship to life and the world (Havel, 1999: 54).

Other pronouncements, from the French in particular, dismissive of what the Third Way claims to offer, tend to be more vehement. Abhorrence at the 'McDisney' package of self-seeking acquisitiveness, mindless consumerism, degradation of indigenous cultures, civic society and community life run alongside the political charges of a definite move to the centre-right. However, as Novak argues by way of correction, the US also has a strong culture of invention: with risk-taking, investing in new technologies and readily available venture capital far more generalized. By contrast, European business suffers from over-staffing and inefficient work rules with fewer incentives to innovate and expand (Novak, 1998: 51–2). To achieve this necessary objective requires further devolution – from state to civil society, from centralized bureaucracies to citizens – to 'make the project of self-government their own' (ibid.: 15).

Structurally, the auguries for implementation have been exceptionally good. During Labour's first two years in office, for most of the time 12 of the 15 EU nations have been governed by parties of the centre-left. The 1998 Schröder–Lafontaine social democratic coalition in Germany signalled a decisive step in a forward direction. Their Neue Mitte programme committed itself to a closely matching programme of modernization within a market economy similar to Britain's Third Way. Lafontaine's early departure from office, coupled with six regional electoral defeats within the first year in office, signal a setback. In and out of office, Lafontaine reflects the social protectionism and statism to which millions of Germans tend to adhere. Concessions to trade union demands for early retirement rights, plus rumblings for a reimposition of a wealth tax are indicative of a shift away from the Blairite Third Way (de Zoysa and Newman, 2000).

*The Economist* October 1999 'Survey of Europe' introduces a useful distinction. 'France', it concludes, 'has long favoured, always instinctively and often explicitly, what might be termed an "essentialist" view: insisting that mixing culture, history and a unique social model determine a European way of life, which governments must continue to nurture.' The main threat now comes from globalization, 'portrayed in France as an American-led process of levelling down in which quantity is allowed to destroy quality and market forces to undermine good government. The correct defence is a Europe rich in protectionism and government control.' In contrast, the British position is 'functionalist'. It allows for national governments 'to do specific and not necessarily connected things that can be done more efficiently on a European basis', of which free trade is the classic example, without there being a ruling European uniqueness presumption (*The Economist*, 23 October 1999: 5–6).

The Blairite concept at present prevails. The Dutch and the Nordic countries (Finland and Denmark in particular) are closely aligned, the Italian government vaguely champions the Third Way, while the German Schröder administration, in fact conceivably strengthened as a result of Lafontaine's resignation, remains faithful – at least in public – to the Neue Mitte facsimile of the Third Way. The determinate factor is, as before, the ultimate trend of the German position. Germany is the determinate 'swing voter'. Since the Common Market's inception – founded as much as anything else to heal the incessant blood-feud – the Franco-German alliance has at all times held firm. Generous subsidization on the part of the latter in return for moral legitimation has served as a sufficient spur. Now, with the return to Berlin as Germany's capital, the 'sleeping giant' may be flexing its muscles. In Chancellor Schröder's words: 'Germany has every interest in considering itself as a great power in Europe' (*The Economist*, 23 October 1999: 4). In geopolitical terms, it is the greatest by far. As Matthew Taylor observes, 'the debate about new forms of social democracy is much more vibrant outside Britain' (*The Times*, 18 November 1999). As the European Union searches for a new role in the twenty-first century, the issue of political structure is gaining importance. At present there is a distinct condition of flux with the field wide open. We identify three leading prospective scenarios for the development of the Third Way, all central to shaping the future ahead. They are:

- the reaffirmation of the long-established Franco-German alliance;
- a merging of the Neue Mitte and the Third Way;
- a EU line-up in accord with French policy, powerful enough to impel Britain to fall into line.

Chapter 8, 'The European Connection', will specifically deal with their consideration; while Chapter 6 will examine the growing body of Third Way critique – firstly, the friendlier more empathetic versions, and then the stronger, more critical sets of objections.

## References

Ash, T.G., 'Ten Years After', *The New York Review of Books* (18 November 1999), 16–19.

Blair, T., *The Third Way: New Politics for a New Century* (London: Fabian Society, 1998).

Clement, B., 'Blair Backs the End of "Us and Them"', *The Independent* (London: 25 May 1999).

de Zoysa, R. and O. Newman, 'The Third Way Alternative: America's New Political Agenda', *Contemporary Politics*, Vol. 6, No. 3 (September 2000).

Finlayson, A., 'Third Way Theory: Politics in the Era of Globalization', *Political Quarterly*, No. 70(3), (July–September 1999), 271–9.

Freeden, M., 'The Ideology of New Labour', *Political Quarterly*, No. 70(1), (January–March 1999), 42–51.

Friedman, T., *The Lexus and the Olive Tree* (NY: Farrar, Strauss and Giraux, 1998).

Froud, J., C. Haslam, S. Johal, A. Leaver, J. Williams and K. Williams, 'The Third Way and the Jammed Economy', *Capital and Class* (Spring 1999), 155–66.

Giddens, A., *The Third Way: the renewal of social democracy* (Cambridge: Polity Press, 1998).

Havel, V., 'Paying Back the West', *New York Review of Books* (23 September 1999), 54.

Leadbeater, C., 'What the Wonk Told the PM', *The Observer* (London: 10 May 1998), 22.

Marquand, D., 'Pluralism v. Populism', *Prospect* (June 1999), 27–31.

Novak, M., *Is There a Third Way? Essays on the changing direction of socialist thought* (London: IEA, 1998)

Smith, D., 'Doing Everything by Thirds', *Sunday Times* (London: 10 May 1998).

Theuret, P., 'Blairism: the Politics of the "Third Way" and the New International of the Centre-Left', *International Correspondence* (NY: Series No. 1, 1999), 32–4.

# 6
# Third Way Critique

Briefly to recapitulate. In the words of Tony Blair, its founder, (following a visit to the apparently keenly interested South African President, Thabo Mbeki), the Third Way rests on three major assumptions:

- Firstly the economy – rejecting the Old Left's belief in a trade-off between growth and inflation, and the Old Right's throwing people at the mercy of change. Instead, we will found growth on fiscal and financial prudence, sort out the public finances, create a new role for government in education, and with small business as an enabler of economic success, establish a tax regime that stimulates hard work and rewards effort.
- Secondly, a modern society which embraces opportunity and responsibility, and combines rights with duties. So we've cut youth unemployment by more than 30 per cent and reformed taxes and benefits, and we're bringing in the working families tax credit to help people who are disadvantaged. But we're also reforming welfare, tackling crime and reshaping the youth justice system. People believe in a strong society. But they want strong rules, too.
- And thirdly, freedom and liberty. A broader idea of freedom than that of the Old Right: a freedom to do things, as well as a freedom from things. Freedom to have better housing and to be able to get a job; freedom enshrined in the rules of law, in a free press, in a modern constitution (Blair, 1999).

In short, a new radical centre, characterized by a unifying ideology of efficiency, common sense and goodwill, distancing none while basing itself on a philosophy of 'what counts is what works'. To all intents and purposes, innocuous enough to offend none, yet since the day of its inception prone to attract a host of critique. We will review under three separate headings:

1. **Centrist/moderate.** Generally sympathetic to the aims and purposes of the Third Way, but critical of specific formulation and/or implementation;
2. **New right/conservative.** Based on right-wing objections, mainly in terms of covert socialism, incitement to class antagonism, big government, and unworkability;
3. **Left: (i) positive and (ii) negative.** Based on left-wing objections, mainly in terms firstly of flawed philosophy and implementation, and secondly of 'sell-out', diversion, and overt deception.

## 1. Centrist/moderate

Probably the best barometer for New Labour's Third Way is *The Economist*. Traditionally synonymous with the interests of business and finance, it is at the same time ever more focused on globalization and Britain's place in the new world. Hostile to Old Labour's anti-business ethos, and commitment to the class war and wholesale nationalization, it became equally antagonistic to Thatcherite xenophobic intransigence, its roughshod modes of addressing dissent, the negativistic performance in Europe, plus an imperialist nostalgia entirely out of place in a postmodern world. The Major government's interlude of vacillation, intrigue and recurrent scandal proved a similar disappointment. New Labour's conversion to enterprise and the market economy appeared as a godsend. It was welcomed as a vigorous new administration committed to modernization, reconciliation, pragmatism plus the restoration of accounting principles within the public sphere. Blair's initial success in simultaneously enrolling the American President as well as the European Union's political elite into the fold of the Third Way held out the promise of a re-cemented special relationship plus a leading role within the EU at one and the same time. Fulsome plaudits to the tune of 'Britain's most successful export' – extolling Tony Blair as 'the standard bearer of a modern Britain', together with his 'emergence as an international celebrity' (28 March 1998: 75) and 'the long honeymoon' (2 May 1998) reflected the sense of delight.

The euphoria soon started to wane. A mere few months later *The Economist* sardonically referred to the Third Way as 'Goldilocks politics' (19 December 1998), describing New Labour in power as 'just Tory government by other means' (2 May 1998: 14), while reminding its readers that in substituting fairness for equality, most of the reformist past had been sold (19 September 1998: 7). The chief plaint is apparent weakness rather than strength. 'A doctrine that says you can have your cake and eat it' (19 December 1998: 75), inevitably raises expectations that cannot be fulfilled, while disregarding dichotomies that cannot be wished away. Hence, while warning all not to be selfish, it claims to have no problems with people becoming 'filthy rich' (Mandelson). It proclaims equality without restricting choice. And while desiring the American market, it reaches out for Western European social cohesion at the same time. Though its fundamental hollowness makes it superficially attractive, its lack of consistency and ideological rigour – as proved to be true of Communitarianism, the Social Market and the Stakeholder Economy – condemns it to a similarly swift end.

The objections find themselves echoed in other quarters. Labour's performance in office has given rise to contentions that the Third Way principles are being betrayed. Empirical evidence does not inspire confidence. In the first place, there are signs that the promise of ending social exclusion has remained unfulfilled. The government's September 1999 Poverty Report, in fact, suggests that the 'two nation' schism is being revived. The divide between rich and poor has expanded, the 'cycle of deprivation' is still unchanged, while inroads into the underclass have not yet been made. Children from poor families are much less likely to attend school regularly and to reach their full potential. As adults they are much more likely to be out of work and living in poverty; while a further half a million jobs have been created, one in five families have no one in employment (*The Independent*, 8 September 1999).

The greatest default lies in the arena of social provision. *The Economist* leads the chorus once again. Blair, 'the greatest Tory ever sold' has visibly abandoned the principles of the Third Way. Rising levels of inequality, deep-seated poverty, plus the iniquities of the welfare–work continuum are cited in evidence. According to the findings of the 1999 *Wealth of Nations* report, 'inequality grows in Blair's Britain', not merely in regard to what used to be termed 'social classes', but equally in the North/South divide, prospering versus decaying towns, employed versus unemployed, and qualified as against those lacking in qualification. Little impact has been made on social exclusion – especially if this is meant to include health, schooling, housing and unemployment – to an extent that 'if the next Labour government has not raised living standards of the poorest by the end of its time in office, it will have failed' (Norton, 1999).

According to the first government report on poverty and social exclusion (*The Economist*, 25 September 1999), when measured in terms of families with less than half of average income, one-quarter of the population at large and as many as 34 per cent of children (compared to 9 per cent and 10 per cent respectively, in 1979) are living below the poverty line. Britain, with 20 per cent of children in households with no working adult (compared to 12 per cent in the USA and 11 per cent in France) is leading the western negative league table. Under the increasing polarization of work, the proportion of totally workless households has risen from 6 per cent to 18 per cent in the past twenty years – documentation damning enough to support the assertion that under the Blair administration, 'Thatcherism rests in safe hands'. Allegedly, there are ominous signs that under the banner of 'modernization, fairness and enterprise', Labour's policies will lead to 'the end of the welfare state'. Measures such as replacing the joblessness allowance (formerly unemployment benefit) by private insurance, emphasizing meritocratic criteria and enlarging the role of private education are considered critical signals in a strategy of eventual retreat.

Furthermore, laudable as the goal to end the 'dependency cycle' may appear, the welfare-to-work scheme might well prove the most intractable task of all. The pitfalls of the American experience are already evident. Most of the workless unwanted are underqualified, lacking in requisite skills, marginally mobile, and even after training confined to a limited range of tasks. They are beset by domestic and personal pathologies that severely limit their earning capacities in today's competitive labour market. Even such widely publicized self-declared triumphs as the American Wisconsin workfare scheme, on closer analysis reveals multiple flaws. Training is costly, opportunities scarce, and employers only too willing to accept subsidies revert to form when they come to an end. Most jobs are low-paid and casual, and in the longer term, 'only 28 per cent of those leaving welfare had projected annual earnings of $10 000 or more for two consecutive quarters. Seventy-five per cent of those who found jobs, lost them within nine months' (Massing, 1999: 23). Surveying the state of 'the welfare society', Lord Dahrendorf concludes that, in the light of current exigencies, in Britain 'something has clearly gone wrong in the process of slaying the giants of Want, Disease, Ignorance, Squalor and Idleness' as the century moves to its end (*The Independent*, 15 February 1999).

## 2. New right/conservative

Conservative objections are less centred on ideology than on political implications. After all, the Third Way, abandoning socialist dogma has located itself firmly within the market philosophy. No more big unionism, proletarian consciousness, class war or public ownership and nationalization. These have been replaced by the stress on individualism and enterprise, plus a market emphasis not merely in the economic sphere, but as the ruling imperative in other arenas – in essence, the very values that traditionally the Right has espoused. Hence, the point of attack has notably shifted. Perceptively, the Third Way has been stealing their clients as well as their clothes. The solid middle class, professional groups, aspiring young people, small business operators, retirees, and not a few amongst the successful and wealthy have transferred their allegiance, for the sake of modernization and unity, throwing in their lot with the striving achievers of the New Age.

While incapable of attacking ideology, conservative critics tend to allude to the Left's notorious inclination to internecine strife and intrigue, their presumed profligacy plus incompetence, their in-built authoritarian streak, and perhaps most of all their sham conversion to moderation, good sense and normalcy. Blair is dubbed a 'control freak' (that is, authoritarianism) out to dismantle democracy, to take every opportunity to upstage Chancellor Brown (that is, factionalism), to squander resources for political ends rather than the national interest, while surreptitiously, under the banner of the Third Way, ushering in a new socialist era of penal taxation, big government central direction, militancy and discredited dogma that had utterly failed in the past. The past chronic cycle of runaway spending that induced inflation, a retrenchment that led to devaluation and internal protest with cries of 'betrayal' by unions and the entrenched left, and finally the 1978/79 'winter of discontent' are still alive in the public mind. The Third Way's abandonment of ideology in favour of managerialism – adopting the slogan of 'what works' – once a Tory prerogative, counts as a plus over the historic attachment to 'the vision thing'. Denouncing 'Blair's third way to elective dictatorship' clearly seems ill-conceived. There is no evidence that changes in the direction of democracy such as greater use of referenda, and the vesting of Labour's leadership election to party members are demoting MPs to 'untrained social workers', nor that 'a system of permanent government' in which 'Mr Blair's own position would be almost unassailable' is already underway. A greater threat, as Harris points out, lies in

Blair's 'large measure of pragmatism' where the 'permanent revisionism's' attempted reconciliation of the dichotomous values of 'patriotism and internationalism; rights and responsibilities; the promotion of enterprise and the attack on poverty and discrimination', installs a permanently shifting Third Way, devoid of principle, and – similar to Clinton's triangulation – allowing infinite scope for rule by expediency and manipulation (Harris, 1998).

There is a distinct sense of ambivalence in regard to the right-wing critique. Blair's adroitness in shifting his ground deprives it of a stable target to aim at. Thus, the Third Way's flirtation with both the Stakeholder Economy and Communitarianism is seen in two different lights. It is, on the one hand, praised for the early realization that the former imposes a heavy drain on corporate management while the latter is inoperable without compulsion in a modern environment. While, on the other hand, the abandonment is cited as evidence of insincerity and lack of conviction. Adverse critique is on safer grounds in regard to the much-vaunted transcendence of the ideological left/right division. While proclaiming the replacement of the socialist dogma of 'the common ownership of the means of production, distribution and exchange' by an uncontroversial commitment to 'a dynamic economy ... a just society ... an open democracy, a healthy environment', Blair at the same time (and to different audiences) professes that 'change can't come about through market forces, it needs active government, local and national' (Applebaum, 1997). Vacillation, often a virtue, can be a vice at the same time.

When, as Blair declared in his French parliamentary address, ideology is considered as dead, the way lies open to the type of opportunistic politics that now prevail in the United States. Shared values, moral beliefs and normative standards no longer count. What matters is the attainment of office and continued electoral success. Goals are picked up and discarded at will, constituencies pursued in all possible quarters, promises have become cheap, while political life turns into a mere marketing exercise. 'Grass root forums', construed as mirroring public opinion, are given pride of place; pollsters are awarded top-rank authority; and the way is then open to an array of spin doctors, personal counsellors and media presenters in shaping policy, while dissenters – 'who have got it wrong' – are relentlessly pushed aside. Under the 'what works' formula, Prime Minister Blair assumes the status of an imperial president, while under its aegis the Third Way can become 'all things to all men' (*sic*) – policies based on expediency, where dichotomous viewpoints can comfortably be combined.

Samuel Beer, doyen of transatlantic analysts, presents a challenging interpretation of the momentum of British socio-political change. As he sees it, dramatic electoral landslides occur with regularity when the time is ripe: 473 Whigs v 172 Tories in 1832 (Lord Grey); 399 Liberals v 134 Conservatives in 1906 (Asquith); 393 Labourites v 213 Conservatives in 1945 (Attlee); and, 419 New Labour v 165 Conservatives in 1997 (Blair). The first three follow an historic pattern, while Blair's victory – new times, new contingencies – emphatically shows up as idiosyncratic. Traditional landslides have ushered in dramatic change: enfranchisement plus free trade; social intervention in economic affairs and particularly under the Attlee administration, a socialist government committed structurally to transform the capitalist state. Blair's New Labour/Third Way triumph is dramatically different: 'a landslide for the status quo'. Overwhelming public approval for a programme that contained little of substance, and even less that was new.

Radical change had taken place under the earlier Thatcher administration. There was wholesale rejection of the socialist pattern of corporatist government, nationalization, union hegemony, the mixed economy – all accountable for chronic industrial warfare, economic decline and stagflation. Simultaneously, but less immediately obvious, was the discarding of the paternalistic and protectionist Tory stance of 'Disraelian conservatism'. The ideal of a 'patriarchal nation' typified most recently by Eden, Macmillan and the Butlerite readiness to embrace social reform was decried. Thatcherism reflected instead 'the pure milk of Gladstonian liberalism: minimal government, the strict market nexus, individualism, promotion of enterprise by means of lower taxation, and rewards that reflected what each and everyone truly deserved.

Yet, for all its intuitive comprehension of the mood of the times, the enactment was seriously flawed. The persistent disregard for those who fell by the wayside, the spread of social exclusion, the denunciation of the concept of 'society' as a figment of leftist intellectuals' imagination, the strident hectoring style and above all the growing evidence of widening inequalities, paved the way for the Blairite Third Way. Basically, an identical subscription to neo-liberal market supremacy, yet modified in vital directions. Firstly, in place of the jingoist 'island fortress' assertion came the drive towards modernization and globalization, the theme of social inclusiveness to temper the 'winner take all' effects of market reality, and most importantly the rupture of the traditional link to what used to be termed 'the working class'. The winding-up of the welfare state package was made palatable by the promise to make opportunity open to all.

Remarkably, as Beer observes, through all the 18 years of Thatcher's demonization of government, the impact of public spending has remained virtually intact, falling only marginally from 44.9 per cent of GDP to 43.2 per cent (Beer 1997) – an equilibrium which, on all present signs, the Blair government appears pledged to maintain. This is a clear affirmation of Beer's innovation–convergence–consolidation thesis of Britain's unique process of coping with change, while coincidentally affirming the Marxist materialist dialectic at the same time. The material substructure, Marxists contend, determines the superstructure of politics, social consciousness and cultural life. If material progress comes to be the supreme goal, then the social consequences of inequality, internal division and exclusiveness follow in train. Both Thatcherism and the Blairite Third Way, in this analysis, perform an identical function: providing the rhetoric ('ideology') needed to reconcile the masses to the fate predetermined for them by the needs of the ruling class. Ostensibly, the expenditure of social reform will be paid for by savings on other parts of the welfare state. Concessions such as the family tax credit, the minimum wage or the remedying of social exclusion will, in all likelihood, be more than compensated through savings derived through welfare to work, without levying additional taxes on the wealthier sections, benefiting disproportionately from the actions of the Third Way (King and Wickham-Jones, 1999; Malcolm, 1998).

The welfare-to-work programme may well turn into an early crunch issue for the Third Way. The Left, as we will set out below, decry it for its relentless compulsion and degradation of the work ethic, while Tories, in turn, predict that the Third Way will inevitably revert to a socialist type of compulsion. Plans will be made, committees convened, statutes enacted, petty bureaucrats vested with power to boss people about, monitors sent out in each and every direction, and chaos imposed upon the conduct of business, only for the enterprise to end in costly failure again. Already, John Prescott, the Deputy Prime Minister, has publicly declared that 'we have decided that public expenditure is there to uphold the economy in the traditional Keynesian way' (*The Independent*, 30 December 1998). While Sir Clive Thomas, President of the CBI, scathingly criticizing government interference and the concept of workplace partnership between employers and trade unions, critically warns that: 'On the one hand, the Government is trying to create a positive atmosphere for industrial relations – the 'Third way' based on partnership. But then one of the partners is forced to the table' (*The Independent*, 29 May 1998).

One further contribution rates mention. Paul Vallely, an active churchman, perceives significant parallels between Third Way principles and the teachings of the Catholic church. British socialism has historically, at all levels, exhibited a powerful religious wing. Now, with Blair a committed Christian, the Catholic church's minimum wage ideas, stakeholding, Third World debt relief, control of global markets and welfare to work, find themselves echoed in the programme of the Third Way, which equally rejects the Thatcherite notion that 'society' is a concept that in actuality does not exist. Instead an ethical framework is offered to business, with canons of social justice in a prominent place, and market norms modified to succour the weak. A parting of the ways however shows up in two different directions. Firstly, in the church's more radical ideas on restricting the momentum of globalization, especially in its effect upon the Third World. And more strongly still, in the concept of work. Whereas the church is more concerned with the self-expanding qualities of work in regard to personal dignity and service to the community, the Blairite Third Way, putting its emphasis on work as duty in return for material benefits, adopts a strictly utilitarian view, disregarding spiritual qualities, downgrading pride in workmanship, and needing to rely on coercive instruments at the same time (Vallely, 1998). The Catholic church offers a moral compass which Blair has adopted in opposition to the scientific convictions of Marxism and the relativism in the ideas of people 'doing their own thing'. Etzioni's vision of communitarianism, Mulgan's 'connexity' and Giddens – all posit this new moralism in which individual responsibility and duties come before rights. Interestingly, John Rentoul's biography of Blair, depicts his social philosophy as embracing a 'social moralism' which invokes the values of solidarity, equality, social justice and a sense of community, based on the inherent social nature of human beings – a far cry from Thatcherite values.

## 3 (i) Left: positive

The public, Blair deplores, has been 'very frustrating' in its response to the Third Way. While externally Britain stands 'at the forefront of the debate about new ideas in modern politics – here in Britain there is very little sense that a major debate about political ideas is going on, let alone that we are in the forefront of it' (*The Economist*, 27 November 1999; Bagehot: 50). Public indifference to grand affairs is far from a novelty. In postmodern society, privatized and depoliticized, it has never plumbed greater depths. Unions have drastically been downsized together with their industrial workforce, big productive complexes are a thing of the past, public housing estates have been broken up, pubs have been modernized, and altogether the once solidaristic working class has turned its mind to other affairs – so much, therefore, for the grass roots.

No less disappointing has been the intellectuals' reaction. The Third Way, they consider, represents a dramatic shift in Labour policies. Goals have become short-term, guided by the vagaries of shifts in public opinion, manipulated by compliant media networks and closely tied to the governing elite and its favoured insiders or cronies. Hall and Hobsbawn – self-avowed Marxists – will be considered in the section below. The others, ex-mainline, are disenchanted with current trends. Ignatieff, concerned with the 'closed language of game specialists', warns that 'the Third Way could degenerate into using liberal (leftist) rhetoric to recruit the votes of the poor to win office and then pursuing fiscal conservatism to betray them in power' (Lloyd, 1999: 24). Dahrendorf chooses to sit as a Liberal Democrat in the House of Lords. Marquand complains that: 'New Labour won control of the party by using "the people" – in the shape of poll findings – as a stick to beat their own activists; and the habit is hard to break. ... Today's populists need not rely on intuition. They can find out, with a fair degree of accuracy what the people want (or think they want) to hear, and they can trim their messages accordingly' (Lloyd, 1999: 25). Pluralism, he argues, is gradually losing ground. The traditional checks and balances are being dismantled, parliamentary sovereignty finds itself undermined, while the populist doctrine – with focus groups as a surrogate for Rousseau's General Will – demotic, sentimental and resentful of excellence seems set to prevail (Marquand, 1999).

The growing body of left-wing critique represents a continuum, where positive and negative evaluations tend to interact. A recognizable dividing line however shows up at two points. In the first place, positive commentators tend to accept the leaders' goodwill, regarding deviation as self-deception, while negativists allege conscious ill-faith. Secondly, well-wishers generally subscribe to New Labour's manifesto, while dissenters remain committedly socialist, identifying still with traditional Labour's allegiance to structural change. Common ground exists in regard to where the Third Way now finds itself. In its quest to transcend the conflict between the dominant ideologies of capitalism and socialism, it has veered into a neo-liberalist *laissez-faire* direction, where the cure might be worse than the disease. The point of departure is clear. Socialism fundamentally rejects the free market, while British Conservative capitalism has historically and overwhelmingly exhibited its paternalistic 'one nation' side. The neo-liberalism, brought about by Prime Minister Thatcher (and shared with the USA) is in essence a return to the Gladstonian nineteenth-century pattern where interference with the free market is taboo. Guidance is proper – equality of opportunity, in fact ranks as a prerequisite – but other than that it is the epitome of the 'invisible hand': set enterprise free, let competition move forward untrammelled, permit the best to succeed, aid the weakest but let deviants pay the price they deserve. Individualism means freedom, and the progress that freedom brings in its wake, permits all to enjoy the benefits to an equal extent.

One might almost speak of three distinct camps:

(i) 'diehards': old-time socialists, prepared to depart from the controlled planned economy but adhering to structural change where equality of outcome remains a prerequisite ('negative');
(ii) benign socialists: adhering to the values of inclusiveness and socialization of risk, generally to the extent of favouring schemes such as citizen's income, social dividend and negative income tax ('positive');
(iii) Third Way postmodernists: putting their faith in pragmatism, modernization, social inclusiveness and equality of opportunity, but fighting shy of redistributive policies (New Labour in action).

The first category stands on its own, basically representing a self-contradictory world view. The other two inhabit much common ground. They represent shared basic assumptions, which at some points decidedly overlap, exhibit mutual respect, and in some instances coexist within some single minds. Accepting the priority of market forces, they stress the necessity of a social conscience at the same time, embodying 'a meritocratic society ... in which the state takes action to raise the level of the talents – which the market proceeds to reward' (Kay, 1998: 31).

In this context the maxim of 'the aim of socialism is to give greater freedom to the individual' is reinterpreted to imply freedom from 'external control' (that is, planning, solidarity or collective action). The emphasis lies on opportunity and accumulation, while the 'state–citizen' status is converted into a 'provider–client' relationship where moral precepts give way to the quid pro quo of market exchange. In place of an ethos where work is seen as promoting creativity and the realization of personal potential, the welfare-to-work programme transforms it into a duty owed to the community in return for services granted and standards achieved (Freeden, 1999). Thus, 'The Third Way turns out to mean a revival of liberalism inside a Labour body ... emphasis on personal duty, fiscal rectitude from the state and above all education, education, education as the key to social progress' (Marr, 1998). The socialist goal of liberation and universalization has yielded to a neo-liberalist economic cult of productivity and profitability, where despite growing affluence disenchantment and discord will always prevail.

Alan Ryan argues that the historical parallel to the current Third Way can be found in the New Liberalism which informed the Asquith–Lloyd George government between 1908 and 1914, and was defended by such luminaries as Russell, Hobhouse, Keynes and Beveridge. This was the original basis for a 'third way' approach, the current version of which he depicts as 'recycling'. However, 'the old third way had an easier time. It was concerned to find productive ways of expanding the state's role, while preserving liberalism's devotion to individual freedom' (Ryan, 1999: 80). Ryan finds much in the Blairite version which is incoherent, illiberal and authoritarian with a much too ready acceptance of the role of the market. And all this at a time when many view the Liberal Democrats as being located to the left of Labour – with their calls for extra taxation to fund educational spending and a higher 50 per cent rate of tax on earnings over £100 000 to tackle child poverty – coupled with their traditional defence of individual rights be it for asylum-seekers or victims of racism.

While it is premature to speak of a backbench revolt – it may never materialize – dissenting voices are already being heard. Barry Barnes, Labour MP, publicly declares that the Third Way's twin objectives of a free market economy and social justice are 'entirely incompatible' (*The Independent*, 15 January 1999), while 44 Labour MPs join ranks to remind the PM that 'you must return to Labour values and discard the neo-liberal values, under which "poverty and gross inequality still disfigure society and destroy life chances of millions across the globe"' (*The Independent*, 20 June 1999). At the time of writing (Summer 2000), Andrew Mackinlay is mounting a challenge to the chairmanship of the Parliamentary Labour Party, on the grounds that its 1997 manifesto is fully implemented 'without trimming'. He couples this with a call for ministers to listen to their own backbenchers far more and insists that strengthening the Commons select committee system of scrutiny will avoid the 'presidential' style of government that some members detect is emerging. This is not a revolt over ideology as such but more one of style.

In a climate where tax rises are ruled out by electoral exigencies, there is limited scope to tackle redistribution in an effective way. Then, the imminent dissonance between democracy and equality will rise to the forefront again (Thomas, 1998). With democratic freedom dictating the free market nexus in economic affairs, social equality considerations are relegated to a back seat. Unequal outcomes, at best, can be mitigated and even then, efforts at equalization will be denounced as infringements of freedom and enterprise. Socialism, for all its empirical failings, at least tackled these issues head-on. The Third Way, attempting to please all the people all of the time, finds itself in a cleft stick. Any sign of a move to the left will alienate the contented electorate, while concessions to wealthier sectors will cause ruptures within the ranks. The neo-socialist Left is – as we will consider below – not short of proposed solutions. The moderate centrist Left – without wishing to belittle the potentially far-reaching constitutional reforms – appears, however, destined to lose further ground. The neo-liberal ethos, as Habermas (1999: 54) observes, of 'a lifestyle attuned to the world market expecting every citizen to obtain the education he needs to become an entrepreneur managing his own human capital' seems a far cry from the objectives that the Third Way set out to achieve.

## 3 (ii) Left: negative

Radical critique starts off with the premise that 'markets cannot be democratized' (Habermas, 1999: 54). Where money counts as the ruling criterion, the wealthy will always exert more than one vote. Decisions are taken on utilitarian priorities, where considerations of fairness or justice cannot have a place. Even if gross exploitation has ceased to be prevalent in western societies, millions remain socially disenfranchised, suffer insecurity and have restricted control over their lives. Moreover, corporate capital's power has grown immeasurably in recent decades. Transnationals, hot money plus international bodies such as the IMF and the World Bank have usurped functions that were previously the preserve of nation states. Pervading the notion that 'there is no alternative' to monetarization and globalization, the Gross National Product has become the symbol of universal well-being and the supreme goal worthy of global pursuit.

The Third Way, *ipso facto*, is part of this silent conspiracy, endorsing the premise of 'the subordination of politics to the requirements of a global society unified by the market' and confining the state's role to imbuing their citizens with all the skills they need to participate actively in the quest for more wealth (Habermas, 1999: 52–3). As Giddens readily admits:

> Social democrats have to shift the relationship between risk and security involved in the welfare state, to develop a society of 'responsible risk-takers' in the spheres of government, business enterprise and labour markets ... Equality must contribute to diversity, not stand in its way (Giddens, 1998: 100).

Converting the world population into an entity of self-motivated work-committed entrepreneurs however is, as Habermas views it, an anomalous project destined to fail. Thanks to the secular process of hyper-technology, 'the end of a society based on full employment', stands well in sight. With work, apart from the relatively small sector of 'symbolic analysts', rapidly turning into a scarce commodity, trends point to 'cost-neutral projects to share the shrinking volume of available work, promote capital ownership among broad layers of the population, or institute a basic minimum wage uncoupled from real earnings and pegged to current welfare levels' (ibid: 53) – objectives, as matters stand, that are a far cry from the momentum of the Third Way.

There are three principal sources of coherent left-wing critique: the special 1998 issue of *Marxism Today*; journal articles in such as *The New Left Review*, *Socialist Alliance* and the *New Statesman*; and a small East London movement contesting local elections under the title of *3W* (Third Way). They do not reject the notion of a Third Way, but with one voice insist that the Blairite version presents a false coinage: a manifest departure from socialist principles, a submission to capitalist policy – *tout court*, a deception, deliberate or otherwise, of the electorate, a set of bland platitudes full of 'management speak' plus an enterprise destined to fail and in doing so, bound to discredit left-wing initiatives for a long time ahead. Capitalism, they argue, for all its capacity to modify in advance of major crises, by virtue of its internal contradictions, is destined to fail. Why become a party to prolonging its lifespan and damage the cause of progress and justice, by giving it a new lease of life? The time has come to learn from experience, and overcome the old Red Riding Hood fallacy: you must not get into bed with the wolf. However amiable on the outside, he will eat you in the end.

Socialist as they are, they need not necessarily reject all that is inherent in capitalism out of hand. Only an insignificant minority refuse to accept that the statist public ownership experiment has dismally failed. Technological progress – anyhow an essential component of Marxist analysis – provides instruments to keep markets in check. Indeed, it provides for progressive forces the potentiality to adapt the market system towards socialist ends. Properly cleansed of acquisitive excesses and directed towards socially committed ends, the social market – encouraging innovation and enterprise, guided towards equalization, removing exclusion while keeping inordinate accumulation in check – can embody a Third Way project where social democracy can flourish free of constraint.

The bulk of critical comment is analytic, decrying the Third Way's theoretical weakness and/or its pragmatic content. Some is specific: with proposals to reformulate the Third Way to meet socialist ends. We will review the former below, reserving specific proposals for the final chapter, devoted to ideas and initiatives to revitalize the Third Way.

Marquand indicts the Third Way as liable for inducing a 'false consciousness'. A specious notion of harmonization, where schisms prevail. 'The central fault line in modern industrial society', he argues, 'is that between the winners and the losers in the global market place. The lion's share of the extraordinary productivity gains associated with the current capitalist renaissance has gone to the owners of capital, to a new techno-managerial elite and to a handful of stars in the global entertainment industries. These are the winners: the new Lords of Creation. They want to hang on to their winnings. Most of all they want to maintain a global economic system in which they can win even more. Confronting them are the losers, the casualties of the same global system: the anxious middle classes, threatened with proletarianization; the increasingly casualized working class; and the burgeoning under-class' (Marquand, June 1999: 10). Thanks to this false ideology, people have become confused and bamboozled, and so act against their true interests.

The *Marxism Today* special 'Blair project' issue turned out to be something of a damp squib. Eminent contributors such as Jacques, Hall, Hobsbawn and Hutton barely make any points that are novel or of serious critical content. The refrain may be 'postmodern', yet the perspectives still closely follow the old-fashioned party line. The proletariat may be defunct, unions near-impotent and public ownership an experiment that failed, but any deviation is still denounced as a treacherous concession to market exigencies, an aim ultimately bound to fail. Talk of 'the new anti-market era that is now unfolding' and 'the death of neo-liberalism' does not belong to a universe where public contentment and depoliticization widely prevails. There are periodic insights such as 'it is now possible to produce the GDP with far smaller labour inputs than before' (*Marxism Today*, 1998: 7), or 'what is required is a complete reconstruction of the world financial system and the principles on which it is founded' (ibid: 29), but whether the cure lies in seeking to restore 'the manufacturing base as a stabiliser of society' (ibid: 8) or 'a world bank that can lend to countries under speculative attack without having to go through the rigmarole of ad hoc IMF-led bail outs' (ibid: 29) is, in the light of recent experience open to serious doubt. For all that, there are some telling points made in regard to the rising level of inequality. As Hutton observes: 'the language of fighting inequalities has disappeared from the public discourse ... New Labour has accepted a broadly conservative hierarchy of values: "liberty ranks first, fraternity second and trailing a very poor third is equality"' (ibid: 35). Yet in relation to the gravity of the indictment, the proposed remedies are remarkably slight: corporate governance plus stakeholding; regulation of public enterprise; the abolition of 'private schools as centres of educational excellence'; or marginal adjustment of taxation at either end of the income scale.

Radical socialists altogether deny legitimacy to the Third Way. Deliberate or otherwise – 'Thatcherism in trousers' is one of their milder epithets – they charge the Third Way with serving the interests of the capitalist class. Disenchanted with Thatcher's divisive confrontational style (and Major's insipid performance), they turned to New Labour to consolidate the fortunes of the Left. However, the 'One Nation' slogan mystifies the working class – increasingly suffering a decline in their living standards, low pay and fear of a loss of employment, whilst believing that education, modernization and globalization will equalize life chances under a government committed to progressive ends (World Socialist Web:1998). The absence of ideology becomes an advantage. Projecting itself as purposeful, well in control and endowed with a macro-perspective, the populace is lulled into an acceptance of policies that subvert its best ends. Meanwhile, the power of nation states to protect citizens' rights is 'withering away'. Market forces are no longer a bargaining interaction of competing forces but subject to manipulated demands, artificially created needs and the desire for a quick profit, while speculative inter-currency financial transactions have reached a daily volume of $1300 billion – 'fifty times greater than the volume of commercial exchanges and almost equal to the reserves of all the "national banks" throughout the world' (Bauman, 1998: 66). Grave as the indictments are – as is equally true of Callinicos's more recent article in the *New Left Review* (July–August 1999), – they tend to be weak when it comes to prescription. When not couched in out-of-reach utopian terms, they hark back to policies that have already been applied and have universally failed.

The most coherent critique comes from the 3W movement, the socialist counterpart of the Third Way. They fail Blair on four major grounds. 'Recreating Community' will not occur under conditions where inequalities have worsened rather than improved: while average incomes have risen by 42 per cent in the past twenty years, the richest 10 per cent have increased by 68 per cent, while the incomes of the poorest one-tenth have suffered a setback of 8 per cent (Northcott, 1999). The state has abdicated its responsibilities and has left it to the voluntary and private sectors to fill the gap. 'Democracy and Decentralization' are not one and the same. While people are depoliticized and debate is confined to focus groups, it matters little whether the emphasis lies on localization or centralization. Parochial administration, subject to lower levels of accountability can, in fact, be more prone to cronyism as well as corruption than central government. A 'Global Vision' is all very well, but while being 'the servant of globalized capitalism' – as it is already proving to be – it represents an ineluctable race to the bottom where indigenous workers are compelled to compete against other work-forces offering cheap labour as their main selling point. Furthermore, environmental safeguards fall by the wayside, and transnationals – lured by tax concessions and subsidies – are allowed to come and go as they please. 'The End of the Welfare State' is the final act in dismantling the advances gained in recent decades. With benefits drastically cut, universalization abandoned, workfare enforced and the poverty trap deepened, millions are left to their own devices under a system where 'winner take all' priorities are set to prevail. Meanwhile, polarization is deepening, while the prospects for social progress are distinctly worse (Harrington, 1998).

The 3W match their critique with concrete proposals on each of their enumerated points. We will review these, together with other relevant contributions in the final chapter, which is directed to projecting an updated version of the Third Way.

## References

Applebaum, A., 'A New Direction for Britain' *Political Quarterly*, Vol. 76 (2) (March–April 1997), 45–62.

Bauman, Z., *Globalization: the Human Consequences* (NY: Columbia University Press, 1998).

Beer, S.M., 'Britain after Blair', *Political Quarterly*, Vol. 68 (4) (October–December 1997), 317–25.
Blair, T., 'My Party Is More Ideologically United Than I've Ever Known It', *The Independent*: Columnists (London, 8 January 1999).
Callinicos, A., 'Social Theory Put to the Test of Politics: Pierre Bourdieu and Anthony Giddens', *New Left Review*, No. 23 (July–August 1998), 77–102.
Freeden, M., 'The Ideology of New Labour', *Political Quarterly*, Vol. 70 (1), (January–March 1999), 42–51.
Giddens, A., *The Third Way: the renewal of social democracy* (Cambridge: Polity Press, 1998).
Habermas, J., 'The European Nation-State and the Pressures of Globalization', *New Left Review*, No. 235 (May–June 1999), 46–59.
Harris, R., 'Blair's Third Way to Elected Dictatorship', *The Sunday Times* (London: 20 September 1998).
Kay, J., 'Evolutionary Politics', *Prospect* (London: July 1998), 31–4.
King, D. and M. Wickham-Jones, 'From Clinton to Blair: the Democratic (Party) Origins of Welfare to Work', *Political Quarterly*, Vol. 70 (11) (January 1999), 62–76.
Lloyd, J., 'Falling Out', *Prospect* (London: October 1999), 22–7.
Malcolm, N., 'The Third Way: No Way', *Sunday Times* (London: 4 October 1998).
Marquand, D., 'Pluralism v Populism', *Prospect* (London: June 1999), 27–31.
*Marxism Today* 'Good to be Back' (London: special issue November–December 1998), 1–39.
Massing, M., 'The End of Welfare?', *New York Review*, XLV1(15) (7 October 1999), 22–7.
Northcott, J., *Futures: Issues and Choices* (London: Polity Press, 1999).
Norton, C., 'Inequality Grows in Blair's Britain', *The Independent* (London: 25 October 1999), 19.
Ryan, A., 'Britain: Recycling the Third Way', *Dissent*, Spring 1999 (New York), 77–80.
Third Way (3W) 'The Third Way – an Answer to Blair', *The Third Way* (London: 1998).
Thomas, R., 'Equality versus Democracy', *Prospect* (London: November 1998), 14–15.
Vallely, P. *The New Catholics: Social Catholic Teaching for the 21st Century* (London: SCM Press, 1998).
World Socialist Web 'The Blair Government and the British Working Class: a year of New Labour's "third way"', Socialist Web Site (London: 6 May 1998).

# Part III
# New Times: the Way Ahead

# 7
# Social Antecedents: Communitarianism, Stakeholder Society and Social Exclusion

'A successful nation will develop new bonds of connection, of community. Even though today's world is individualised, the age of mass production over, diversity in lifestyle much more prevalent, people need communities. People need to feel a sense of belonging.'
Tony Blair, Trimdon Colliery Community Centre, Co. Durham, 29 December 1999.

## Introduction

In his New Year speech addressing his Sedgefield constituency, Tony Blair advanced the notion of Britain becoming 'a beacon for the world' in the twenty-first century by harnessing its genius for innovation, liberty, enterprise and tolerance. Future success would depend on utilizing e-commerce; developing educational excellence; strong bonds of community; a global outlook and multiracial tolerance. In outlining his vision, achievement would be a central value, creating the sort of society that 'take(s) those values that have made us great in the past and put(s) them to work making Britain succeed in the future'. One measure of ensuring achievement and pivotal to New Labour's policy has been the creation of their flagship New Deal, including the Social Exclusion Unit set up in the Cabinet Office. This combines the departmental interests of several government agencies by focusing on that most intractable of problems – the limited opportunities available for those who leave school without qualifications, in a world where new knowledge-based industries require specialized skills. The unit's initial aim of getting some 260 000 unemployed 18 to 24-year-olds off benefits and into work through the Welfare to Work scheme was warmly welcomed, and now extends to older unemployed workers.

In offering vocational training and job experience so that the 'socially excluded' compete more effectively in the labour market the unit has achieved some success, especially in enhancing 'employability' skills. However, the gain in permanent full-time jobs is limited. Critics argue that falling numbers of young people in the population at large, plus a growing economy would, in any case, have secured the desired result. Drop-out rates remain high, with 'churning' from one training scheme to another commonplace, while the quality of the jobs secured are often unsatisfactory. Two further caveats need noting. Many new jobs are incapable of sustaining a living wage with access to affordable transport and child care; and disturbingly, over 160 000 youngsters have simply 'disappeared' from official figures. Youth unemployment epitomizes the very antithesis of community cohesion and vitality, leading to out-migration of those seeking work elsewhere, or to the negative values accompanying social alienation and dislocation.

The socially excluded is Labour's less contentious notion of what Americans call the underclass – an undifferentiated term implying, within the US context, a somewhat misleading racial dimension, and divorce from mainstream society, by those whose behaviour is socially deviant and often welfare dependent. In the UK, better welfare support has limited the extent of exclusion, and the concept lacks the overtly racial dimension, but it does imply a failure of those on benefit to take up what opportunities are available. By definition, the excluded tend to be less powerful, and so less able to challenge the stereotypes attributed to them by government or media. The complex roots feeding inequality and exclusion rarely fit any neat social categorization. The suspicion remains that Labour is converting a former wider concern with equality, including the idea that some degree of equality of outcome is necessary for future opportunity, to one narrowing the vision to a politics of inclusion. Targeting absolute poverty, rather than the relative position of the poor leaves, unchecked, growing income disparities.

The preceding years of Conservative rule focusing government policy on incentives and tax reductions relatively neglected this growing problem. A refrain uttered by the Left, and also by 'one nation' Tories, was concern with community fracture and the erosion of tradition by the creative destruction of newly unleashed market forces. The 'excluded' were far more heterogeneous than at first realized: ranging from poor single mothers, and pensioners struggling on inadequate state support, to city-based youngsters and redundant industrial workers prematurely 'retired', and those stuck on dispirited post-war council estates on the outer fringes of the major metropolitan areas chronically lacking amenities and jobs. Many suffer from the sheer confusion of coping with the myriad problems thrown up by today's society, and distressingly find themselves pitted against each other in order to survive. Working-class solidarity is no more. The enormous economic and industrial changes between 1979 and up to the present, saw unemployment peak at over 3 million. Even today, when that figure has been halved, residual pockets of severe social disadvantage are still evident. Labour identified this as a major problem to be tackled, along with Blair's wider promise to eliminate child and family poverty within twenty years, by delineating 40 indicators of poverty – both relative and absolute – by which government progress would be measured.

The new Chancellor acted quickly to tax the windfall profits of the privatized utility companies, funding what in effect is a policy innovation and key modernizing element of Third Way reform. The New Deal's stress on opportunity allied to work (including the new National Minimum Wage), incorporates ideas on welfare reform which owes something to American experience, as does the new means-tested Working Families Tax Credit, rewarding those who stay employed. In doing so, it secures the crucial political approval of the middle class who believe in supporting individual effort. Increase in child benefit is coupled with better provision for Ofsted-inspected child-care facilities under the Sure Start programme. The emphasis is on self-reliance, and a more structured and dignified life, made possible through work and its discipline. The more positive image this promotes, within family life and parental role-modelling, is central to building successful communities, whilst recognizing the disappearance of the traditional nuclear family and the idea of secure lifetime employment. It moves Labour's social policy into more politically acceptable territory, beyond the blanket commitments associated with past social democracy, and the more narrowly conceived individualistic agenda of the New Right.

These ideas once formed part of an earlier, and perhaps more ambitious project that Labour flirted with when in opposition – on the one hand, the communitarianism of Amitai Etzioni, and on the other, the German notion of stakeholding advanced in the United Kingdom by Will Hutton. Both have been eclipsed in recent Labour thinking by a more pragmatic and deliverable political agenda. Before analysing further the policy on social exclusion we must consider these earlier influences on Labour thinking, as the former ran counter to the grain of traditional Labour centralism, while the latter may have reinforced it.

## 1. Communitarianism

Following the unprecedented changes to the economies of the USA and UK during the Reagan–Thatcher era, commentators worried over the deleterious consequences that unleashing a more market-led approach to economic management might bring about. The negative impact on communal life, threatened by downsizing and company relocation, guaranteed that communitarian criticism was given wide press coverage. The causal agents of change are, it must be noted, not just rampant capitalism *per se*. Other identifiable agencies included the rise of the information age, female liberation and the widespread influence of television – both as a moulder of opinion and as a means of furthering active disengagement from social life. In the USA, Amitai Etzioni brought the issue of communitarianism to a wider public by focusing on the notion of greater social inclusion and community cohesion, at a time when both were under duress. In challenging the ruling liberal rights-based agenda, his critique extended to the growing selfishness of an American society, exclusively concerned with individual self-realization, at the expense of the wider society. By the mid-1990s, many of the leading political figures in the West were under his spell, in particular the emerging star of New Labour – Tony Blair. Yet for all that, the influence of communitarianism in practice has been muted in the marketplace of party politics, and little of substance has emerged from its early flirtation with the political leadership class.

One obvious drawback has been the continuing vitality of the market in securing relatively low levels of unemployment in both societies, and the limited 'common sense' agenda endorsed by communitarian analysis with its tendency to romanticize the past. Another limitation is that this type of analysis fits an American individual rights-based context better than the more dirigiste-collectivist traditions operative within European society. President George Bush, in his inaugural address, mysteriously proclaimed 'a thousand points of light' would act as a beacon, offsetting the evident lack of government support at local level by encouraging the compensatory mechanism of voluntary endeavour. Similarly, President Clinton endorsed, albeit briefly in 1993 the so-called 'new covenant', which addressed the economic fears of middle America by proclaiming many radical communitarian objectives, including support for a new volunteer spirit. The programme, as such, never really developed, and the early failure of health-care reform was a mortal blow, but his success in generating sustainable employment won him many plaudits, yet without any real redress of widening levels of inequality.

Communitarians focus on the loss of community life, of the decline in moral worth and the commodification of society's values at the expense of older internalized virtues, such as a belief in order, religious observance and family stability. Gertrude Himmelfarb in *The De-Moralization of Society* (1995) sharply criticizes the emergence of contemporary values at the expense of Victorian virtues, which were expressive of self-reliance, thrift, hard work, patriotism and family life. Excessive 'liberal individualism' promotes values which are ego-dictated, can be assumed and discarded at will, and are the necessary accompaniment to a rapidly changing materialist way of life that is destructive of communal existence. A rights-based culture does little to sustain the mutual bonds of obligation and duty that all of us owe to each other, and to the society we live and work in. Another peculiarly American element is the collapse of class politics and its replacement by the zero-sum game of identity politics – along the lines of race, ethnicity, gender, age group or sexual preference which, according to Michael Piore in his aptly named *Beyond Individualism*, have destroyed rational planning, undermined social cohesion and even threaten national identity (1995). By contrast, communitarians stress the social perspective, and the practical responsibility of rebuilding communities (and families) at local neighbourhood level. By mobilizing churches and encouraging voluntary support agencies – the infrastructure of civic society – they can act as important building blocks of cooperative activity and trust, so providing the necessary key to social harmony. This sustains localized democratic control and responsibility, while channelling upwards citizen demands into the national arena against the all-powerful central state. The emphasis is determinedly on what works eschewing liberal abstractions.

Jonathan Freedland of the *Guardian*, suggests that this represents America's own version of the Third Way. Historically, power flows up – in true de Tocqueville fashion – from the grass roots and not down from the top, as is true of Britain together with other western democracies. The separation of powers, and weak party structure, linked to traditions of local elections right down to minor posts, expresses the principle of popular sovereignty far better than leftist utopias, which at the very least involve disruptive change. For Britain, Freedland argues, acts such as the abolition of the monarchy to get rid of the 'hierarchical pyramid', a second elected chamber, a written constitution with a charter of rights, plus devolution right down to the grass roots would serve the cause of social equality far better than structural tinkering, which would revive the agonies of the class war (1998). Labour has partially moved to accommodate this prescription with its devolution agenda. However, as Robert Putnam argues, much is amiss as other factors impinge on the problem. Ubiquitous television ownership since the 1950s, with the average American watching at least four hours daily, has led to active civic disengagement, with a fall in political participation, less socializing outside the home and with fewer joining voluntary organizations in an increasingly privatized society (1996); trends equally discernible in the UK. Organizations such as the Boy Scouts, PTAs and other volunteer activities are in free fall, replaceable by anonymous professional fund-raisers. Even participation in organized worship, despite its apparent stability, shows signs of waning, especially the outward-looking main-line churches that are losing ground to more evangelical, but inwardly focused, congregations. Moreover, diminishing social capital – the erosion of formal and informal 'social connectedness' – is evidenced by stressed-out families and isolated individuals 'bowling alone', and made more visible as the attitude that formed the Second World War 'civic generation' fades from memory. Employers and policy-makers urgently need to develop family-friendly and community-congenial policies – as much out of self-interest as with a need to restore civil society – because diminishing trust and civic-mindedness have been replaced by more lawyers, police and other agencies of law enforcement to combat rising crime and disorder (Putnam, 2000).

Both Thatcher and Reagan in the 1980s attempted to reinstate 'Victorian virtues' as a way back to 'the world we have lost' and achieved some success within the economic and political spheres. Yet in regard to the moral dimension their injunction fell on deaf ears, with critics understandably decrying the unrelenting drudgery and toil of Victorian society, coupled with its moral hypocrisy and denial of opportunity for so many excluded categories of people. Yet few today remain indifferent to some of the more negative counter-cultural effects of wide-open permissiveness, moral relativism and mockery of public norms which have indeed been inimical to community life and which Himmelfarb ascribes to a 'values society'.

One important influence on the communitarian debate has been the writer Francis Fukuyama. His work emphasizes how social trust precedes any worthwhile economic transaction by providing the necessary social capital which people draw upon to sustain a rich associational existence. Without social cooperation and agreed ethical standards, company formation and voluntary effort are impossible. His writings criticize the excesses of the late 1980s, when patterns of cooperation between owners, employees, customers and suppliers were wantonly destroyed by the new prevailing economic dogmas. The most extreme antithesis of community is seen by 'the contemporary black underclass in America today represents what is perhaps one of the most thoroughly atomized societies that has existed in human history' (Fukuyama, 1995: 303). Within the inner city there are few functioning intermediate-level organizations that usually play a vital part in cohering the social order such as mainstream churches, clubs or libraries. Life is the Hobbesian nightmare characterized by lawlessness and brutality, where no one trusts anyone, and where communities rot through lack of work, investment, morale and opportunity. William Finnegan's research in the USA, similarly depicts a bleak constricted 'cold new world' for many youngsters, lacking connection to anything, except the ephemeral community of the gang, which makes their eventual reintegration into the mainstream difficult (1999).

In Fukuyama's *The Great Disruption* (1999), the central concern lies with the family and the changing position of women in society. From the mid-1960s until the early 1990s, most western industrial societies experienced a similar pattern of declining social and moral cohesion. The social indicators were: steeply rising crime, divorce and illegitimacy rates spiralling upwards, fragmenting family life, diminishing fertility, and a general loss of faith in public institutions which were being more challenged than ever before, and so became legitimate matters for public concern. The one linking explanation for this calamitous loss of moral and social trust lay in the transition to the information age. He writes as follows:

> ... the Great Disruption was an updated version of the transition from *gemeinschaft* to *gesellschaft* that occurred during the nineteenth century, only this time taking place as we move from an industrial to an information economy rather than from an agrarian to an industrial one. ... Changes in technology – the substitution of mental for physical labor, information for material product, services for manufacturing, as well as medical advances that allowed people to live longer and to control reproduction – laid the basis for the enormous shift in sex roles that has taken place in the second half of the twentieth century (ibid.: 128–9).

One of the casualties in the transition has been the erosion of 'social capital' defined as:

> a set of informal values or norms shared among members of a group that permits cooperation among them. If members of the group come to expect that others will behave reliably and honestly, then they will come to *trust* one another. Trust is like the lubricant that makes the running of any group or organization more efficient' (ibid.: 16).

Central to understanding the 'Great Disruption' has been a culture of individualism taken to excess, and increasing life expectancy. But perhaps most critically of all, it is the growing participation of women – now enjoying more freedom and opportunity – in gaining employment in the growing service sector coupled with their new-found ability to control their own fertility. The Pill enabled women, like men before them, to engage in sexual adventurism both within and outside the family, but without courting the risks of unwanted pregnancy. Furthermore, working women with their own family now felt confident enough to raise their children alone if need be, without being reliant on the economic contribution of a male partner. As family life fragmented so it impacted negatively on all, while poorer younger males whose expectations of future secure employment were vanishing became disproportionately locked into criminality. Fukuyama argues that the normative basis of social existence can be reconfigured, regenerating both trust and social capital by acknowledging that moral changes in behaviour, though cyclical over time, can be enforced when necessary through public concern and action. Thus severe social dislocation in early Victorian Britain and the USA was met by evangelical re-moralization, instilling more strait-laced 'Victorian values' which resulted in a more orderly society later. Emperor worship in Japan during the Meiji restoration acted in a similar fashion, as do the ascription of 'traditional' roles to women in Japan today.

Today a similar catching up of moral and cultural change, set against the pace of technological advance, is necessary and may already have been occurring since the mid-1990s. For example, many of the factors cited such as increases in crime (notoriously difficult to gauge with accuracy) and family breakdown have been self-correcting. Fukuyama himself recognizes that crime statistics have fallen dramatically in the USA in the last five years, as have other indices of social pathology, indicating that the Great Disruption is drawing to an end. The unresolved question is whether re-moralization has already begun, as individualism becomes reined in by public action, or have we become more acclimatized to the new normative requirements of the information age, as we learn to adapt and become flexible? Many feminists are dismissive of this interpretation with its imputed threat to their hard-won freedoms, a hostility which extends to much communitarian analysis.

Central to this debate has been the influential contribution of Amitai Etzioni. His work stands mid-way between market-based individualism, and older conservative notions of order, centred around tradition and community respect. His 'golden rule' invokes respect for, and the upholding of, society's moral order, as you would have it respect and uphold your autonomy, plus the good society needs an equilibrium of order and autonomy with neither maximized at the expense of the other (1998). He articulates a community of communities in which people have multiple and fluid memberships which can be changed if autonomy is threatened. In attacking self-centred, me-istic orientations he proffers 'a set of 'do's and don'ts, a set of moral values, that guides people toward what is decent and encourages them to avoid that which is not' (1994: 24).The movement's aim is 'shoring up the moral, social and political environment. Part change of heart, part renewal of social bonds, part reform of social life' (ibid.: 245). The specific prescriptions seem limited – reducing the cost of running for office, more public scrutiny, rebuilding communities and intermediate associations and restoring family life. Predicated on ideas of self-help and individual responsibility, the enemy is as much the central state as the unfettered rule of the market, glorifying consumer choice, but nowhere is the logic of structural change and economic reform faced squarely.

Within the communitarian movement priorities are divergent within its in-house journal *The Responsive Community*. Some would restrict individual freedom, others would control divorce to sustain the two-parent family, or refocus attention on the marginalized underclass. However, Etzioni himself is clearly against compulsion, but how then can miscreants be made to conform if their behaviour is merely anti-social rather than illegal? How can individual and social responsibility be encouraged? In *The Limits of Privacy* (1999), privacy, as an individual right, should not be accorded a privileged status in formulating government policy, but viewed as one good among others in determining the common good. The greatest threat to privacy is not government, but the private sector, operating and compiling secretive dossiers on us as consumers. What we need, he argues, is more access to how this information is obtained and recorded, balancing individual rights with social responsibility.

In Britain the banner of communitarianism was held aloft by David Selbourne. He argues that liberalism is corrupted and socialism overtly state-dominated and epitomized by claims of duty-less rights, demand satisfaction (the economics of benefits), and ego-gratification through unimpeded freedom of action. In championing the rebirth of duty as the sovereign principle of civic order 'usurped from above' by supranational bureaucrats and state apparatuses, and from below by the undermining of the civic bond by the increasing dominance of the a-civic and anti-social 'universal plebeian' (1994: 40), Selbourne advocates a new civic-social-ism which is neither left nor right, as a means of warding off civic disaggregation of the citizen-turned-stranger. In a similar vein, John Wallis from within the Ecumenical movement, has called for a fusion of politics with morality, of reconnecting personal values with public morality in a new 'politics of community' (1995). Meanwhile, John Gray vigorously argued for a reinstatement of 'one nation' politics against the then prevailing Conservative practice (1994). In all of the above sincerely felt concern, there is a fear of the social order becoming anomic. While the critique hits the target regularly, the prevalence of widespread inequality, though deplored, is nevertheless left with an inadequate response. Correspondingly, critics either see the movement as one identified with the professional middle class (Gerber, 1995), or dismissively by *The Economist* as 'nostalgia for a partly imaginary past'. For others it represents in its anti-liberal authoritarian invective a threat to civil rights and non-conformity, especially towards women (Coote, 1995).

Communities can just as easily be oppressive and insular – be they based on allegiance to workplace, religion, social grouping or place – while also offering a retreat rather than greater involvement in the wider society. Furthermore, current trends in family and community life are, if anything, in reverse. People work longer hours, with dual family employment, longer commuting, experiencing rising levels of stress, are employed on limited work-time contracts, often without recourse to adequate benefits, all of which are hardly conducive to family stability and community participation. Time becomes a scarce commodity not readily traded for voluntary activity. Community values and a sense of 'being amongst one's own' often only take on real meaning for people over 40, as persistent high levels of youth unemployment ravage community life leading to outward migration, dislocation and alienation (Vallely, 1997). At a more prosaic level the rise of the out-of-town shopping mall or supermarket, coupled with growing suburbanization, reflects the ubiquity of car ownership, but has a deadly knock-on effect for the 'traditional high street' both in the USA and United Kingdom.

With deference gone, a sense of belonging being eroded, traditional authority challenged and middle-class professionalism becoming subject to external scrutiny, the readily 'taken-for-granted' consensus, is now much more difficult to engender in today's pluralistic and divergent culture. Clearly communitarianism has tapped into a well of discontent, but its panacea is much too voluntaristic to succeed. The means to rectifying analytically defined problems are left to a 'social compact', which locates power at the grass-roots level and is too vague to have any meaningful confrontation with the status quo. In the final analysis, is the movement one of personal regeneration, or does it involve structural change, and a challenge to establishment interests beyond moral prescription and symbolic action? Much of Labour's agenda is conventionally conceived in governmental terms, paying little attention to newer radical social movements, such as feminism or environmentalism, which employ newer forms of voluntaristic localized democracy beyond the traditional remit of the state. By way of contrast, Labour in moving into the 'one nation' territory, so successfully monopolized by the Conservatives, promotes the language of personal responsibility, self-help and economic common sense, while demonizing irresponsible behaviour, employing containment politics and falling prey to charges of authoritarianism (Swanson, 2000). Thus early attempts at welfare reform focused on the disabled and on vulnerable single parents struggling with young children, where inadequate state support does little to alleviate poverty and family crisis. Opportunity to work is important, but equally paramount are the needs of the young family, and getting the balance right is vital.

Communitarian discourse is inadequate if it ignores persistent poverty and structural inequality. The fear of anomie and desire for social cohesion is dependent on forging a moral consensus, which communitarians rightly see the market as singularly incapable of developing by itself, a dilemma still unresolved for New Labour. At a time when significant sections of British industry from cars to textiles have been hit by plant closures resulting in redundancy, following foreign-owned corporate decisions, the knock-on effect for the local community is devastating. The work community has a centrality in most people's lives which are becoming noticeably more stressful, as work and social/family life become squeezed by growing employer demands.

Flexibility within work, granting employees some autonomy over their own time management, is crucial to reducing stress and enhancing family cohesion. Communitarian discourse needs to address this concern as much as it attends to moralistic questions. If economic reform is talked of then complementary ideas of stakeholding can be invoked, but, like communitarianism, only by way of passing reference, and rarely in a consistent manner, despite the preparatory work of Liddle and Mandelson (1996) emphasizing the idea of teamwork in companies, local neighbourhoods and wider society.

## 2. Stakeholding

> 'At the heart of the stakeholder concept lies the simple proposition that property must discharge obligations to the wider community as well as to its owners ...'.
>
> David Marquand, *The Independent*, 15 January 1996.

Much political debate since the collapse of communism has been over what type of market capitalism should be adopted, and where exactly the remit of the state should extend in terms of regulation, mindful that its operations are constantly judged by the global financial markets. The British left flirted with French indicative planning in the 1960s, Swedish-style social democracy in the 1980s and today German ideas of stakeholding based on security and inclusion are influential. Given the communitarian concern over social solidarity, frayed by economic individualism, a new means to resurrect social citizenship values as denoted by T.H. Marshall becomes imperative. Basically Marshall argued that earlier won rights to individual freedom (the civic rights secured in the eighteenth century) and access to political power (the political rights won in the nineteenth century) needed supplementing in the twentieth century by social rights – a modicum of welfare and security, a share in the social heritage, plus enjoyment of the life of a civilized being according to prevailing standards (Marshall, 1965). This latter category in particular is seen as being under threat as universal welfare rights are curtailed, and income and wealth becomes more unequal. The question raised for New Labour and other proponents of the Third Way, is whether a new role can be found for the state – not in terms of public ownership – but by building on the creative resources of the people in which the state becomes a long-term shareholder, cajoling where necessary, investing for growth and directing human capital to offset incipient insecurity.

In a speech in Singapore in early January 1996, Blair spoke approvingly of the stakeholder economy 'run for the many, not for the few ... in which opportunity is available to all ...'. This umbrella term was the benchmark by which new policies would be assessed, although its meaning was by no means clear. Initial Conservative reaction either castigated it as a sop to the unions and other interests by restoring their former powers, or as something Mrs Thatcher had previously advocated with her ideas of widening share ownership and the sale of council housing. On the left, the strongest advocates of this approach are John Kay and Will Hutton. John Kay in *The Foundations of Corporate Success* views stakeholding as capitalism with a social conscience, providing a necessary ethical dimension which the importation of American-style capitalism under Thatcher had eroded. He advocates a form of social accounting in which the responsibilities of directors of companies would be to improve the skills of their employees and suppliers, while enhancing the provision of quality goods and services at fair prices to the company's customers.

Will Hutton has led a similar crusade from the pages of *The Guardian* and later *The Observer*, both papers approvingly owned by trusts. With his best-seller *The State We're In*, he rigorously attacked Britain's financial system and attempted to rebuild the case 'for redistributive taxation to achieve public purpose and relieve the growth of poverty'. Central to his writing is the interplay between constitutional questions and redefining adequate modern citizenship rights along with their accompanying cultural values. Hutton is anxious to move away from the reductionism of *homo economicus* and individualized consumption by stressing our social natures within the workplace and society at large. Later, in a summary of his, *The State to Come*, six stakeholding propositions were advanced: 'the same value systems apply in employment and other spheres of life; macroeconomic policy needs to tighten the demand for labour; a market economy needs democratic institutions that generate social capital, particularly trust; businesses function best on the basis of internal commitment and trust; "intermediate institutions" like universities need to generate social capital and provide a long-term perspective; and systems of social insurance and distribution of risk must be fair and inclusive' (Hutton, 1997: 1).

The Anglo-Saxon economies place a central role on choice, on maximizing shareholder value often, it is alleged, at the expense of company employees, customers, suppliers and the local community within which the firm is located. This breeds short-term attitudes, fuelled by a stockmarket culture fed on mergers and take-overs, which are not conducive to developing the long-term interests and growth of the firm, its employees or nation. The institutional framework is one of deregulated labour markets, a system of training and education mostly independent of company interests within a highly competitive environment. British and American experience of corporate purpose, solely serving the interests of investors, is compared unfavourably with the German model. There the board of directors consult widely all interested partners and not just shareholders, as many are represented on supervisory boards and workers' councils in larger companies. The rationale for building long-term investment strategies and training is made possible, as the capital markets are less intrusive in decision-making.

Stakeholding is not a return to the corporatist state, but is one of shared problem-solving or co-determination, in which no one – including even the bankers – is dominant, and where employees have a stake through enhanced security, training and participation. In the United Kingdom this would mean sharing managerial power and the responsibility that goes with it, so that for example, the debilitating trade union/employer confrontations of the past could be avoided. Trade union power in the 1970s threatened other stakeholders, whereas the later Conservative reforms tilted the balance too far towards shareholders as seen by the upward rating of share prices following on company rationalization where employees became first victims of any downsizing. The model of German (or Japanese) stakeholding, carefully nurturing company formation and success through building a corporate culture of trust and loyalty, finds an echo in the UK, where more enlightened companies have already developed along these lines. However, many companies would need the active spur of new legislation – tax breaks to sustain long-term investment, more accountability, stakeholder rights involving consultation, if such a system were adopted here.

Critics of stakeholding suggest that most people prefer clear property rights, and an enhanced shareholder role, to those of simply being another voice in decision-making, where the responsibility of ownership becomes confused so that no one is accountable to anyone and where genuine conflicts of interest may well exist. In the new information age a vibrant entrepreneurial culture offers more to newer footloose companies than last year's model, based on a male-dominated lifetime employment pattern. Thus, nearly three-quarters of US growth in 1999 was generated by new sectors of the economy which did not exist a decade earlier, by a plethora of companies developing commercial applications for new technology (McRae, 2000). German or Japanese-style capitalism is more heavy-industry dominated, and umbilically tied into its banking system for long-term finance, with a history of relationships stretching back over many years, than the more decentralized Anglo-Saxon service sector economy where capital is usually raised through the market. In building long-term cooperative relationships, Germany (and Japan) promote seniority, lifetime employment and in-house training for their core employees. Companies also develop a web of cross-shareholdings binding suppliers and customers together (the Japaneses *keiretsu*), and focus on coordinated planning and investing long term.

All of this is now under severe pressure as the 'New Economy' replaces the old. Nothing is more illustrative of this than Vodafone's successfully contested bid for Mannesmann of Germany in early February 2000, where the 60 per cent of foreign-held shares was decisive to the result. Since then the capital gains tax on the sale of large shareholdings has been abolished, paving the way for the break-up of Germany's large conglomerates. Developments such as this, coupled with the achievements of the Neuer Markt and the newly proposed merger of the Frankfurt stock market with London, easier access to venture capital and the first stirrings of corporate and income tax reform, indicate that change is coming. However, recent research indicates that Germany is not yet a globalized economy, nor is it adopting the Anglo-Saxon model, and even with more decentralized industrial relations still operates within a social partnership framework. Affiliates of TNCs are now given greater autonomy and a more decentralized network of operations suggesting that incremental 'hybridization' is becoming the norm (Lane, 2000).

Across the EU, shareholder capitalism is rapidly taking hold: hostile take-overs, leveraged buy-outs, mergers (worth \$1.2 trillion in 1999, a rise of 50 per cent on a year earlier), foreign stock market listings to raise cheaper capital and also a general pull-out of corporate lending by banks. There is still some way to go as inward foreign direct investment (FDI) still favours the Dutch or British model of flexibility. The former has, as the OECD 2000 Employment report confirms, some 29.1 per cent of its workforce part-time, as against an EU average of only half of that. In Britain, FDI is eight times that of Germany.

Economic growth was higher in the Anglo-Saxon economies during the 1990s, with markedly lower levels of unemployment including higher job creation, more opportunities for women, growing availability of stock options, faster company formation and, especially in the

US, a 'can do' flexible attitude coupled with a low corporate tax rate. The UK benefits from low employment costs and greater labour flexibility which negatively translates into a large pool of non-unionized relatively cheap and unskilled labour. This is often at the expense of good technical training – so much an achievement of German industry – where the fear of poaching skilled workers deters extensive in-house schemes. The emphasis in the UK on the 'new economy' of knowledge-based 'thin-air' services, focused around information and communications technology, is epitomized by the 'portfolio worker': self-employed, subject to frequent job change and often employed outside the older corporate world. Commentators attribute sluggish economic growth until recently in Germany, to an over-regulated social market economy, high domestic wage costs, lack of labour mobility, and an over-dependency on a manufacturing model ill-suited to 'the weightless world of new technology, of soft skills and service jobs that will be the wealth-creators of the twenty-first century' (Smith and Bischof, 1999).

In the light of the CDU scandal engulfing the former Chancellor Helmut Kohl, the German public is understandably outraged at the close links forged between big business and the political system. This involved slush funds and secret funding of parties, with links extending to foreign countries and their companies. In both Germany and Japan notes *The Economist*, a recognition that stakeholding conceals problems that more rigorous Anglo-Saxon accounting systems reveal, and increasing global competition exposes, is leading a return to shareholder value. The 'ageing of the Japanese population ... is likely to create a huge demand for cash from the pension system, which will be forthcoming only if firms pay higher dividends' (10 February 1996: 25). The meltdown in the Far East has impacted negatively on Japan's already faltering economy. It is suffering from endemic deflation, rising government deficits and negligible growth, and has ignominiously been given the sobriquet of 'crony capitalism' because of a patent lack of transparency and a reliance on 'old boy' networks of influence which act to shut out effective outside criticism and scrutiny.

Critics further suggest that stakeholding would resurrect the directive role of the state into all areas of life, and is too authoritarian in seeking new ways to enforce community obligations in a more diverse society. David Green charges that Hutton's ideas on social inclusion are coded reference to maintaining public sector monopoly – destructive of diversity, individual initiative and family responsibility. The avoidance of centralism allows experimentation at the local civic level by reinvigorating voluntary effort, and organizations such as friendly societies would once again flourish (Green, 1997, 1998). The experience of existing mutual organizations, be they building societies or financial organizations where customers in effect own the business, have if anything, been following a policy which is the opposite of stakeholding by seeking ways to demutualize in order to raise new forms of capital more effectively and enhance efficiency.

In the USA, stakeholding ideas associated with the work of Robert Reich, the ex-Labour Secretary in Clinton's cabinet, are a means to expanding the 'social responsibilities' of large companies, at a time when the state is being downsized and is no longer trusted to run new training programmes. Thus costs are hidden by passing them on to consumers, even though it may result in a loss of business competitiveness. However, many of these critiques are disfigured and limited by the assumption that everything private is positive and the public *per se* is bad – even though it is underpinned by democratic legitimacy.

Finally, some sections of the Left remain unconvinced. Stakeholding is depicted as an ideological construct, masking the power of capital, and is wedded to the market and its insoluble contradictions. Thereby an exaggerated role is assigned to the 'stake' workers and trade unionists supposedly command in corporate governance. By the 1990s, to sustain competitiveness with the advent of globalization, corporations downsized a supine labour force, bereft of adequate trade union protection, even within stakeholding German companies. By decentralizing wage bargaining to the level of the firm and aligning costs more closely to their needs, they undercut trade union membership which fell from 33 to 25 per cent of the workforce in the 1990s (Budd, 1997).

Clearly such a change in the United Kingdom would involve worker representation on company boards, diluting shareholder rights which New Labour would not countenance. It would need radical changes in corporate governance so that all stakeholders, including existing shareholders, would be viewed as legitimate partners. Change would even extend to local and central government as the former enjoyed greater economic freedom to encourage local enterprises. So far Labour allows a 'public interest' criterion when takeovers are threatened, has toughened competition and regulatory rules, and employs more watchdogs on the privatized utilities which enjoy near-monopoly status. The delayed response on stakeholder pensions, designed to attract younger, poorer workers, lacking a company pension scheme, and solely reliant on their national insurance contributions to give them a state pension when they retire, is becoming urgent as the state pension is grossly inadequate, unless supplemented further. But for the moment stakeholding is not central to Labour's programme, nor is there much evidence that directly incorporating this model into company law will ever take place. If anything, New Labour has shown little interest in the wider picture. Its 'big ideas are at the level of superstructure, not base' being more pragmatically interested in what works and enabling people to help themselves (Lloyd, 1999: 27).

On the periphery some stakeholding ideas, like those of communitarianism, have influenced the mind-set of Labour politicians, but as yet there is little direct action. Constitutional reform devolving powers away from Whitehall will allow for more local initiative, but the deeper truth is that uninterrupted economic growth since 1992 is hardly propitious for proponents of change. Why change a winning strategy and would it ever 'fit' the differing cultures of the United Kingdom (and USA)? Thus, as noted (in Chapter 4), the one major study actually recommending stakeholding in the USA of course viewed it differently. Give every high school graduate $80 000 to finance college, set up a business or use it in any way they choose in what would constitute a new form of economic citizenship. This 'stake' though eventually repayable would equalize opportunity and positively influence the behaviour of the young (Ackerman and Alstott, 1998). Nearly half of all Americans now have an 'equity stake' through wider levels of share ownership, facilitated by the onset of Internet dealing, and this acts as a spur to maintaining managerial efficiency, without recourse to the cumbersome apparatus of further state regulation. The huge net increase in jobs at over 22 million in the Clinton era, fuelled by easy access to venture capital, with private sector investment at record highs, has finally 'trickled down' employment opportunities to the underclass. Admittedly this has not brought social equalization, in fact the reverse. But it does afford some legitimacy for staying with the present market-led approach, despite growing evidence of the limits to environmental sustainability and a lack of social justice which all centre-left governments are wrestling to contain, and were vividly brought to the world media's attention at the Seattle WTO meeting in 1999.

## 3. Social exclusion

The 1990s saw the publication of a series of major reports on the problems of growing poverty, wealth and income distribution, including reference to the problem of social cohesion: the Commission on Social

Justice (1994), Rowntree(1995) and Dahrendorf(1995). All three reports influenced Labour thinking on social exclusion. All three reports while highlighting that inequality of opportunity and structural barriers to achievement, damage long-term economic prospects, offered what Levitas calls a basically 'social integrationist discourse'. The focus has gradually shifted away from economic redistribution to questions of a lack of work, low pay and the behavioural (or moral inadequacy) of those seeking or avoiding the work that is actually available. Unpaid work, though recognized as important, has became downgraded as economically unproductive, though admittedly vital to social cohesion (Levitas, 1998). Poverty is concerned with economic distribution and a lack of resources, while social exclusion is as much about relational issues following on from a lack of power and a perceived lack of social efficacy. Economic disadvantage and deprivation are becoming spatial, with cities fragmented by ghettoised council estates lacking amenities and served by failing schools, yet existing alongside the gentrifying splendours of urban renewal. Women in particular suffer constraints through inadequate child-care provision, often compounded by dual household unemployment ('workless households' comprised some 18 per cent of the total in 1999), or alternatively if employed were subject to low wages (Smith, 1997). At the bottom of society many women bear the burdens associated with dysfunctional families and often without adequate support from their partner if children are involved. This has placed enhanced responsibilities on the schools as primary agents of socialization as they try to compensate for inadequate parenting.

Social exclusion and the 'new poverty' is associated in the European Commission's eyes with widespread economic restructuring, new family formation and social networks which have 'informalized' much of the labour market. Social exclusion is about process and what exactly leads to marginalization, and is not simply connected to poverty. Many of the poor are socially included (such as pensioners), while there are those outside of poverty excluded because of racial prejudice or social stigmatization. Poverty is usually central though expressed in many ways, and reconnecting people to the mainstream via income or employment or other social supports is crucial. EU social policy is concerned with the 'inadequate realization of social rights', not just a lack of income, with access to a decent standard of living including health care, housing, education and general household participation. Thus social exclusion means the inability to fully realize citizenship rights, although the actual provision and definition of these rights varies enormously across the EU. Beneath Labour's 'flexibility' rhetoric the government has in fact signed up to the EU social chapter, including directives on working time, parental leave, new union and individual work rights which redress some of the insecurities built into the individual work situation. More critically, however, the setting of the new minimum wage at an unrealistically low level, opens them to the charge of adopting a strategy of two steps forward but one step back.

Keynesians argue for an adequate system of income support available through social security to sustain the unemployed. But the bureaucratic costs, imputed disincentives to work and welfare dependency so consistently argued from the political right have curtailed many such welfare rights. The political battleground is how far the state should compensate for, or mitigate, market and individual failure through the welfare state. How far should benefits replace average earnings following on from an involuntary lack of work with de-commodification a realistic alternative? De-commodification is defined as 'the extent to which individuals and their families can sustain a normal, socially accepted standard of living regardless of their ability to participate in the labour market' and in effect is a measurement of the strength of citizens' rights and entitlements. The United Kingdom is relatively generous in terms of housing and child benefit, but unemployment benefit is abysmally low with the most vulnerable being single or unemployed couples (Fawcett and Papadopoulos, 1997). Social protection has been notably limited over the past two decades, with a 'residual' model of welfare adopted despite the widespread economic restructuring. Against this background Labour assumed power in 1997 and quickly reacted to widespread concern with the growing problem of a youth 'underclass'. This is a highly loaded term and one not simply conceptualized in deviant terms, as causation and motivation are complex. Commentators as a rule argue that the 'underclass' is embryonic rather than fully developed, but could one day become so (MacDonald, 1997).

The multicultural complexity and fluidity of British society defies any easy identification of those groups at risk of poverty and its 'multiple' deprivations. Disadvantage is positively correlated with a lack of qualifications, disproportionately associated with ethnic minorities, single pensioners and lone parents, and is often highly localized. Securing a national agenda which in itself is inclusive, while paying attention to local and more targeted programmes, is a difficult task made more so by governmental departmentalization and increasing fragmentation through the 'contracting out' of many services.

Professional barriers need eliminating through joint training, and a recognition of 'joined-up policies' so no one slips through the cracks. Plans have already been announced for merging the Benefits Agency with the Employment Service, facilitating an American-style 'workfare' system. This is ostensibly tailored to meeting individual needs through personal advisers in 'one-stop shops', thereby inculcating personal independence and responsibility amongst claimants. Many new initiatives have already started including: Crime and Disorder Partnerships, Supporting Families Initiative, Sure Start, Family Literacy, Employment action zones and a new national Children's Fund.

The New Deal is more concerned with enhancing employment than securing income support. Welfare to work is a central element of this strategy involving public/private sector cooperation and community enterprises, and also building voluntary community level supports through encouraging self-help ideas, ideally without the 'community' element simply being an 'add on'. A neighbourhood renewal programme, concentrating on the most deprived estates, aims to establish neighbourhood wardens and learning centres, support for business with some selective demolition of run-down housing and rehabilitation. Much emphasis is laid on the idea of labour flexibility, often expressed uncritically, and for those involved may mean a regression to part-time work and limited contracts embodied in a 'hire and fire culture'. The tax structure too can encourage forms of participation and lift people out of the poverty trap by easing the transition between paid work and subsisting on benefit.

In addition, educational reforms are designed to concentrate on numeracy and literacy by constantly testing and monitoring standards nationally, so that all children leave school properly equipped to deal with the challenges of modern life. Whether sufficient extra funding has in fact been made available to realize these eminently worthy objectives without penalizing mainstream spending on schools is contestable. Much spending has been illusory, dependent on new forms of creative accountancy and spun by rhetoric (Davies, 2000), as the government maintained its tight grip on public expenditure (following the guidelines set down by the previous Tory administration). Now into its third year in office substantial real increases in funding, in what *The Economist* dubs a 'loosening of the belt', have finally been earmarked for education, health, transport, housing, defence, the Home Office and the war on poverty.

All reform comes at a cost, but government spending will still remain 'prudent', hovering around the relatively low level of 40 per cent of

GDP, despite the £43 billion plus increase announced in the Comprehensive Spending Review (CSR) in July 2000. By European standards this is modest and much remains as a 'catching up' exercise. In Sweden the state accounts for 58 per cent of GDP, in France 55 per cent, while in the USA it is only 30 per cent. The Third Way trumpets the modernization of public policy and service delivery as a key objective in its attempt at re-legitimizing government activity. Simply throwing money at problems is no solution, as past experience of thwarted expectations, 'stop–go' policy and the blame mentality of the 'cuts' all demonstrated. Defining tight performance indicators, and encouraging innovative thinking amongst public sector managers, are necessary means to improving public services, but difficult to achieve as morale is low through past neglect, relatively low pay and an erosion of the public service ideal. Policy rightly needs to be attuned to achieving smaller, more manageable targeted goals within a constantly changing economic landscape, where the welfare state is but one agency amongst others in tackling problems (Oppenheim, 1999). Yet in admitting this, better pensions plus affordable housing are still an unrealizable dream for many still heavily reliant on the state. And while 'the government talks incessantly of poverty, but rarely of money', much will remain unresolved (Benn, 2000: 315).

A significant boost to NHS spending was outlined in the Chancellor's March 2000 budget with annual 6.1 per cent real increases extending over the next four years. Thus key reforms planned for the NHS require: standardization across regions and localities to end health inequalities, less demarcation between professions, further dismantling of the unpopular internal market for a system of incentives, and reaffirmation of the principle of a tax-funded system, free at the point of delivery, while envisaging a role for private sector facilities where appropriate. The culture within the NHS needs to be changed from one that is producer driven to one that reflects patient needs. Education also received a similar spending increase (6.6 per cent) in the CSR, accompanied by plans to divert more funds to schools directly, especially at secondary level to help drive up standards. One of New Labour's difficulties has been holding on to its newly acquired allies in the middle class by stressing its inclusive approach to social justice, which the New Deal and other reforms were designed to accomplish. While long-term and youth unemployment have been significantly reduced, the resources needed to tackle these and other problems have involved some mild forms of redistribution, necessitating limited increases in taxation. Another equally important objective, has been to re-legitimize the principle of state provision, by improving standards for that broad swathe of 'middle Britain', worried as to its quality at a time when the private option is increasingly out of reach.

The commitment to increase funding substantially for public services, announced in the CSR, eschews further major tax cuts and is a step to fulfilling expectations of what a Labour government, be it New or otherwise, can do. The limited 1p cut in the standard rate of income tax in April 2000 acted to ward off more ambitious tax-cutting promises from the Conservative opposition. Nevertheless, half of income tax revenues are now paid by the top 10 per cent of earners, only 20 years ago this raised one-third, indicating that the redistribution was made possible by fiscal drag through generating higher economic growth. If Labour can demonstrate qualitative improvements in public services then the downsizing/privatizing of the state may be suspended. If it fails then the lure of tax-cutting and further private sector involvement in welfare will become normative. This finally exposes a clear ideological division between the political parties on which the next election will be fought.

## 4. The new citizenship?

'Call it community, call it civic patriotism, call it the giving age, or call it the new active citizenship, call it the great British society – it is Britain becoming Britain again', Gordon Brown's speech on advancing new measures to encourage charitable donations. Quoted in *The Independent*, 10 February 2000.

It is too early to determine whether stakeholding will ever be the lynchpin of the Third Way, although it appears doubtful, as it smacks too much of 'Old Labour' in its negativity towards capitalism (Plender, 1997). The traditional society it once addressed is fading away as the information age takes root, undermining the former established hierarchy of big unions and big business. However, the unedifying spectacle of whether or not the government knew in advance of BMW's closure of Rover in March 2000, suggests that Blair's earlier successful vigorous opposition in 1997 to an EU directive giving staff the right to know in advance of intending closure, was wrong. This would have avoided charges of governmental impotence, as prior consultation would have been mandatory for all interested parties. Commenting on this, and the coincident Barclays Bank closure of much of its rural network, Will Hutton argues in *The Observer* that 'pursuing shareholder value and maintaining a reputation for responsible behaviour are increasingly incompatible objectives' rectifiable by an annual social audit of companies and their legitimate stakeholders (Hutton, 9 April 2000: 30).

It is also well to remember that one of Blair's intellectual advisers is Charles Leadbeater, a strong advocate of the new mobile 'dot com' economy and the place of mutuals within it – organized for and by their members, although non profit-making. Currently, though some decline is apparent with the demutualization of the building societies, some 30 million people in the United Kingdom are members – ranging from agricultural co-ops to friendly societies and pre-school learning groups – with the new economy spawning newer ones such as Linux's software challenge to Microsoft. The new economy is generating novel methods of organization encouraging employee share ownership and innovative social enterprises. This could extend into traditional state sectors so that welfare, for example, would be delivered by a limited number of mutually owned providers, organizing everything from pensions to unemployment benefits (Leadbeater and Christie, 1999).

In a similar vein, Frank Field suggests that the all-or-nothing view of the state is too restrictive. Pre-Beveridge, welfare was secured by the approved societies and unions. Today, the state's role could be one of organizing rather than providing welfare, establishing an efficient framework through bench-marking, and encouraging a more fruitful collaboration between the state and individual (Field, 1998). Gordon Brown is keen to encourage voluntary effort, including enhanced corporate funding, and developing networks of social entrepreneurs active at neighbourhood level, in partnership with government. Whether this would be a relationship based on equality and pluralism, or one of subservience to central political control is, as Melanie Phillips remarks, problematic. Partnerships often end in failure, with innovation and local enterprise subjected to stifling local officialdom and central government definition (*Sunday Times*, 13 February 2000: 19).

Stakeholding, it is well to remember, extends beyond economic control to embrace new ways of involving people in the decision-making process. Labour's record to date is somewhat equivocal. Devolution and the mayoralty election for London generated passion and interest, but attempts by government to maintain control over candidate selection and stifle debate have resulted in charges of manipulation and 'control freakery' that questioned their commitment to the whole process. One critic talks of an emerging 'partyless democracy' – the abandonment of majoritarianism to a more depoliticized, consensual, populistic and plebiscitary form – where real alternative choice has been marginalized (Mair, 2000); while another sees the re-emergence of a 'Dual Polity' – that is, central government handling national 'high politics' while local and regional peripheral 'low politics' are kept separate. In this scenario, single-party Baldwinesque dominance can be more easily established, as expectations become narrowed including any potential criticism of government (Marquand, 2000).

Labour understandably has concentrated much of its early efforts on maintaining macroeconomic stability. It has encouraged people back into the labour market by making work pay, so that the option of subsisting on benefits becomes unattractive and increasingly unavailable, and to enhancing individual 'employability' which becomes the basis for any notion of reciprocity between state and individual. There is, though, a social cost to this endeavour. Family life and community cohesion suffer if too much emphasis is placed on the employability of young mothers, rather than addressing the needs of young children, or if insufficient recognition is given to that legion of unpaid carers, performing essential community tasks, yet receiving few status rewards by way of compensation.

Certainly the language of aspiration that communitarianism expresses is one readily embraced by the Prime Minister. Critics unfairly portray this as a lurch into moral majority populism and remain suspicious of his rhetoric and motives. Yet a loss of interest in the public realm of politics as participation declines, coupled with an erosion of trust and civility, replaceable by the fickle values of consumerism, are indeed a legitimate cause for concern. Perhaps communitarianism seems too vague and nebulous and maybe a tad too American to be realized here, although the idea of community long associated with the Liberal Democrat's agenda, means that any moves to strengthen the rapport that exists between them and Labour, will only promote this notion further. Additionally, and much beloved of the Liberal cause, the incorporation of the European Convention on Human Rights into United Kingdom law (it comes into force in October 2000) will promote equal access to rights, by making government and its agencies more disciplined and accountable, while defining how the needs of the wider society should also be considered. To that extent the Human Rights Act is communitarian – involving both rights and responsibilities. In 1997 Labour's victory received the backing of only 31 per cent of those entitled to vote in the lowest turnout since 1945. New Labour's initial focus is on what works and is deliverable in policy terms so the 'big picture' tends to get clouded. A hundred years earlier, Bernstein defined evolutionary socialism in similarly morally regenerative terms, as the sum total of successive reforms. Retrospectively perhaps, the Third Way will be seen as an updated and cumulative attempt at practical modernization, guided by the notion of a fairer more socially inclusive society.

Social class acts to define a world of social advantage, although one increasingly conditioned by gender, ethnicity and race. Community, even if articulated only rhetorically, implies the idea of all of us meeting as equals, enjoying equal dignity and a right to respect. In rejecting the liberal calculus of individual self-interest, Michael Prowse argues for a stronger notion of community embodying ideas of civic equality, and one moreover, expressive of Blair's deeply held beliefs in our common moral obligations. Further decommodification through pursuing quality of life issues, promoting public services, and the availability of public space that all would be expected to share, implies additional limits to market freedom curtailing economic inequality. Downgrading the dominance of the sovereign consumer, and cash nexus, would remind us that economic inequality is as much a consequence of past institutional development, law and custom, as it is of exceptional individual merit. Many feel the balance of interests has swung unfairly against the ordinary citizen (Prowse, 2000). In the sharing of risks in a more interdependent economy, the rewards (and responsibilities) appear too one-sided, as public sector wages are held back by state limits on spending, while tax breaks favour new share-option holders and venture capitalists.

Economic growth is never an end in itself but acts to extend freedom and choice, and so far Labour has targeted work as a panacea with some success, although the problems of jobless growth have not gone away. The Third Way, in modernizing social democracy, requires a new theory of fairness building on Labour's economic achievements. By extending individual equality of opportunity and defining admissible limits to outcomes; in recognizing that unequal rewards are generated by intergenerational family advantage (or its lack); in accepting that the state's role involves monitoring as well as some service delivery often in partnership with the private sector; that the needs of the lowest are recognized beyond a mere 'trickle down' rhetoric, but without at the same time hammering the rich so they take flight in the sinews of the global market, a start has been made. But can the circle be squared without further economic redistribution beyond the 'taxation by stealth' strategy, now that common ownership is off limits? Can the idea of tax as a public good providing for a modernized public service be re-legitimized? If tax increases on income are off limits, then new inheritance taxes could, for example, 'level up' opportunity via a bond (Fabians) or capital grant (IPPR) available to all youngsters to give them a more equal start in life. The Ackerman–Alstott stakeholding ideas promoted in the USA have already met with a positive response in the United Kingdom, with the suggestion that the £22 billion windfall from the sale of mobile telephone licences could provide an endowment fund offering a grant to all 18 year olds (Prowse, 2000). As Samuel Barnett, founder of Toynbee Hall in 1884 once remarked, 'God loveth a cheerful tax-payer.'

As 'winner-take-all' societies continue to generate extremes of wealth and inequality, it may be difficult for Labour's managerial politics to countenance their long-term perpetuation unchecked. Inadequate state control over the economy is consequential to their adoption of neo-classical monetarism. Labour's focusing on a politics of inclusion linked to notions of personal responsibility paradoxically means that forms of exclusion, resulting from hierarchy and widening inequality, continue to disfigure their achievements. So more consideration of the philosophical basis of the Third Way needs articulation, with a greater recognition of Labour's past history, what it constitutes and how the new agenda builds on that achievement. T.H. Marshall's vision of universal citizenship conferring an automatic social right to resources, has been replaced by a third way conditional form. Raymond Plant calls it 'supply-side citizenship', dependent on achievement not status, while discharging obligations to the wider society. Communitarianism implying fraternity may one day be central to this vision, along with a redefinition of the social rights of citizenship, but not one pared down to only a minimum achievable standard. A start has been made but the road ahead is long.

## References

Ackerman B.A. and Alstott, A., *The Stakeholder Society* (Yale: Yale University Press, 1998).

Benn, M., 'New Labour and Social Exclusion', *The Political Quarterly*, Vol. 71, No. 3 (July–September 2000), 309–18.

Budd, A., 'The Contradictions and Crisis of State-holder Capitalism', *Contemporary Politics*, Vol. 3, No. 2 (June 1997), 151–69.

Coote, A., *The Independent* (23 June 1995).

Davies, N., 'Schools in Crisis', *The Guardian* (7 March 2000), 4–5.

Etzioni, A., *The Spirit of Community: the Reinvention of American Society* (NY: Touchstone, 1994).

——, *The New Golden Rule; Community and Morality in a Democratic Society* (NY: Basic Books, 1996).

——, *The Limits of Privacy* (NY: Basic Books, 1999).

Fawcett, H. and T.N. Papadopoulos, 'Social Exclusion, Social Citizenship and De-Commodification: an evaluation of support for the unemployed in Europe, *West European Politics*, Vol. 20, No. 5 (July 1997), 1–30.

Field, F., 'Inside the Whale: Redrawing the Line between State and Government' *Political Quarterly*, Vol. 69, No. 3 (6) (July–Sep 1998), 252.

Finnegan, W., *Cold New World: Growing up in a Harder Country* (London, Picador, 1999).

Freedland, J., *Bring Home the Revolution* (N.Y: Fourth Estate, 1998).

Fukuyama, F., *Trust: Social Virtues and the Creation of Prosperity* (New York: Free Press, 1995).

——, *The Great Disruption: Human Nature and the Reconstruction of Social Order* (London: Profile Books, 1999).

Gerber, C., 'Coming Glued: Left Communitarianism vs Communitarianism of the Professional Middle Class' in C. Gerber (ed.) *Radical Politics in the Post Communist Era* (Amherst: 1995).

Gray, J., *Beyond the New Right* (London: Routledge, 1994).

Green, D., *Benefit Dependency: How Welfare Undermines Independence* (London: IEA, 1998).

Himmelfarb, G., *The De-Moralization of Society: from Victorian Virtues to Modern Values* (London: IEA, 1995).

Hutton, W., 'Six Stakeholding Propositions', *Business Strategy Review*, Vol. 8, No. 2 (3) (Summer 1997), 7.

——, *The Stakeholding Society: Writings on Politics and Economics*, ed., David Goldblatt (Cambridge: Polity Press, 1999).

——, *Stakeholding and its Critics* (London: IEA, 1997).

——, *The State We're In* (London, Jonathan Cape, 1995).

Lane, C., 'Globalization and the German Model of Capitalism – Erosion or Survival?', *BJS*, Vol. 51, No. 2 (June 2000), 207–34.

Leadbeater, C. and I. Christie, *To Our Mutual Advantage* (London: Demos, 1999)

Levitas, R., *The Inclusive Society? Social Exclusion and New Labour* (London: Macmillan, 1998).

Liddle, R. and P. Mandelson, *The Blair Revolution: Can New Labour Deliver?* (London: Faber, 1996).

Lloyd, J., 'Falling Out', *Prospect* (London: October 1999), 22–7.

MacDonald, R. (ed.) *Youth, the Underclass and Social Exclusion* (London: Routledge, 1997).

McRae, H., 'Can Europe Ever Catch America?', *The Independent*, The Thursday Review (27 January, 2000), 5.

Mair, P., 'Partyless Democracy: Solving the Paradox of New Labour?', *New Left Review* No. 2 (London: March/ April 2000), 21–35.

Marquand, D., 'Revisiting the Blair Paradox', *New Left Review*, No. 3 (May/June 2000), 73–9.

Marshall, T., *Citizenship and Social Class* (NY: Anchor, 1965).

Oppenheim, C., *The Inclusive Society: Tackling Poverty* (London: IPPR, 1999).

Piore, M.J., *Beyond Individualism* (Cambridge: Harvard UP, 1995).

Plender, J., *A Stake in the Future: the Stakeholding Society* (London: Nicholas Brealey, 1997).
Prowse, M., 'Mind the Gap', *Prospect* (London: January 2000), 30–5.
——, 'How to Spend It', *Prospect* (London: June 2000), 36–40.
Putnam, R., 'The Strange Disappearance of Civic America', *The American Prospect* (Winter 1996), 34–48.
——, *Bowling Alone* (NY: Simon & Schuster, 2000).
Selbourne, D., *The Principle of Duty: an Essay on the Foundations of Civic Order* (London: Sinclair-Stevenson, 1994).
Smith, D. and B. Bischof, 'Is Germany now the Sick Man of Europe?', *Prospect* (London: July 1999), 18–21.
Smith, Y., 'The Household, Women's Employment and Social Exclusion, *Urban Studies*, Vol. 34, No. 8 (July 1997), 1159 (19).
Swanson, J., 'Self-Help: Clinton, Blair and the Politics of Personal Responsibility', *Radical Philosophy*, 101 (May/June 2000) 29–38.
Vallely, P., 'Defining the New Jerusalem', *The Independent* (2 September, 1997).
Wallis, J., *The Soul of Politics* (London: Fount Paperbacks, 1995).

# 8
# The European Connection

It is highly unlikely that Britain can establish the Third Way all on its own. Some of the elements, such as modernization or social inclusion can well be developed, but in other respects the advent of globalization and especially the implications of EU membership put the goal beyond reasonable reach. A larger, more extensive context seems essential. Two different options appear as the evident alternatives. Firstly, the goal of an updated revived Atlantic Alliance or secondly, achieving integration of the Blairite Third Way into the European Union agenda for the future ahead. Each of the pathways offers attractions as well as constraints.

The Atlantic Alliance option offers the benefits of a common language, civic institutions and legal system; a politically literate electorate; a closely similar employment structure with the service sector increasingly dominant; an emphasis on hyper-technology plus informatics; and last but not least a cultural predisposition towards accommodation and compromise. Yet for all that, it would be a distinctly unbalanced partnership. The days of the special relationship lie decidedly in the past. A greatly diminished ex-Empire matched with the mightiest, wealthiest sole superpower, would leave the former in a clearly subsidiary position – some argue, little more than a fifty-first state (Soetendorp, 1999). Moreover linked to a nation where even Liberalism ranks as anathema, all left-wing content would need to be excised from the Third Way. Coming to equal the American model of triangulation, with its accent on expediency and accommodation, one is left wondering whether altogether the exercise would have been worth while.

The European connection is dramatically different. There is not only no one common language, but divergence in a whole range of institutions from customs and law to culture and education. Add to this, the long history of feuds, intrigues and bloody open hostilities and the case for British insularity appears virtually self-evident. Yet more than a quarter of a century of close integration and cooperation has built up confidence. Out of the original six-strong Customs Union (with Britain well on the sidelines), has emerged a cohesive EU community with a 15-nation member establishment (soon to be 20 and then 28), with a population of some 374 million, its own parliament and executive body in the commission, its new world currency and a soon to be added military and security dimension. Britain, which for all its ambivalence, has at all times been a part of the leading triumvirate has good cause to give thought to strengthening the bonds that already exist. Above all, the left-centre thesis of the Third Way will find itself on safer ground. With four-fifths of the membership governed by left-centre parties, the prospect is there to develop a shared ideology, fundamentally based on the principles of the Blairite Third Way.

The present chapter will examine the pros and cons of seeking to integrate the Third Way within the structural framework of the European Community in the new century, while the following one will direct its attention to the prospects within the United States.

## A Europe divided

There could hardly have been a more propitious start. Virtually coincidental with New Labour's election, centre-left parties gained power within twelve out of the fifteen European Union states. The most spectacular result was Gerhard Schröder's victory in the 1998 German election. In tandem with his overtly socialist inclined foreign minister Oskar Lafontaine, he put forward his Neue Mitte (New Middle) agenda that is in essence almost identical to the Blairite Third Way. Lafontaine's early resignation, if anything, strengthened the Chancellor's hands. Freed from the inherent pull to the left, Schröder felt able to march in step with the British proposals to implement the goals of the Third Way throughout the varied EU states. The November 1999 heads of states Florence meeting, attended by Tony Blair, Lionel Jospin, Gerhard Schröder, Massimo D'Alema of Italy, Fernando Cardoso of Brazil as well as President Clinton seemed to augur well. As Will Hutton, noting the decidedly cool British reaction, observes: 'Yet in the rest of the world, the Third Way has provoked a thunderous response. It has been the principal focus of the German SDP's Values' Commission.' The joint paper by Schröder and Blair last summer is debated almost daily in the German press. It is the new fault line on the Italian Left. It is how the Brazilians hope to modernize their country and Latin America. It is the political world view which Bill Clinton hopes will become the new core position of the Democrats (Hutton, 1999).

Nevertheless, the expected advance has not occurred. The main obstacle has been French prime ministerial overt disdain, substantively echoed by the German SDP's Values' Commission. In their view, the Third Way 'offers no effect on inequality, weakens trade unions, creates a two-tier welfare state in which the middle class has no stake and excuses the business class and business from social responsibilities' (Hutton, 1999). In other words, promoting a 'get rich at any cost' entrepreneurial mentality at all social levels, it has failed to implement positive change.

Palpably, the Third Way has not made the headway that proponents expected. Opposition has come more from the socialist left than from the political right. The main voice of rebuttal is that of Lionel Jospin, the French Prime Minister. His contention is that it is just another version of Thatcherism, more insidious still for misleading its traditional constituency with a myth of social reform. 'Jospinisim', instead preserves the values of 'solidarity, justice and liberty', even in a climate where redistributive taxes and state ownership are no longer advocated. The 'new alliance' uniting the working classes, the middle class and the 'exclus' (the unemployed, the poor and under-educated) expresses a common will where the motto of 'yes to the market economy, no to the market society' will be allowed to prevail (*The Independent*, 27 September 1999).

The radically innovative 35-hour week has attracted the most attention. Designed to cut back unemployment by sharing available work, it is strongly opposed by the business community. Headlines such as: 'It wasn't meant to work out like this', referring to the 'big rush for the subsidies' plus the unintended consequence of enforcing American-type flexibility (*Sunday Times*, 21 November 1999); 'French bosses threaten end to welfare state' – indicating that 95 per cent of the employers' associations voted 'to walk out of the [welfare state] system that has managed health care, unemployment and pensions since the Second World War' (*The Times*, 19 January 2000); and, 'French firms flee Jospin for Britain', setting out the brain drain exodus to 'Europe's tax El Dorado' in Britain (*The Times*, 22 February 2000), signify the persistent disapproval of the business community. However, for all the protestations, the economy in the Summer of 2000 is one of the fastest growing in the EU. Its health system lauded, literacy high, unemployment falling fast and at last below 10 per cent, with France becoming a major player in corporate take-over activity across the EU, and embracing the new Internet-based economy with relish.

Officials too paint a positive picture. Martine Aubry, the employment minister, claims that some 21 000 new jobs have already materialized, that with the policy now mandatory another 40 000 are expected in the following year (Lichfield, 1999). Subsidies are projected to be exceeded by savings in unemployment benefits (not to speak of relief within the criminal justice system), and that whatever the ultimate financial equation, the social benefits of a fairer share-out of jobs plus enhancement of free time and greater flexibility will make the project amply worth while. Bourdieu's contribution to the debate, well brought out in Callinicos's recent article in the *New Left Review*, puts the emergent neo-left philosophy well into perspective (Callinicos, 1999). Uniquely, the French intelligentsia still safeguards its role in the socio-political firmament. In contrast to Britain where Blair is seen as having surrounded himself with a host of professional academic quasi-businessmen – as is similarly true of most other advanced societies – 'the French intellectual occupies a position quite different from his lonely counterpart in Britain or America, condemned to isolated struggle and individualism. He is part of a recognized group, a power in the land' (Brandon, 1999: 17). Socio-cultural critics stress the necessity of preserving the values of 'civilization' over the hegemony of capitalist acquisitiveness. The compulsive race to raise the GDP to ever more dizzy levels is a part of the system's 'symbolic violence' that neutralizes social dissent. Consumerism and commodification added to the now permanent condition of insecurity caused by 'mass unemployment, the growth of contract labour and flexible production, the *deterritorialization* of enterprise now freed from any specific attachment to region or nation' (Callinicos, 1999: 89) combine to disarm resistance on the part of the working class. The remedy, to say the least, is unusual. In a context where hyper-technology and materialist living are making ever more extensive strides, Bourdieu reaches back to the 'ethic of conviviality' that recalls more simple, less stressful days. He commends a return to a proletarian consciousness that, in an age of shared deprivation and misery, by clinging to the values of association, spontaneous pleasure and fun, bonded communities together and helped compensate for conditions prevailing outside (Bourdieu, 1999).

The fact that neither Schröder's *Neue Mitte* nor the Blairite Third Way acknowledge the potentialities of the New Age, is a distinct deficiency.

Especially so when the New Left – the first to focus on the implications of the demise of the Fordist age – were the first to identify what, thanks to hyper-technology, could be achieved (*Marxism Today*, 1988). Scarcity, under conditions of rational planning and management, as far as the advanced nations are concerned, could in the foreseeable future be overcome. Then the pre-eminence of the work ethic would yield to new social arrangements where paid employment would take its place alongside the values of social commitment, cooperation and self-fulfilment within the context of greatly expanded free time. With accumulation and acquisitiveness no longer yielding extraordinary rewards, associative and other-directed qualities could foster a climate of social peace (Gorz, 1999; Newman and de Zoysa, 1999; Rifkin, 1995). Bordieu's analysis, inherent no less in Jospin's perspective as well as the innovation of the 35-hour week, thus ideologically makes France the odd man out within the EU triumvirate.

For the first time the Franco-German alliance, the bedrock of the EU, is facing a serious test. Germany, throughout the willing paymaster as a quid pro quo for acquiring moral legitimacy, is flexing its muscles. Under the aegis of the *Bundesbank* (now metamorphosed into the new European Central Bank) which is masterminding the common currency and political enlargement to almost double its size, is bound to enhance its position. Chancellor Schröder's August 1999 declaration that Germany 'has every interest in considering itself a great power in Europe in the future' induces *The Economist* to conclude that: 'If any power can lead Europe in the future it can only be Germany' (Europe Survey: 23 October 1999: 3). Politically, Germany stands closer to the British functionalist concept perceiving the European Union primarily as a trading community where inter-governmentalism remains normative rather than the French vision of an eventual political super-state. In regard to the Third Way, the rift is wider still. In their strictly centrist position, the unconditional acceptance of the market economy, financial reform of the welfare state, and public intervention confined to the poorest, the Anglo-German versions are closely alike. Bourdieu's neo-Marxist projection – evoking memories of the inter-war Frankfurt School (Benjamin, 1999) – may even domestically be a minority choice. Yet, the cultural priority substantively echoes the Jospin critique. The wage concessions made to the public sector and health workers, in such light reflect deliberate policy rather than 'Jospin's retreat' (*The Times*, 22 March 2000). France has long subscribed to the view that 'there is not merely a European territory, but also a European way of life, mixing culture, history and social model. ... Wise governments must nurture that way of life and protect it from outside threats' (*The Economist*: Europe Survey; 23 October 1999: 5). The main threat now comes from American-led globalization, undermining good government while destroying the quality of life – a way of critique which Germany and Britain (and presumably most of the other members) fail to accept.

France and Britain, the two rival protagonists have defined their position. Germany, the leading power and likely arbiter, remains ambivalent. At the time of writing (Summer 2000), the entire EU scenario is clearly in flux. The options that confront Germany are manifold and could potentially give rise to unity as much as to further discord. Regarding the prospects of the Third Way, we perceive two distinct pathways. Firstly, reaffirmation of the Franco-German axis as the predominant motor force of the EU. And secondly, the alternative of Germany electing to move towards the British perspective, rejecting the French option and presenting a common front linking the Neue Mitte and the Blairite Third Way.

Traditional forces are compellingly strong. Under the aegis of the Franco-German alliance the EU has unquestionably been one of the political success stories of the post-war years. Strong as the ties have become, the new common currency, the euro, provides a new link in the chain. Potentially it could lead in various directions, though logic dictates that those who were centrally involved in its origin and are now crucially committed to its success, have every interest in remaining in step, hence, on major issues, presenting a Franco-German common front. In May 2000 the German Foreign Minister spoke approvingly of moves to a 'parliamentary federation' for the EU while yet insisting it remains 'a Europe of nation-states'. The German idea of federalism in fact means devolving power to the regions or *Lander* and not a move to further centralization as is understood in Britain's unitary state. This opening up of the debate was closely followed by the French President who argued somewhat differently that a core pioneer group could push ahead in key areas of mutual advantage. Internal reaction in Britain implicitly assumed that continued membership meant relegation to a slower lane, rather than the idea that advanced cooperation in some areas, such as defence and foreign policy, is already occurring and one where Britain takes a leading role.

As it happens, Germany is the world's third largest economy while France ranks as fourth (with Britain a close-ranking fifth). Acting in concert they have already achieved a great deal and seem capable of no lesser success in the future ahead. Given the human and technical resources of the EU, the future seems virtually boundless. Britain, in or out, is almost irrelevant. Admittedly, it serves as a potential conduit to the vibrant US market economy. Yet conversely, Britain has proved a notoriously fickle participant in the common enterprise, after a period of some twenty-eight years still tangential in membership, choosing to critique the European currency from the sidelines, preaching a social accord dogma at odds with its own market-oriented political actions, while antagonistic to the more traditional social democratic programmes adopted by both France and Germany as well as many other EU states. Social protection, co-determinate styles of management, emphasis on socio-cultural values plus preservation of social accord are considered fundamental within most states. In their structure of high income but high unemployment economies, a concern for the dignity of labour – abandoned within Anglo-Saxon societies, they are closely alike. Indeed, the German stakeholder pattern awarding a wider, more diverse voice throughout industry, matched with France's tradition of venting grievances by direct action might well blend into a new effective socialist praxis towards an EU Third Way. Designed to preserve the workforce from the downsizing and casualization pressure prevalent within the Anglo-Saxon economies, its 'consensus capitalism' is likely to attract wide-based support (Whittam-Smith, 1999).

Individually, Chancellor Schröder may well have a preference for the British Third Way. It matches his Neue Mitte ideology better than any alternative project. Yet politically the path ahead appears set. The Franco-German axis dominates as a compelling contingency. Internally, strong pressure in a diverse direction emanates from the Left. While, beyond its own frontiers – taking account of the newly fledged euro together with both deepening and expansion of the Union – the agenda calls for unity among the leading protagonists. Strategic wisdom points in one single direction: a move towards Jospinism and with it, the socialist left.

The alternative option however does not necessarily represent a lost cause. Inherently the Schröder and Blair ideologies are closely alike. They furthermore share the fortunate coincidence of their opposition parties' penchant for shooting themselves in the foot. The Christian Democrats' cash scandals are tantamount to political suicide, while the Conservatives' infighting – predominantly focused on the EU – has damaged their political credibility beyond early repair. Britain has consistently denounced the Common Agricultural Policy's annual ritual of 'food mountains and wine lakes' as an exercise in waste, consuming, as it does, one-half of the EU's budget while serving the sectional (predominantly French) interest in subsidizing now well-off small-scale farmers at the expense of tax-payers abroad. For long, a sole voice in the wilderness, now confronting enlargement with Poland's 27 per cent peasant-farmer workforce (compared to the EU's 4 per cent) and other potential subsidy candidates, a rethink will need to take place. Germany, the prime paymaster, is increasingly restive. Both deplore the profusion of red tape, the vast over-manning, the growing intrusiveness of the Commission, and not least, the ultimate threat of a super-state. But at that point, agreement stops. Britain – the perennial 'outsider' – where even today 69 per cent are opposed to joining the euro, while an astonishing 46 per cent want to leave the Community altogether (Pierce and Landau, 1999) – can hardly claim the privileges of primary membership. Not having gone through the deck-clearing experience of the Thatcher/Reagan monetarist revolution, for good or ill, Schröder's room for manoeuvre is circumscribed. Political reality demands his pursuit of the 'Rhenish model' of corporate governance, industry-wide collective bargaining, high wages and job security (Gray, 1998: 93–4), although admittedly this is increasingly interpreted more flexibly. Ideologically as well as strategically, there is every sign that the Franco-German axis will coalesce.

That does not however mean that moves towards convergence are ruled out for ever. Both France and Germany, find themselves increasingly impelled in the direction of the free market economy. In Germany tax cuts on personal income and on corporations are in place and privatization is proceeding rapidly, while even the collective bargaining system is being changed at the level of the individual firm where greater flexibility is becoming operative. Schröder's reforms, claims *The Economist*, 'are in the right direction, and they may add up to something impressive' (8 July 2000: 28). *Time* magazine talks of a 'French Renaissance' with Stanley Hoffmann arguing that: 'State policy, under Gaullist as well as under Socialist rule, has freed France from chronic inflation, practiced monetary rigor and either privatized state enterprises or made them competitive' (Hoffmann, 2000: 82). Protectionism is being dismantled and globalization embraced. Conversely, the Blairite Third Way, though still meticulously excising 'socialism' from its vocabulary, is perceptively moving towards redistributive policies. Blair's five new 'key pledges' of: full employment, educational excellence; making the National Health Service the best in the world; eliminating child poverty; and making Britain a 'beacon' nation for the world (Abrams, 2000), decidedly demand intervention as well as redistribution of wealth. After the first two years of tight expenditure limits, Labour enjoys a budgetary surplus and is committed to extensive public sector spending to approximate levels operating within the EU, not to engineering further tax cuts. The idea and vision of social democracy seems alive and well. Without wishing to minimize the force of the schisms, the signals pointing towards convergence cannot be ignored. They will be considered in the section below.

## United but separate

We will, in this section, initially consider the ongoing European Union developments. They are: firstly, the establishment of the euro; next, internal integration and expansion to widen membership; then the case argued by Eurosceptics in Britain; and finally, the forces indicating a Third Way convergence within the European Union, as the new century gets underway.

### Internal developments

The euro is bound to prove a major landmark in EU history. The planned assimilation of eleven out of the fifteen national monetary systems into one unified single currency must, taking the magnitude of the task into account, rank as a major event. Already common tax policies, interest rates, macro-management of the economy, planning and development, together with labour and employment policies are taking effect. Shared policies are bringing the nations ever more closely together, leading both to common economic initiatives as well as deepening interrelationships, and will be discussed under the heading of 'Integration' below.

Objectively, the euro has not been an unqualified success since its inception in January 1999, as its value has fallen steadily. Depreciating by 20 per cent against the dollar in its first year (Whittam-Smith, 1999), and by a further 3 per cent against the pound in the course of the first three months of 2000, its market stability is open to doubt. While exports have benefited through the low exchange rate, the central commitment to internal price stability and high tax rates to cover the cost of social policies are deterring investors. A net ouflow of some £250 billion during the first year of operation is raising questions as to the capacity of the 'consensus capitalism' model being adequately equipped to hold its own in a climate of neo-liberal competitive globalization (Whittam-Smith, 1999). Job maintenance, costly social provision, plus a stakeholder economy that impedes modernization have for some time been projected as obsolete. Now the *Bundesbank*-inspired 'sound money' paradigm, promoting growth and job creation through economic stability and budgetary discipline that also shaped the terms of the EMU treaty under the Maastricht provisions, similarly finds itself subject to adverse critique (Dyson, 1999: 199–201). With the euro set to become the sole legal tender amongst the 11 participants in 2002, the future status of the euro as matching the dollar as a leading world currency appears open to doubt.

Yet, for all that, internal developments point in the reverse direction. The euro area's far more self-contained structure, the favourable trade/GDP ratio, plus the large current account surplus of the euro-11 provide a sound enough counterweight to what might turn out to be a mere short-term exchange rate decline. What counts even more is the newly gained mechanism of forward planning, consistent extension and growing air of confidence inducing 'more takers' to apply for membership of the single-money club. Greece – the sole original reject – has already formally reapplied. The Danish government has set a referendum date for their decision. The Swedes are likely to follow suit. And, 'even the stay-away Norwegians, much farther back in the queue, may again, now that they have a centre-left government start thinking about joining the EU. And if they did join, the pull towards the euro zone', speculates *The Economist* (25 March: 51), 'might also eventually prove irresistible – leaving only Britain, in the EU, outside'.

Integration meanwhile is steadily moving ahead. Nothing else promotes future achievement as effectively as previous success. And overwhelmingly, the European Community is a story of signal success: from modest, not altogether hopeful, beginnings, it now presents, as the new century gets underway, the prospect of a united Europe no longer beset by chronic dissent and war, but prosperous, powerful and cohesive with a common passport, one currency, free movement of trade, peoples and services, together with common policies regarding social affairs, set to create a framework of coexistence and cooperation that will lead to a deepening of common identity all of its own. Add to that the planned, deliberate endeavour of policy makers to strengthen the ties, formal and informal, that bind the nations together and the future seems clear: even if not a superstate or, in one way or another, a federal association with its own independent machinery of state, then a body that, to all intents and purposes, has assumed much of the essential appurtenance of a fully fledged state.

The outlines are there. To take one example, the European Court of Justice is perceptively acquiring the powers approximating the US Supreme Court. Assuming jurisdiction over Human Rights is, according to an inter-governmental Commission's note equivalent to becoming 'the genuine supreme court of the Union', prompting *The Economist* to raise the question of 'could an EU constitution be far behind' (ibid.: 50–1).

The common defence initiative exhibits a similar trend. Shared security and military capabilities might potentially evolve out of the military presence in Kosovo and similar troublespots where embryonic EU formations are already extant. Pragmatic reasoning alone makes the cause of a European military union compelling. 'Europe', as Richard Medley, a leading global military-political analyst, states, 'desperately needs an excuse for a robust employment program, and a "European" defense initiative is a made-to-order solution ... designed to bring the EU into a more level footing with the United States and improve Europe's economy in the process' (Medley, 1999: 20). Related developments (foreshadowed by leading agenda items for the December 2000 inter-governmental conference), refer to the creation of an 'enterprise Europe', the imposition of European-wide taxes plus social security payments, immigration measures and labour laws, as well as proposals to eliminate most national vetoes, and are indicative of the deepening momentum (Prescott and Gray, 2000).

Though formally not the 'unified superstate' that critics abhor, the message seems clear. Even if falling short of the early planners' projection of 'the union of the peoples of Europe' as the ultimate end, the EU is launched on a deepening project directed to making it, as Tony Blair and Antonio Guterres (the Portugese Prime Minister) both fervent advocates of the Third Way – have put it, 'the world's most dynamic and innovative area by 2010'. Within that overarching concept however opinions differ. Britain is virtually alone in setting its face against measures such as the removal of the unilateral veto power and tax equalization that others consider essential towards making integration a meaningful step.

Enlargement is a less contentious matter. European Union membership, according to current plans, is planned to have grown from the existing 15 to 28 by the end of the decade. Seven nations – Cyprus, the Czech Republic, Estonia, Hungary, Malta, Poland and Slovakia – are scheduled to enter by 2005. Three more – Latvia, Lithuania and Slovenia – will follow two years later. Bulgaria and Romania will be integrated by the end of the present decade. While Turkey – still needing to set its house in order regarding democratization – will be confined to the waiting line until 2012. Transforming its 'rich man's club' character to a more inclusive, diverse entity, consonant with the 'Europe' connotation, will of necessity call for re-evaluation in several directions. The main items of change are likely to be the following:

- It seems highly unlikely for the Common Agricultural Policy (CAP) to retain the form it has had since inception. Set up to cushion small peasant communities on both economic as well as cultural 'quality of life' grounds, it has been perpetually costly (consuming close to one-half of the Community's budget) and slanted towards a shrinking, now typically prosperous group. It is furthermore manifestly protectionist, prone to all kinds of schemes of corruption and fraud creating a persistent bone of contention between Britain and the rest of the Community.

The expected enlargement will inflate the CAP's cost exponentially. Agricultural-based nations – most notably Ireland and Portugal – were admitted on past occasions. However, these were countries with low population levels, on the threshold of modernization and so limiting the extra costs to the Community. Now, with Eastern Europe claiming admission, the task looks quite different. Poland alone has a population of some 39 million with a heavy concentration of small-scale farms lacking even simple machinery, plus an ineffective transport system that would add to the costs. Subsidizing economies of this order to anywhere near matching levels would make inordinate demands on existing resources well beyond the level of public support. Germany, the primary paymaster for past costly indulgence and now morally re-legitimated, has been increasingly restive in recent years. With Britain, for long agitating to close down the programme once and for all, clashes are clearly looming ahead. However, the issue as to how structurally backward some nations are, short of substantial aid to effectively accommodate their membership, will at some stage need to be faced (*The Economist*, 8 April 2000: 53–4).

- New rules to cap the size of the European Commission, and to rebalance voting powers in the Council of Ministers are also imminent. Majority voting rather than the unilateral veto power has already been touted as an essential amendment (*The Economist*, 15 January 2000: 52). While the European Commission, at present consisting of 20 members from 15 countries will, under expansion, require the big countries to give up their numerical privilege. The main changes foreshadowed are as follows:

(1) The Council of Ministers voting system already favours smaller nations. The larger countries will demand a correction before permitting new members to join and before they concede their

right to a second commissioner. Weighted voting schemes, designed to avoid some of the pitfalls of the UN – a hazardous exercise – are already under consideration.

(2) The principle of unanimity, embodied in the veto power, appears insupportable with the expected near-doubling of membership. Majority voting is bound to replace it. However, with countries, particularly the larger ones, reluctant to be overruled in matters of 'serious national concern' (a notoriously indefinable contingency), it will in all likelihood be confined to relatively innocuous areas such as those of industry, transport and cultural policy. The methods of how to deal with macro-issues in the political, economic or social fields remain enigmatic – and for the sake of ongoing accord, barely discussed (*The Economist*, 12 February 2000).

With that many issues in flux, the prospect of delayed implementation cannot be dismissed. Increasingly the 'big bang' view of enlargement is gaining momentum. Postponed entry for a further three of four years would allow the contestants to make up lost ground and then for the entire group to be ready for equivalent membership when entry time comes. It would equally allow the more laggard applicants to adjust to coming constraints, while preparing the ground for internal reform at the same time (*The Economist*, 8 April 2000).

The leading three nations' preferences differ in regard to implementation. Implicitly, Britain favours widening over deepening. France wants the opposite, while Germany wishes to press on in tandem with both initiatives. The 'big bang' solution, avoiding confrontation, seems the likeliest candidate. Following the EU tradition of deferring head-on collision, it would equally allow it to set its own house in order at the same time. Neil Kinnock, the Commission's Vice-President, has undertaken to tackle the problem of 'Eurosclerosis' without fear or favour. It will not be an easy task. As he alleges, amongst the 22 000 staff, 'it is difficult to find anyone with the slightest sense of responsibility'. From the Commissioners down to the lower bureaucratic levels staff have managed to surround themselves with lavish allowances plus tax privileges to an extent where the democratic process is impaired. The evidence of flagrant corruption that compelled the entire body of the Commission to resign in 1999, has further aggravated the climate of cynicism and apathy. A successful outcome to Kinnock's initiative to modernize the machinery, cut back on overstaffing, return some of the tasks to national governments, and 'bring Europe back to the people'

(Castle, 2000), could do much to restore public confidence. Further ideas for reform, with one suggestion gaining particular ground, is for a second chamber – comprising a European senate of national parliamentarians which would have some real oversight over law-making thereby offering a real challenge to bureaucratic deal-making and secrecy (Siedentop, 2000).

## Britain and the EU

New Labour has solidly affirmed its commitment to deepening European Union ties. The government has repeatedly declared that joining the euro is vital to Britain providing certain economic tests have been met prior to holding a successful referendum. Integration, though not wholeheartedly embraced by the Blair administration, is regarded as necessary and, subject to safeguarding sovereignty, equally in Britain's best interest. While expansion – opening the door to rightfully entitled nations decidedly empathetic to British values as well as contingent in social philosophy – is to be welcomed as a move in the right direction.

In contrast, public support stands at a nadir. According to an April 2000 European Commission report, 'the proud British distrust the EU' (*The Times*, 4 April 2000). Fifty-nine per cent (4 per cent higher than six months ago), are opposed to the single currency as against an EU average of 32 per cent. Merely 29 per cent consider membership beneficial, while 24 per cent are unconditionally negative. Furthermore, 'awareness' of EU institutions – standing at 44 per cent as against the next in line, Italy's, 52 per cent – is lowest of all. An earlier survey revealed that while 57 per cent are prepared to accept the status quo, a rising proportion of 46 per cent want to leave the Community altogether as soon as they can (*The Times*, 29 December 1999). No wonder that within the continent, New Labour's late-day conversion is viewed in a cynical light. Giddens's Third Way, still the policy blueprint, gives the EU only the scantest attention. What there is, does passingly refer to it as a potential model for UN expansion while expressly pointing to its undemocratic character, as summed up in the tart observation that 'it has to be said that if it applied to join itself it would be refused entry, because it isn't democratic enough' (Giddens, 1998: 142). Britain's putative 'Trojan Horse' role, especially highlighted by the French veiled accusation of serving as a stealth instrument of 'dictatorship by ugly America' (*The Times*, 21 April 2000), inhibits stable relationships. Particularly so, when Anglo-Saxon capitalism speaks and acts with one voice in matters of the economy, communication, modernization and globalization.

Nostalgia for reviving the 'special relationship' is by no means extinct. Even though Britain's reduced circumstances rule out anything like an equal balance, influential sectors are advocating a total withdrawal from the EU in favour of a new Atlantic Alliance. The far looser construct would not infringe on sovereignty; the 'mighty pound' would not find itself hamstrung by restrictionist policies (*The Economist*, 29 January 2000: 65); the prohibitive costs of euro conversion (estimated at a staggering £36 billion) would not need to be faced. Furthermore, the prospect that France and Germany, the dominant forces driving towards a federal Europe, will treat Blair like a third partner in a *ménage à trois*, and 'they'll cheat all the way to suit their books while he sticks to the rules' (*The Times*, 23 February 2000: Opinion) will be out of the way; while 'Eurozone Woes' of 'powerful cartels formed by unions and employers and regular intervention by the State' (*The Times*, 18 March 2000) that vitiate the workings of the market economy and free enterprise would cease to apply.

Agendas are distinctly diverse. The *Global Britain* pressure group, made up of prominent Conservatives, explicitly sets out to sever all ties with the EU. Closely in touch with Republican Senators led by the former presidential candidate Phil Gramm, they are promoting a plan to join Britain with Canada, Mexico and the US into the North Atlantic Free Trade Association (NAFTA). Michael Fabricant, a Tory MP who has tabled several Bills calling for closer transatlantic ties, draws special attention to the benefits deriving from the 'special relationship' in regard to communality of language, legal system, political structure and cultural traditions (*The Times*, 20 March 2000). In a quite different vein, it is being asserted that 'Blair's third way leads to New York'. As Sydney Blumenthal, one of President Clinton's closest advisers has put it: 'With Great Britain we have forged a 21st-century alliance, as the President called it, based not only on all our traditional mutual interests but on our common conviction of the necessity for a new social contract.' Purportedly, the Third Way is 'simply the latest buzz phrase being used to give some intellectual ballast to New Labour's rightward drift' (Castle and Usborne, 1998) – an interpretation that, for all their adherence to a close transatlantic relationship, Blair and his co-leaders of the Third Way, would repudiate as complete travesty.

Eurosceptics run a gamut of shades. From those who aver that they 'want to be in Europe but not run by Europe', to the more extreme refusing 'to be governed by foreigners'. The Tory party consensus has perceptibly shifted in a Eurosceptic direction. Already a dominant factor in the downfall of the Major administration, since the advent of the euro the momentum has spread. John Redwood, one of the party's leading voices has recently delivered a stark warning that the European Union treaty, due to be signed in December 2000, will bring about 'a European army, European taxation, European frontiers and a European criminal justice policy' tantamount to a 'superstate, bound to blow up parliamentary government in Britain' (Webster, 2000). Additionally the veto abolition, introduced under the innocuous sounding terminology of 'flexibility' or 'enhanced cooperation' will make EU structures even more undemocratic than they already are, while providing an 'open door' to masses of indigent asylum seekers, encouraging military adventures and reinforcing the negative impact on British trade. To make matters worse, the financial scandals currently engulfing the German Christian Democrats, giving rise to allegations that 'many key players who forced the euro on to the statute books were crooks' (Laughland, 2000) are adding fuel to latent flames.

Though currently less vociferous, it would be wrong to presume Euroscepticism to be a prerogative of the Right. Open-door policies – as is equally true of intensified competition on the part of the appellant states – would after all more severely impact on the employment, housing, environmental and public service standards of the less privileged sectors than on the Tory hierarchy. At the grass-roots level, unease is intense. Amongst Labour activists, not least parliamentarians, there is equally criticism of EU membership as well as the politics of the Third Way. As these will be critically considered in the final chapter, directed to the future of the Third Way, analysis is being deferred.

## Convergence

As the new century gets underway, the European Union is both established and weak. As Smith and Wright sum it up: 'Over four decades after the Treaty of Rome (1957), the European Union with its 370 million inhabitants has some of the key characteristics of a large modern state, even if they are underdeveloped. It has an executive civil service, the European Commission, that draws up specific legislative proposals. Political direction is provided by the Council of Ministers. There is also a European Court of Justice, an elected parliament, European citizenship with the symbols of a common passport, an anthem, a flag and a common European currency. However, there is another side to the coin. The sense of a shared European identity remains relatively weak, and national feelings – the strong sense of being French, British, Spanish, German and so on – are still extremely powerful' (Smith and Wright, 1999: 14–15). Membership is virtually unquestioned but a European self-consciousness, comparable to patriotism, as yet barely exists.

Chryssochou (1998) contends that for the EU to evolve beyond the institutional level, it needs to integrate an autonomous shared participatory ethos all of its own. 'Blair's Plan for Europe' suggests that the Third Way philosophy has the capacity to supply the missing element. 'Unlike the Europsceptics', *The Economist* (19 February 2000: 55–6) adds, 'he is not spooked by the vision of a European superstate'. What Blair advocates is a 'move away from the heavy-handed intervention and regulation' to an agenda of 'jobs, competitiveness, economic change and dynamism' with life-long learning equipping all to participate on equal terms. Neither qualified voting nor enlargement are considered barriers to progress and unity. Conversely, the Third Way itself needs a canvass beyond the traditional nation state. Widely perceived as a mere palliative for privatization and globalization, it has in its narrower focus failed to arouse interest on any scale. Significant state functions have already withered away. With more to follow, the European Union, democratized and made representative, could reciprocally provide the vision that the Third Way needs. Blair's five 'key pledges' for the decade ahead could fit the bill. They are:

- Full Employment.
- Educational Excellence.
- Making the National Health Service the best in the world (that is, aiming for excellence in matters of public health).
- Eliminating Child Poverty.
- Making Britain a 'beacon nation' for the world (that is, making the European Union a model for social equality plus a quality of life commensurate with existing resources).

The contention expressed in Leon Brittan's (ex-senior British Commissioner) recent book that Europe is 'moving our way' is not a view widely shared on the continent (Brittan, 1998). Britain has historically ranked as an 'awkward partner' (George, 1990), and the persisting mode of hesitancy, reluctance and outright hostility has done little to reconcile doubters and enemies on the other side. The euro comes first. 'Membership of the Euro Club', Krieger insists, 'is the entry ticket to top-tier EU influence, and the UK cannot sustain equivalent influence as a free rider' (Krieger, 1999: 168). Britain cannot forever opt to remain on the sidelines: chronically carp at the loss of sovereignty; threatening withdrawal whenever it does not get its way; eyeing the Atlantic Alliance as a more congenial resting-place; and while obstructing progress, claiming the privilege of the veto at the same time. Blair's consistent endorsement of American economic strategy, plus his emphasis that, under today's changed circumstances, enterprise and fairness go hand in hand (Grise, 1999) is typically interpreted as a sign of recidivism.

The best hope lies in the fact that just as the Third Way needs a larger stage, the European Union equally seems at a dead end, faced both with the dilemma of apathy and indifference. The absence of vision (as the lamentable turnout at the last parliamentary election vividly underscored) represents a vacuum that needs filling. While at the same time, hampered by an inflexible labour force and an onerous system of social benefits, both Jospinism plus the Rhenish model are undergoing modification. There are evident signs of a gradual rapprochement. The omens are positive. Schröder's 'Neue Mitte' and Blair's Third Way are fundamentally alike, the centre-left holds office in most EU states, and, as noted, the French are exhibiting greater flexibility. Jospin has publicly acknowledged that 'as a system, and above all a system of production, socialism no longer exists' (*The Times*, 10 December 1999), and as *The Economist* observers: 'Even the French now talk of "making work pay", a favourite Americanism borrowed by Britain's Chancellor.' The idea of an 'active welfare state' in which the unemployed are encouraged to come off benefits and into work is another increasingly shared conviction. 'Lifelong learning' and making use of the Internet is a further Blairism that now crops up in Commission circles.

Britain's Third Way, in turn, will need to move towards the Left. Blair's critique of the effects of the unfettered market hegemony and 'ruthless profit-hunting on the stock market' seems a step in a forward direction. The French initiative in favour of 'a charter of basic rights' might equally prove a positive step (Bremner, 2000). And more specific safeguards for workers' rights might be enough to mobilize a new concept of the Third Way. Within the EU a pattern of adjustment to the new global realities will ensue, but one which retains something of the old order as the protective walls of the Community help ward off more serious challengers. What Britain cannot do is simply promote the virtues of the single market with a limited vision of an enlarged Europe constituting no more than a free-trade area along the lines of NAFTA. The Third Way vision of a post-industrial future borrowing 'best practice' from American experience, if suitably modified, could provide the vision Europe currently lacks.

Social inclusion – an item strangely absent from Blair's above pledges and a concern widely shared across the continent – and initiatives such as the French 35-hour week (which the Dutch have apparently adapted to work in a smoother way) seem primary candidates for a common Third Way policy within the European Union. We will expand on these and other innovative potentialities in the final chapter, having first considered the issue of 'The American Third Way'.

## References

Abrams, F., 'Blair: We Were the 20th Century's Civilising Force', *The Independent* (London: 28 February 2000).

Benjamin, W., *The Arcadian Project* (Cambridge, MA: Harvard University Press, 1999).

Bourdieu, P., *Acts of Resistance: against the New Myths of our Time* (Cambridge: Polity Press, 1999).

Brandon, R., *Surreal Lives* (New York: Grove Press, 1999).

Bremner, C., 'France to Lead EU Drive for Basic Rights Charter', *The Times*: Europe (London: 5 May 2000).

Brittan, L., *A Diet of Brussells: the Changing Face of Europe* (New York: Little Brown, 1999).

Callinicos, A., 'Social Theory Put to the Test of Politics: Pierre Bourdieu and Anthony Giddens', *New Left Review*, No. 236 (London: July/August 1999), 76–102.

Castle, S. and D. Usborne, 'Blair's Third Way Leads to New York' *The Independent:* UK News (London: 19 September 1999).

Chryssochou, D.M., *Democracy in the European Union* (London: Tauris Academic Studies, 1998).

Dyson, K., 'Benign or Malevolent Leviathan? Social Democratic Governments in a Neo-Liberal Euro Area', *Political Quarterly*, April–June 1999.

*Economist, The*, 'Germany: Rebirth of a Salesman' (London, 8 July 2000), 23–8.

——, 'The Union Pauses for Breath' (12 February 2000), 49–50.

——, 'Who Will be Joining Europe's Club – and When?' (8 April 2000), 53–4.

George, S., *An Awkward Partner: Britain in the European Community* (Oxford: Oxford University Press, 1990).

Giddens, T., *The Third Way* (Cambridge: Polity Press, 1998).

Gorz, A., *Reclaiming Work* (Cambridge: Polity Press, 1999).

Gray, J., *False Dawn: the Decline of Global Capitalism* (New York: New Press, 1998).

Grice, A., 'Chancellor Admits to Relocation of Wealth', *The Independent* (23 March 2000).

Hoffmann, S., 'From Decline to Renewal', *Time* (NY: 12 June 2000), 82–3.

Hutton, W., 'Up, Up and Away', *The Observer* (London: 21 November 1999).

*Independent, The*, 'A French Strike at the Heart of Blairism' (London, 27 September 1999).
Krieger, J., *British Politics in the Global Age: Can Social Democracy Survive?* (Cambridge: Polity Press, 1999).
Laughland, J., 'Many Key Players Who Forced the Euro on the Statute Book Were Crooks', *The Times*: Opinion (London: 25 January 2000).
Lichfield, J., 'A French Strike at the Heart of Blairism', *The Sunday Times* (London: 7 March 1999), 5.
*Marxism Today*, 'New Times' (London: October 1988).
Medley, R., 'Europe's New Big Idea', *Foreign Affairs* (New York: September/October 1999) 18–23.
Newman O. and R. de Zoysa, *The American Dream in the Information Age* (London: Macmillan 1999).
Pierce, A. and J. Landau, 'Support for the Euro Hits New Low', *The Times* (London: 27 March 2000).
Prescott, M. and S. Gray, 'Britain Vet New EU Push for a Unified Superstate', *The Sunday Times* (London: 19 March 2000).
Rifkin, J., *The End of Work* (New York: Putnam 1995).
Siedentop, L., *Democracy in Europe* (London: Allen Lane, 2000).
Smith, D. and T. Allen-Mills, 'It Wasn't Meant to Work Like This', *The Sunday Times*: News Review (London: 21 November 1999).
Smith, D. and S. Wright, 'The Turn towards Democracy', in Dennis Smith and Sue Wright (eds), *Whose Europe? The Turn towards Democracy* (Oxford: Blackwell 1999), 1–18.
Soetendorp, B., *Foreign Policy in the European Union* (London: Longman, 1999).
Webster, P., 'Mandelson Warns We May Miss the Euro Boom', *The Times*: Politics & Government (London: 20 April 2000).
Whittam-Smith, A., 'Mr Schroeder, It's not the British but You Who Has Let the Euro Down', *The Independent*: Comment (London: 6 December 1999).

# 9
# American Exceptionalism Again?

## Introduction

One of the great unsolved mysteries of American capitalism and society was why the US largely avoided the challenge to its legitimacy of a sustained socialist alternative. It was not as if capitalism was uniquely benign compared to developments elsewhere, nor without recourse to repression of trade unions and workers struggling to survive. Socialism did develop but only in a pallid version of the great struggles occurring in Europe at roughly the same time, and this in a country which had by the last decade of the nineteenth century the most advanced capitalist economy of them all. Just before the outbreak of the First World War, the socialist vote peaked at a mere 6 per cent, and the relative absence of a mass working-class party is reflected today in the weaker regulation of industry, less welfare, weaker unions, greater inequality and less government of all kinds (Lipset and Marks, 2000). The difference between developments in the USA and elsewhere is referred to as 'American Exceptionalism', and has prompted much academic historical enquiry. The reasons advanced range from: the lack of a feudal past, individualism as a powerful corrective ideology, ethnic and racial diversity fuelled by constant immigration which acted to inhibit collectivism and party organization within a powerful two-party system based on a first-past-the-post voting system, and last but not least, plentiful employment providing a degree of security and 'affluence' throughout much of the nineteenth century.

At different times in American history it looked as if political change favoured the adoption of European-style social democratic practice, most notably with Roosevelt's New Deal reforms carried forward later by Lyndon Johnson's 'Great Society' programmes in the 1960s. The adoption of Medicare and Medicaid and other 'entitlements', coupled with a commitment to alleviate the poverty of many newly enfranchised African-Americans, bore the hallmarks of embryonic social democracy, only to be waylaid by the mounting inflationary costs of the Vietnam War and subsequent criticisms of bureaucratic, wasteful, top-down solutions associated with too much 'big government'. Since those heady days little political headway has been made in reinstating these broad-based commitments, as faith in government has receded, while faith in the market mechanism became the panacea for solving societal problems. The Democratic Party has been fighting a rearguard action to protect the best of what remains of this legacy against recurring demands to curtail activist government.

However, the argument that America was indeed exceptional has been overstated. In his extended discussion of why US historical change took a different turn, Eric Foner suggests that 'what needs to be explained is the coexistence in American history of workplace militancy and a politics organized around nonideological parties appealing to broad coalitions, rather than the interests of a particular class' (Foner, 1990: 252). The assumptions underpinning the failure of US style socialism are also flawed. Comparatively speaking, there was no great social transformation in advanced capitalism either in the US or Europe. Trade union economism, working-class incorporation and voting for bourgeois parties was strong and 'normal'. This was evidenced, for example, by the support given to the British Tory party by a third of working-class voters throughout much of the twentieth century, and again given more contemporary prominence by the emergence of the Reagan Democrats in the 1980s. If one accepts these strictures, then Foner raises the intriguing possibility that the future does indeed lie within the New World – that is, American-style advanced capitalism, based on mass consumption and mass culture, dissolved class identity and ideology, as it did later in Europe. This may indicate that future European radicalism will focus more on libertarian and moral questions, will be more about gender and ethnicity and less concerned with the politics of class, the central preserve of Socialist belief. Foner concludes: 'Only time will tell whether the United States has been behind Europe in the development of socialism, or ahead of it, in socialism's decline' (ibid.: 276).

Today, the American radical tradition and activities of the left are even further marginalized. This is despite evidence that inequality and poverty are more severe with the US operating a system of welfare, described by Robert Solow, as 'lean and mean' than in other comparable states. As *The Economist* notes, the official poverty rate in 1998 at 12.7 per cent for a family of four, is still higher than in the 1970s, but a little lower than the peak of 15.1 per cent in 1993. Poverty is concentrated in urban areas, especially amongst families headed by single women, the majority of whom work for low wages supplemented by growing public assistance programmes, such as the Earned Income Tax Credit and tax credits for child care (20 May 2000). The cosmopolitan upper class, according to Rorty, gain their particular dominance due to the political ineffectiveness, plus cultural irrelevance, of the New Left. Eschewing economically based class issues and demands for redistribution in favour of debates over religion, ethnicity or minority rights, they have forgone their heritage and found themselves stranded in a 'sterile vacuum', where their focus is on theoretical cultural debate, rather than active political engagement. Politics, thus a matter of short-term expediency, becomes just another cost benefit enterprise (Rorty, 1998).

One central element of the Left's failure, in the absence of a popular mass 1960s-type movement, notes Barbara Epstein, has been the retreat into a poststructuralist discourse which ignored questions of economic redistribution. In denial of 'essentialism' or the belief in any inherent quality, including that of the 'good society', in relativizing interpretations of reality, it imparted a degree of scepticism which equally undermined the validity of the left's agenda as well. The result has been an impotent, authoritarian, left-wing sectarianism, often located in academia where 'campaigns to police language stand in for more substantial efforts throughout the left' (Epstein, 1997: 157). Tom Wolfe simply derides it as 'Rococo Marxism'. Within the mainstream Democratic Party there were also few grounds for optimism. A response to repeated electoral failure, became viewed by some activists as being beholden to a politics addressing only the core constituencies of labour, minorities and intellectuals, but without generating new appeals to a more suburban and white collar electorate. What emerged came later to be known in programmatic terms as the Third Way. This prompted much soul-searching, galvanizing a section within the party to force the pace of change and reform, while equally motivating others to resist. In the discussion that follows, the 'solution' to Democratic failure will be analysed, along with the successes and failures of the Clinton years, coupled with a critique of centrist politics and an examination of the likely future direction a more progressive politics both within the USA and beyond may take.

## 1. The struggle for the heart of the Democratic Party

Political defeat concentrates the mind wonderfully. But whether the lessons of defeat lead to a correct analysis of why things went wrong is perhaps more debatable. One such analysis now proving irresistible is that of the Democratic Leadership Council (DLC). By the 1970s, the New Deal coalition was fragmenting, compounded by the divisive fractures exposed by the Vietnam war, and replaceable by the 'New Politics' of issue activists, such as campaigners for feminist rights, homosexual reformers and environmentalists. They had profited from the changes in the electoral machinery for party nominations, as the contests were now more open with the adoption of primaries and delegate quotas, thereby displacing many former party officials. Their control of the institutional machinery of the party and of Congress was to become dominant. Over time the intra-party struggle that ensued was to change the nature of the party itself and how it was perceived by the wider electorate.

Into this battleground of New Left versus the old 'interest group Liberalism' stepped the DLC, founded in 1985 by Al From, in the wake of Reagan's stunning re-election win. The DLC was based on ideas, not broad-based constituency groups, and formed around an extra party elite whose support lay amongst more conservative elected officials and governors, moderate southerners, westerners and neo-liberals (those within the party in favour of government reform, 'growing the economy' to provide for social relief and comfortable with the new technologies). They initially believed the party hierarchy was already moving in their direction, but were not really prepared for the hostility and suspicion they encountered. As Baer notes, the New Democrats believed: 'that minorities, New politics issue activists, and labor should no longer be at the centre of the party's national coalition. The DLC was prepared to challenge the political strategy that had dominated Democratic thinking in the postreform era' (Baer, 2000: 67). Above all, what worried them was the possibility of a fundamental electoral realignment entrenching the Republicans as the majority party, formed as a consequence of Democratic ineptitude, irrelevance and rigidity of ideological belief encapsulated in the now derisory term of 'tax and spend' Liberalism. Critics within the party simply saw them as Democratic conservatives.

The DLC has now been active for over 15 years and over that time has modified its tactics and appeals – from an all-inclusive 'big tent' which diluted their message of reform, to one where they became more adversarial. They established their own think-tank, the Progressive Policy Institute and magazine in1989, their own state chapters, networks and conventions, and focused their efforts on support for a winning presidential candidate who could transform the party from the top down. A keynote statement of policy *The Politics of Evasion*, followed the electoral presidential débâcle of Dukakis in1988. This policy noted that even if all its traditional core supporters were mobilized the party would still have lost, and they were losing the northern ethnic and southern Protestant vote, especially male. To repair the damage the Party had to drop 'Liberal fundamentalism', with the caveat that continually losing the presidency would result one day in sub-presidential 'trickle down realignment', that is a haemorrhaging of governors and state officials. The prognosis advanced was to re-align the party with the mainstream values of 'individual liberty, equal opportunity and civic enterprise', thereby recapturing the centre, despite an organizational party structure which had most congressional Democrats remaining under Liberal control (Baer: 129–33). The DLC also embraced the ideas associated with the 'information age' and with it the need to attract new 'wired workers' to their progressive agenda. In programmatic terms, this translated into a strategy for: economic growth, not redistribution; an expansion of opportunity, not government; budget deficit reduction including subsidies and entitlements; a commitment to international trade including NAFTA; communitarian 'reciprocal responsibility'; a tough agenda on crime and a strong defence. In other words a listing of priorities at variance with traditional Democratic concerns.

In March 1990, the up-and-coming governor of Arkansas, Bill Clinton, took the chair of the DLC. The following year and with their endorsement he made the decision to run for the presidency. Clinton was in some ways an odd and ironical choice representing, as Martin Walker observes in his biography, so 'emblematic (a) figure of that antiwar and liberal current' which the DLC wished to oppose (Walker, 1996: 18). His 1992 presidential victory (with only 43 per cent of the vote) was fought on a New Democrat platform. But paradoxically, the success of the party in retaining narrow control of Congress and with it a majoritarian Liberal emphasis, meant that they were to be a source of opposition to the 'New Covenant' Clinton had sought. In Baer's words 'he lacked the political capital that would compel these legislators to follow his policy lead' (op. cit.: 220). Unable to build a new coalition he was forced leftwards, governing largely as an Old Democrat (including even raising gasoline taxes), with his one major concession to an increasingly demoralized DLC, being the passing of NAFTA with considerable bipartisan support in Congress.

Clinton's salvation as president and the revival of the DLC platform lay in his party's stunning defeat in the mid-term elections of 1994 to a revitalized, radicalized and ideologically driven conservative party, led by the incoming House Speaker, Newt Gingrich, and his 'Contract with America'. The Republican victory was made complete by their winning control of both houses of Congress for the first time since 1954. Within the inner court of the Clinton White House the ensuing ideological, and personality struggle, to reposition him in the centre, became a contest of epic proportions for the soul of the party, and one moreover dominated by spin control. This meant that substantive issues became increasingly sidelined to the process of managing news dissemination itself, a problem that New Labour also suffers from (Stephanopoulos, 1999). Prior to the presidential election of 1996, the DLC through the Progressive Foundation issued their *New Progressive Declaration*. This explicitly endorsed a Third Way 'new progressivism', by acknowledging the central role of the new knowledge economy and globalization, and the profound changes wrought to traditional state activity under threat from external agencies, such as international NGOs and regulatory bodies, and from below (by revitalized state and local authorities including the wider civic society). Public effort, they argued, should be as much about wealth creation as about its redistribution. In its broad-based appeal to progressives of any and all political persuasions, discussion within the DLC, disenchanted by Clinton's earlier failure to adopt their programme, flirted with the possibility of establishing an independent third party. In the event, Clinton eagerly adopted the DLC philosophy of 'opportunity, responsibility, community', with an enabling not mandating role for government symbolized by a commitment to balancing the budget and welfare reform.

The president's successful re-election in 1996 with an increased vote (49 per cent), along with his famous state of the union speech announcing 'the era of big government was over', epitomized the extent of the DLC victory. However, Liberals, with some justification, claimed that his defence of entitlements against further Republican cuts was the key to victory, along with their activist grass-roots support and financial help. This was despite the earlier unsuccessful concerted effort of the AFL-CIO in opposing NAFTA. The continuing control of Congress by the Republicans, though with narrowing majorities after 1998, meant that Clinton had to reach out and build bridges across party lines if he wished to see his programme enacted. Burns and

Sorenson characterize his role and leadership as a transactional not transformational president, one who fixes deals but lacks a new vision for his country (1999). Given the constraints he operated within this is hardly surprising. They are listed by Walker as follows: a budgetary fiscal crisis, mounting national debt (4 trillion dollars in 1992), including interest payments to service this greater than the actual defence budget in 1996, inherited caps on discretionary spending, and finally a sense that the need for an imperial-style president and corresponding executive branch was as defunct as the Cold War itself (Walker: 1996).

Admittedly, some of the constraints were partly self-imposed, brought on by Clinton's own disreputable behaviour with Monica Lewinsky. Two special prosecutors investigated his conduct, most notably that of Kenneth Starr, who pushed for impeachment. The long, complicated investigation into Whitewater (producing no evidence of criminality), and the intertwined nature of both investigations, has prompted one critic to bemoan the lack of objectivity in the way the case was reported. Much of the scurrilous evidence was funded by Clinton-haters, such as the Scaife family, although in more reasoned terms William Bennett accuses Clinton of 'reckless and irresponsible private behaviour; habitual lying; abuse of power ... defiled the office of the presidency ...'. Character matters (Bennett, 1998: 5). In his defence Anthony Lewis claims the case mounted was political '... plotting in secret to achieve a political overthrow by legal subterfuge'. Threats to witnesses, abuse of the separation of powers by an unaccountable prosecutor, and a criminalization of politics. Lewis concludes by stressing: 'the danger of misusing the criminal law for political ends is the lesson, finally of Kenneth Starr' (Lewis, 2000: 29).

A climate of hatred, fostered by shock jock radio talk and demonization by the Christian Right of Clinton personally, has been relentless in providing a constant background chorus of disapproval to his presidency, and one moreover reflected in Congress. More sober-minded Republicans were no doubt furious that his political skills in avoiding impeachment, plus his ability to sense the national mood, were coupled with his capable economic oversight over the economy. Whether this can be attributed to a defining Third Way politics, or is more the result of expediency and pragmatism as critics attest, the outcome has nevertheless been dramatic. Since 1998, the budget has been balanced and buoyant fiscal revenues are producing growing surpluses. Unemployment is at about 4 per cent and some 22 million net new jobs have been created since 1992, of which half are highly skilled 'wired workers'. Crucially, annual labour productivity between 1995 and 1999 rose to 2.9 per cent, double that of the previous twenty years, thereby helping further to improve living standards while keeping inflation under control. These impressive results have kept his approval ratings in positive territory. Indeed Republican irritation is precisely because of his adoption of some of their key ideas (especially welfare reform and slimming down or 'reinventing' government), while distancing himself from many traditional features of the Democratic programme. Dick Morris, who developed his electoral strategy in 1996, has termed this 'triangulation'. This involved the four e's: economy, education, environment and stigmatizing republican extremism.

Clinton's successes in social policy have been in governmental fine-tuning, thereby keeping partially alive the notion of activist government, and not in any grand new initiatives, such as the earlier abortive failure of health-care reform. However they are important, affecting the lives of many 'middle Americans' through such initiatives as extending Head Start, the family leave law, a new ratings system for television, new programmes of immunization, more police on the streets plus, in his first term, the restriction on hand gun sales. That inequality has increased on the stock market boom, should not detract from the fact of falling poverty since 1997. At last rising incomes for those at the bottom of the social hierarchy are being recorded, furthered by the earned income tax credit and a raising of the minimum wage. More needs to be done, and is achievable without recourse to extra taxation which remains the leitmotif of all parties today. He has moreover, in his personal ease with minorities and in his appointments to public service helped in building community links with government.

As the centre of power in the US migrates towards the west and south and away from the old Democratic city heartlands to the suburbs, so it reflects the changing demographic and sociological contours of American society, with more women working and smaller-sized families. Even more speculatively, as *The Economist* reports, 'By 2050, one in four of the 400m who will then be living in the United States will be Latino – and if you add in the Asians, their joint share will be one in three' (11 March 2000: 3). The political implications will be profound, as these 'New Americans' with their numbers fuelled by continuing immigration, begin to make political demands commensurate with their new-found status, especially in California and Texas. Clinton has assiduously ridden these changes, as demonstrated by his clever defusing of the affirmative action row over positive employment policies for minorities against white discontent in 1995, by suggesting the correct response was to 'mend it not end it'. Americans today are far more morally and socially tolerant than even they themselves suspected. The majority dislike of politicized religion coupled with non-judgmental attitudes about women's rights and civil rights extends to personal private standards of behaviour, and even stretches into the Bible belt (Wolfe, 1998).

Clinton's past electoral success amongst newer immigrant groups, minorities and women defines an agenda for his successors. Few of them will be able to escape from his shadow and influence, and so lies the continuing appeal of a Third Way agenda. Opponents like George W. Bush now mouth consensual 'centrist'-sounding platitudes, such as 'compassionate conservatism', but his policy prescriptions though far removed from invoking much direct public engagement are still some distance from Reaganism. One further indicator of how far the DLC has gained prominence is through the complementary formation of a Republican Leadership Council, formed to combat the right and redefine the Republican agenda. If, as Walker suggests, Clinton helped forge a new post-Cold-War consensus around lean government at home and free trade abroad (China has now won House approval to join the WTO), then the New Democrats may one day soon be welcoming as allies their New Republican counterparts, in opposition to both old-style Democratic Liberals and the Christian Right and their socially conservative agenda.

The remoulding of the Democratic agenda has diminished their past 'liberal' image amongst the electorate, but whether this could be described as reinstating a postmodernist form of social democracy is far from certain. James Fallows quotes Michael Sandel, a professor of government at Harvard, who is puzzled by how:

> 'Today's accumulation of enormous wealth is unparalleled since the last Gilded Age. But the Gilded Age of a century ago brought in its wake a wave of progressive reform and public investment – in parks, libraries, schools, and municipal projects. Today's gilded age, by contrast, hasn't generated any comparable resolve to ease the effects of inequality by strengthening public institutions' (Fallows, 2000).

Once there was nation-building allied to a sense of national interest and mutual responsibility, while today the rise of the global market differentiates the knowledge elite or 'overclass' from the many, and from sharing a common citizenship.

In answer to the question 'How far has Clinton moved the progressive agenda forward?' – critics answer barely at all, pointing to the glaring inadequacy of health-care coverage. For good measure, they also accuse him of opportunism and lack of principle. But given the opposition and narrow mandate, his 'small agenda' which included the construction of a more progressive income tax, has enhanced the prosperity of the vast majority of Americans. However, Clinton's constricted vision never really defined what a new progressive politics could offer. Paying off the national debt early on the back of growing budgetary surpluses, takes priority over promoting initiatives such as adequate child care, universal health insurance, protection of workers' rights and a communitarian commitment to repairing a weakening civic society.

## 2. Critics of Clintonism and the Third Way

Critics of the Clinton agenda and by implication the Third Way, range from across the political spectrum. Of greatest interest are those closer to home. Left Democrats are disillusioned by the movement into the centre and the curtailing of their hopes for a social democratic future transplanted in the USA, while their hopes of realization are further threatened by advancing globalization with its downward pressure on domestic wages and employee security. On the right, critics focus on moral questions and family instability, claiming that Clinton is an exemplar of all that is currently wrong with American society, while a few also concentrate on his embrace of globalization.

The most vituperative criticism from the left comes from the pen of Christopher Hitchens (1999). His argument characterizes US politics as 'the manipulation of populism by elitism', typified by triangulation or 'the benefit of the "lesser evil" calculus' (ibid: 23, 26). Clinton, positioned equidistantly between left and right, thereby secures the approval of both, but in reality delivers only opinion poll rhetoric to the former while 'the Right gets deeds'. Thus, Hitchens dismisses the welfare reform of 1996 as an essentially Republican class measure when 'being tough on welfare was more important than being correct'. The consequence was 'the creation of a large helot underclass disciplined by fear and scarcity, subject to endless surveillance, and used as a weapon against any American worker lucky enough to hold a steady or unionized job' (ibid.: 65). However, the rising numbers of the working poor, assisted by the earned income tax credit (a subsidy to employers to pay low wages, according to Hitchens), are now perceived more sympathetically by the American public as the stigma of welfare dependency is removed. As Massing observes, improving benefits for those prepared to help themselves by addressing the question of a proper social wage is, once again, on the political agenda (Massing, 1999). Equally condemnatory in Hitchens's polemic is Clinton's foreign policy. Thus, the air raids on Afghanistan and Sudan are depicted, as in the film *Wag the Dog*, as a ruse to redirect attention away from the Lewinsky scandal. Nothing is positive and his presidency has further dishonoured a largely co-opted left.

Less partisan, more measured, but still negative, are critiques that chart the abandonment of the Left's traditional terrain. Jeff Faux accuses the Third Way of being amorphous and incoherent, lacking a plausible strategy of renewal and inadequate in its rejection of the Old Democrat platform. For a start, the Third Way is seen as a tactical adaptation to electoral failure in the early 1980s, but based on a misreading of the party's history. Democratic governments are, and were, fiscally responsible. It was Reagan who ran up the largest deficits ever recorded. The presidential victory of 1992 was won not by adopting 'conservative issues', but by focusing on the bread-and-butter issues of the economy, and relying on traditional supporters to get the vote out. The danger as Faux reminds us, is that the New Democrats have already 'conceded the imagery, fostered by conservatives for decades, of the Democrat party as a nest of left-wing extremists' and so are forced to mount a rear-guard defence against further shifts rightwards. If that is indeed the case, then the Third Way in the USA is a dead end, as it lowers expectations of what public action could be capable of, and narrows the policy debate to safe issues. Faux writes: 'political compromise is built into electoral democracy, but principled compromise starts with the principles, not the compromise' (Faux, 1999: 70, 75). Furthermore, the lack of a principled opposition to market excess and globalization leaves many workers defenceless, undermining their trust and replacing it with a belief that government is largely supportive of the big business battalions. This latter refrain, that the imperative of the market implies a minimal role in government regulation, and indifference to market outcomes, is echoed in much of the criticism of US-style Third Way politics. David Henwood, no less a severe critic, argues that the adoption of such an overtly pro-market position by a Democratic president has meant that: 'advocacy groups for the poor, unions, environmental organizations, and the liberal weeklies were all silenced' (Henwood, 1997: 169). This was written, however, some two years prior to the WTO meeting in Seattle when a combination of protesters totally disrupted the proceedings.

In a similar vein, Chait argues that the Third Way implies a one-directional step-by-step move to the right, with the left consistently compelled to give ground for the sake of retaining the centrist position. The conundrum is the basic asymmetry where the proponents of the Third Way essentially come from the camp of the left. As left-centre policy is their starting point, their advocacy of the middle way impels an *a priori* shift to the right. Their opposite camp's lukewarm response changes the calculus once again. In order to retain the centre, the Third Way as time goes on, shifts more and more to the right. As Chait remarks: 'It is a contradiction, and also the best definition of Clintonism' (Chait, 1998: 19). One feature of Clinton's non-ideological politics is an over-reliance on focus groups and polling data, none of which suggests that a clear vision or commitment to principle has been embraced unlike his opponents who know exactly what they want from government.

Curiously there is a significant overlap between the agendas of the radical right and the radical left in some major policy areas. When it comes to globalization or the role of the nation state, the two opposed movements' declared policies are similar. Patrick Buchanan, once a leading figure on the right of the Republican party but now apostate, is the presidential nominee for the Reform Party of Ross Perot. Buchanan for many years acted as a key spokesman for the Christian Right, and was vociferous in his denunciation of the pro-choice lobby, and other Liberal moral failings, associated with the godless excesses of the 1960s. His most recent book largely constitutes a diatribe against free trade and takes up a conservative-populist stance (Buchanan, 1998). The prevailing attitude of 'there is no alternative' to globalization is firmly condemned as inimical to the national interest. The continued sovereignty of the nation state is perceived as essential to best safeguard public interests, while protecting the weak from their otherwise dire fate. Transnationals, speculative money, plus the mass export of jobs to low-wage economies are identified as prime threats. The huge trade deficits, derelict productive sites, decay in social capital together with the abandonment of the lower-skilled to a workless existence, are cited as too high a price to pay for 'economic progress' that apparently enriches the wealthy and powerful while depriving the masses still further.

To a lesser degree there is also a growing tendency to isolationism amongst some Congressional Republicans, expressed in their hostility to external regulatory bodies such as the UN and IMF, and committing US troops abroad, even for peace-keeping measures such as Kosovo.

Traditional notions of Wilsonian morality and 'of making the world safe for democracy' are rejected unless vital American military or economic interests are involved (Judis, 1999). Clinton, after a hesitant start, promoted a policy of engaging with and enlarging the world's market democracies, although incongruities remain, most notably in his vacillation over China and human rights abuse. While no clear and consistent grand strategy emerges in the post-Cold War era, few commentators admit to one either, although criticism of the administration for sending the wrong signals to adversaries and allies alike at different times is commonly made (Hyland, 1999). For Buchanan and others, similarly ideologically disposed, an 'America First' rhetoric is a return to the politics and class analysis of earlier times, but it also poses a very real dilemma for Third Way proponents. While constraining globalization and adopting protectionism may well protect the lower privileged and the lesser skilled at least in the short term, it equally militates against the modernizing agenda and commitment to open trade that the Third Way espouses.

The USA, as the leading First World economy, with the highest productivity of all OECD nations and as the world's only surviving superpower, naturally finds itself most comfortable with the New Economy and technologies which are gradually encompassing the world. At a time when the US domestic situation is almost totally positive – with higher living standards, a cleaner environment, better health, an emerging black middle class, falling crime – all of which fuel ever-rising expectations, Gregg Easterbrook remarks, 'as pragmatism supplants ideology, society will get better at fixing things' (Easterbrook, 1999). Clinton has long been accused of lacking vision, a criticism similarly made of the Third Way, but the fine tuning skills he has brought to his presidency have helped secure this unparallelled prosperity.

Anthony Giddens, Britain's leading Third Way analyst, defines its politics as 'concerned with restructuring social democratic doctrines to respond to the twin revolutions of globalization and the knowledge economy', it is not simply an attempt to secure a middle ground between socialism and neo-liberalism (Giddens, 2000: 163). As good a summary of Clinton's endeavours could hardly be bettered. The leading transnational corporations (TNCs) are American and the rising industries of the future are similarly dominated by American corporate interests. Globalization is largely viewed as a promise rather than a threat, notwithstanding the short-term adjustments necessary to accommodate older economy workers who suddenly find their traditional skills redundant. With trade union membership falling to only 14 per cent of the workforce, the AFL-CIO has led the charge against NAFTA and globalization, often on the self-seeking grounds of defending international labour standards, whereas the reality is to keep out cheaper goods manufactured by foreign workers whose only hope of a better life is through access to the US market. This is not a 'race to the bottom' but a form of nationalist pseudo-protectionism (Amsden, 2000). Clinton has been mindful of these concerns with his stress on education, retraining and 'employability', but so far the matching funds to retrain and redeploy those left behind are inadequate.

According to WTO figures, in 1999 the US share of total world exports was 12.4 per cent and worth some $695 billion, thereby ranking the US as the world's single largest exporter of goods. By contrast, the total EU share was greater at 18.9 per cent, but opinion is far more divided over the merits of continuing globalization. The American critics, Petras and Morley, decry the dominance exercised over the economy and federal authorities by the largely unaccountable powerful TNCs, ably assisted by the foreign policy and political elite and the financial resources of Wall Street, pitted against an undernourished and troubled Main Street (Petras and Morley, 1995). But of greater significance, is that the balance of critical commentary within the US tends to favour globalization, and the operation of world-wide free markets as a force for democratization and modernization, and as the only effective means of eliminating endemic world-wide poverty (Bergsten, 1997; Friedman, 1999; Yergin and Stanislaw, 1998). It also implies US control without the exercise of military power. Within the more protectionist European Union, however, judgment is more equivocal. Dismissed by one eminent critic as promoting a 'false dawn', the advent of global technologies facilitates an unregulated and anarchic international state rivalry for global market dominance, disruptive of domestic social cohesion and cultural unity (Gray, 1998) – while two notable German writers talk of the 'global trap' and its assault on democracy and prosperity, and the desperate need to reform currency markets, speculative capital flows, and asset price inflation (Peter-Martin and Schumann, 1997). Despite the debate, the question of how really globalized the world has become is still unsettled, as the Asian economic crisis of the late 1990s, had remarkably little effect on the economies of the USA and Europe.

In his final State of the Union address to Congress in January 2000, President Clinton fully endorsed America's final frontier – globalization.

> To realise the full possibilities of this economy, we must reach beyond our own borders, to shape the revolution that is tearing down the barriers and building new networks among nations and individuals, and economies and cultures: globalisation. It's the central reality of our times.

He envisaged a new trade consensus based on open markets, as the best way to improve living and environmental standards, while a policy promoting democracy and peace would also facilitate and sustain the reform movement in China and Russia. A second emphasis, was on the need for domestic security against conventional enemies, with the US acting as international peacemaker as the occasion demanded, including too the policing of international terrorism and criminality. There was no apologizing for America's commitment and endorsement of the global market and what he saw as the progress and prosperity that it had brought to American citizens. Clinton went on to remark, 'we should be filled with awe and joy at what lies over the horizon. And we should be filled with absolute determination to make the most of it.' Yet despite the hubris, the President has been unable to restore public respect, trust and engagement with government. The political culture has not been reinvigorated by a sense of difference, of a new defining public project – beyond a cafeteria mix of policy called triangulation – to which Democrats can point with pride. Clinton has been a brilliant counter-punching tactician, but always lacked a coherent strategy (Rochman, 2000).

## 3. The race for the year 2000 presidential election

The impeachment of President Clinton has left deep scars with no winners only losers. The institution of the presidency has been weakened, along with claims to 'executive privilege', while the Office of the Independent Counsel is deeply compromised. An American public if not scandalized, is appalled that such indiscretion could be so liberally reported world-wide by an apparently insatiable media anxious for detail, much of it prurient. Republicans, on the defensive after their electoral reversals in 1998, were defeated yet again after losing the impeachment vote in an acrimonious and partisan debate in the Senate in February 1999. However, they quickly sought to repair the damage by promoting an outsider and 'moderate' in George W. Bush to become their presidential nominee for 2000. Meanwhile, the Democrats will seek vindication in the coming election to assuage the shame of impeachment, by reinforcing their argument that it was indeed a vast right-wing conspiracy – illegitimate and partisan in nature and unworthy of such draconian reprisal – in what was essentially private misconduct. With only six seats needed to regain control of both the House and the Senate, an intense and possibly bitter electoral battle in the aftermath of impeachment is likely.

The promise of tax cuts no longer has the allure it once held. With jobs plentiful, and over half of all Americans owning shares, many feel wealthier on the back of the stock market boom. The burden of taxation is now lower on 'middle America', and while voters naturally want lower taxes, many realize that growing budgetary surpluses since 1998 should be used for sustaining the long-term financial stability of Social Security and Medicare, both subject to long-term negative demographic trends, and also to reducing the interest payments on the national debt. Gore proposes to pay off the national debt by 2012. This might be the more prudent political agenda as too rapid a cut in taxation will overheat an already booming economy. The contest between Bush and Gore will determine whether Bush's commitment to cut taxes significantly, increase Pentagon spending, and use part of the social security surplus to fund private investment accounts within the retirement system is the more attractive option for voters. In any case, as Martin Walker observes, the four leading presidential candidates at the beginning of 2000 more or less agreed on the big issues: no tax increases, no changes in the abortion law, a commitment to free trade, and with former 'wedge' issues like welfare now effectively settled. The result has been a blurring of issues, with Congress once again authoritative, and more power devolved to state and local government, especially in regard to welfare initiatives (Walker, 2000).

Given this context, the race for the presidency threw up unconventional challenges. Senator McCain, running against the Republican front-runner George W. Bush, campaigned for a ban on 'soft money' in campaign finance and the corrupting role of corporate lobbyists, coupled with 'responsible' tax cuts. For good measure, he added a riposte against the intolerance of the Christian coalition. His Vietnam war record, 'character' and anti-establishment stance proved equally popular with many independent-minded Democrats whose support Bush will need to win if he wishes to become president. Bush's own political base is, like Clinton before him, out of the governor's mansion. His campaign, although ultimately successful, tactically veered towards the Right so forcefully condemned by McCain. Described by *The Economist* as 'a composite of unpopular boilerplate Republican positions' (11 March 2000: 61–2), following his early 'Super Tuesday' victory, he quickly moved towards the political centre to re-establish his more 'compassionate big-tent conservatism'. However, the political centre is more open, fluid and demographically diverse than ever before. Voters appear more socially and morally tolerant, which gives politicians greater freedom from too overt a media scrutiny of their private lives. And Clinton has reminded Americans of what government can achieve and so has partially restored their belief that it can deliver quality public service.

This presents a dilemma for Bush, and the Democratic nominee and establishment figure Al Gore, the victor over Senator Bradley who had campaigned on a more traditional 'left' Democrat platform, by advocating an extensive health insurance scheme. If both presidential contestants are seen as too beholden to their party's 'special interests' (Gore, for example, has close links with the powerful teachers' unions; Bush is supported by the Christian Right), along with their capacity to mobilize vast monetary resources and campaigning foot-soldiers, then both may have difficulty in winning majority approval. The paradox is that it takes money, and lots of it, to run an effective campaign which creates cynicism amongst an electorate wanting someone in the White House whom they can respect, and perhaps place on a pedestal. And all at a time when party ideology and the big issues are losing relevance to more pragmatic problem-fixing agendas, along with a nebulous belief in the power of a candidate who can somehow display independence, principle, 'character' and personality. Now where does this leave the Third Way? Recommitting the Democrats under a Gore presidency to improvements in public services and to extending Clinton's 'small agenda' is welcome in itself. But in eschewing larger tax cuts demanded by the Republicans leaves unquestioned the limited interventionist role assigned to government by the 'conventional wisdom' of the Right, and does little for developing a progressive 'all-inclusive' agenda.

## 4. A progressive future and changing demographics

No political environment remains static. Yesterday's wooing by Clinton of the relatively affluent suburban 'soccer moms' marching in Washington for more effective gun control has garnered some limited support for the Democrats, offset no doubt by NRA gains among traditional blue-collar workers. But what about the majority of Americans who are neither rich nor poor and have a distrust, or at least scepticism, towards government and its accomplishments? For critics like Greider, the New Democrat label promotes a Faustian pact with finance and globalizing big business in exchange for 'soft money' to fund public support. But in reality it lowers public expectations as to what government can do providing a 'cul-de-sac for the party that claims to speak for the working class and the poor' (Greider, 2000: 12). With household debt rising to over $6.3 trillion and only 7 per cent of Americans owning shares worth over $10 000, the hyperbole surrounding the 'trickle down' effects of the new miracle economy needs unmasking. The victor has been big money and its negative non-decision-making whereby 'money doesn't just talk in politics, it silences' (ibid: 16). Walter Dean Burnham writing in *The Nation*, detects discontent below the surface. The political contradiction of a centrist electorate that 'on the ideological plane, government is perceived in conservative terms, but operationally, there is a liberal mode that favours continuance of domestic programs that only Big Government can provide' (17 April 2000: 12). Clinton never won a popular majority of the total votes cast in a political landscape largely conditioned by Reagan, leaving the Democrats exposed as they have to satisfy not just their traditional vote, but also the out-group claimants vulnerable to the jibes of the 'silent majority'.

Decreasing voter turnout disproportionately hits the Democrats hardest, making their task of maximizing potential support through expensive television advertising and rallies ever more dependent on raising money. So a vicious cycle of dependency on 'special interests' is maintained. This is much to the disgust of the consumer champion, Ralph Nader, now the Green Party candidate and well able to siphon off independent-minded Democrats to his cause, especially in the key state of California. On the conservative far right, Buchanan will attract some limited support for the Perot-funded, but bitterly divided Reform Party. However, both Buchanan and Nader raise vital issues, such as the real impact of global trade on working families or continuing corporate welfare abuse, ignored by the mainstream. As a general category, independents are a growing constituency and, as Judis remarks, have some characteristics reminiscent of the Progressives at the turn of the century. Located primarily within the middle-income white middle class with a minimum of a high school education, and geographically located from California to Maine and New Hampshire, they are socially liberal but dislike big government, and most of all abhor the 'special interests' influence on Washington. They comprise some 15 per cent of the electorate, and from supporting Perot in 1992, switched to Clinton in 1996. Moderate in outlook they reportedly dislike Gore's campaign fund-raising (Judis, 13 March 2000).

By the time the political psephologists have delved over the electorate, subdividing and categorizing them into their likely voting constituencies, the one segment that appears to be neglected or taken for granted is the 'forgotten majority'. The great dividing line of real American prosperity is the acquisition of the increasingly expensive four-year college degree, the lack of which defines the new white-collar working class. As Rogers and Teixeira note 'the suburban electorate is in fact composed mostly of members of the forgotten majority: two-earner families of low to moderate education and income, generally working in low-level white-collar, service, and skilled blue-collar jobs' (Rogers and Teixeira, 2000: 70) They comprise some 55 per cent of the white electorate which in total is still some four-fifths of all adult voters. For many of them, stagnant, or declining incomes, until very recently have left them frustrated, while government has failed to rekindle their aspirations which a growing budgetary surplus could now satisfy. A Democrat leadership tied into fiscally conservative values, with a perceived failure to address the long-term problems of inadequate health-care coverage, of satisfactory pensions rewarding hard work, affordable child care, decent wages and quality education and training, could be ruinous. The party's base in the trade unions and minority vote, while geographically concentrated on both coasts and the industrial Mid-West, is too narrowly conceived. They need to enlarge their support especially amongst men.

The Republican dilemma negatively mirrors the Democrats, needing to recruit amongst unorganized whites especially women, and geographically extend beyond the South, Plains and Rocky Mountains. 'The missing middle' as Skocpol terms a majority of middle-class women, now work longer hours to sustain the family budget, at a time when their partner's income has effectively been cut in real terms since the 1970s. Social policy has concentrated on the needs of the old or very poor, so ignoring their urgent requirement for more child-care support coupled with tax breaks (Skocpol, 2000). Whichever party can link the forgotten majority's economic experience to new activist governmental programmes will win a durable majority.

The picture becomes more opaque when the assumption of the South acting as a bulwark of republican conservatism is questioned.

Demographics can unravel many a political career. David Firestone, writing in *The New York Times*, notes that new migration into the south fuelled by moderate northerners is realigning the suburbs towards the centre. The new political agenda is more concerned with education, transport, technology, new jobs and managing growth – issues favouring the Democrats incorporating a degree of activist government – rather than tax cuts and crime. Quality-of-life issues are assuming a greater prominence (3 June, 2000). However, this may just as easily favour the new breed of Republicanism offered by Bush, promoting the values of bipartisan government and educational choice, as it does for Gore.

The pressures for centrist conformity in this post-ideological age are at a premium for electoral party success, which means that many issues become relatively ignored, such as the war against drugs, which increasingly targets minorities. Additionally, many moderate Republicans feel squeezed, and at congressional level this bodes ill for the party as the disproportionate influence of evangelical Protestantism and frontier individualism, gathers apace. Bush is all too aware of the danger, but what independence he can muster to forge a broader alliance is heavily conditioned by the Christian Coalition's renowned ability to get the vote out. His advocacy of 'compassionate conservatism', notes *The Economist*, is not a purely rhetorical device and has a degree of intellectual consistency. Bush accepts limited government in principle, but in targeting poverty, for example, would offer a tax credit to locally based 'faith-based organizations' to re-moralize the indigent while re-engaging the community (and parents) in the welfare of their errant children (29 July 2000: 27–9). This strengthens his support with Christian groups and acknowledges long-standing communitarian concerns. Thus, the Republican platform at the Philadelphia Convention could declare: 'for every American, there must be a ladder of opportunity, and for those most in need, a safety net of care'. Some ideas of the Progressive Policy Institute are now co-opted by Republicans, such as 'digitizing government', whereby an information tsar would force government bureaucracies to adopt new information technologies, and ideas on educational choice also owe much to this source. In addition, Bush has radically advanced ideas for Social Security by diverting part of the payroll tax into individual accounts invested on the stock market; and he also promotes a new 'star wars' defence option, both of which Gore deems 'risky'.

For the Democrats, the dilemma remains that the DLC issues on which it has campaigned for the last few years have become a new political orthodoxy. They are looking stale, and so logically the party needs to reassure its grass roots that a new progressive agenda – based as Teixeira and Rogers suggest on a universalistic, transracial programme, that focuses on economic class issues, relevant to all working families – is achievable in an era of near full employment and rapidly growing budgetary surpluses. This will involve more accountability within schools, remoulding Social Security to ward off putative attempts at privatization, more fiscal targeting to aid working families, boosts to public spending via 'trust funds' on health, environment and education; and a recognition that the sway of the market has finally reached its limits. The focus is decidedly economic not cultural or sectional. Gore's emphasis on prudence and opting for the status quo make him appear conservative, although somewhat schizophrenically, he invokes a populist (Old Democrat) class rhetoric in his speeches attacking major corporate interests. He is offering large tax credits to subsidize individual retirement accounts in addition to the basic Social Security, a major boost to public education spending, environmental sustainability programmes, gun control, plus the promotion of health care for children lacking insurance. Whether the Democrats will move against the corporate interests that feed them appears unlikely, but this essentially political problem will one day have to be tackled. Having partially restored faith in governmental competence it would be ironic if they could not capitalize on their success by promoting those issues so central to the 'forgotten majority'. Without it a new progressive agenda cannot be formulated.

## 5. America's influence: a threat or promise?

Despite the post-ideological drift of Third Way politics in the United Kingdom and Europe, very real differences still exist between different sections of the Left in most societies. Within the United Kingdom, it is not just between old and new Labour, but also over the future direction of the EU. The decision on whether Britain should join the euro is undecided, and on hold until after the next election. Andrew Marr observes that for many in Europe the common enemy is the globalizing role and power of the USA, and the threat it poses to European notions of cultural integrity and the welfare state. In this scenario, the Commission and the promise of a more integrated Europe provides an oasis of sanity against a world run by American global corporations. Whereas in more euro-sceptical Britain the perceived 'enemy' are the centralizing powers of Brussels, represented by an unelected

Commission challenging parliamentary sovereignty and a traditional way of life (Marr, 2000). By contrast, the political debate in the USA seems almost prosaic and settled. One consequence, noted earlier, is that some conservatives suggest that the United Kingdom should join NAFTA in an 'English-Speaking Union'. However, this would run counter to traditional American interests urging the United Kingdom to be more centrally involved in Europe, acting as a powerful voice promoting open free trade rather than protectionism.

In some ways it would be natural even for a New Labour government to favour closer links with Washington. On policy issues much has been copied, including even the exchange of academic personnel. From the early decision granting independence to the Bank of England, to adopting zero-tolerance on crime, welfare to work, public–private partnerships, and even to the mechanics of winning elections plus a host of other initiatives, Labour owes a great debt to Clinton and the New Democrats. The emphasis on education and getting everyone hooked onto the Internet strongly echoes the 'new economy' culture of the US. This is a far cry from Old Labour and past attitudes. During the dark years of Thatcherism, Labour sought salvation in the EU, with its legal protection for citizen and labour rights, identifying with the spirited defence of social democratic practice against the new market realism, and as a way out of their own impotence. America under Reagan's leadership, the arch apostle of deregulation, offered nothing for them. Indeed by the late 1980s, critics, notably Paul Kennedy, were writing of the decline of the American economic empire through 'imperial overstretch', as de-industrialization had not yet been offset by the productivity boost of the new technologies associated with the Clinton years, years which were formative in New Labour's evolution.

Today, Labour is enamoured with the success of the US economy, in terms of its employment record, productivity growth and low inflation, encompassed in the catch-all phrase of 'the new economic paradigm'. By contrast, the early to mid-1990s in Europe witnessed the reverse. A slowing down in growth, chronic structural unemployment and a failure to adapt quickly enough to the new technologies, although the corner now seems to have been turned. However, much in the American experience is unsatisfactory and has been catalogued by Bok in his 'state of the nation' assessment: a lack of a national health system (the WHO currently lists the US system as 37th in the world), inadequate job training, with a welfare state grossly deficient by European standards and generating much insecurity amongst the people (Bok, 1996). There is much disquiet over the long-term effects of the Welfare Reform Act of 1996, as many former recipients and their families have simply disappeared from the rolls, or those in work struggle on low wages with often insufficient child-care support.

The problem for Labour is how much can be adopted from US practice, but without at the same time sacrificing that which is unique to British cultural experience, and also whether in the long run our ties to Europe, are and will be, of more lasting import. Are the British the 'Trojan horse' for importing, via their backdoor, all that is American into Europe, that De Gaulle once so feared British membership would bring in its wake? On this question, Labour's Third Way analysis has so far argued the familiar mantra of flexibility, employability, low taxes, and promotion of the new technologies to secure the necessary global dynamism to compete with the USA, a country increasingly turning towards the Pacific Rim economies and to developing its South American links by including Chile within NAFTA one day soon. Labour secured a notable success at the Lisbon Summit in March 2000, prompting much soul-searching in Europe afterwards. The attitudes of many left-of-centre governments, especially that of Jospin in France, are more equivocal towards the USA. American 'soft power' influence over many international NGOs is resented, as overtly biased and too pro-market, being less concerned with the rights of trade unionists and labour in general and undermining of solidarity. The EU, it is argued, must integrate further to provide a degree of regional stability, by promoting intra-regional trade which the adoption of a strong single currency can command.

One other, somewhat paradoxical, difference is that in the USA the question of national identity, posed by de Crevecoeur, of a new emerging American identity in the eighteenth century and reinforced in daily affirmation in American schools since, is now a hotly debated issue for both the United Kingdom and EU. Whereas, in the USA, economic success has brought greater acceptance and pride, in the EU doubts are justifiably raised by the new centralizing, federalizing structures comprised of top-down bureaucracies which stifle consent, democratic accountability, diversity and legitimacy. The vision which produced the balancing act of the American constitution is still sadly lacking for the European venture (Siedentop, 2000). In the United Kingdom the devolution to the new Scottish Parliament, Welsh Assembly, and power-sharing Stormont, coupled with a newly elected mayor for London, with others soon to follow in the major conurbations, have raised the question of British identity and also that of the

'English question'. Peter Hitchens, in a parallel to the culture wars debate in the US, argues that Labour's cultural values 'of classlessness, anti-racism, sexual inclusiveness and licence, contempt for the nation state, dislike of deference, scorn for restraint, and incomprehension for the web of traditions and prejudices which were revered by the other side', now dominate against older conservative values which 'stretched back into a misty past' (Hitchens, 1999: xviii). In a more temperate tone, Marr sees the possibility of an English parliament emerging with a second chamber devoted to the federal issues of its four constituent members (Marr, 2000). Whatever the result, the question of the break-up of Britain is real.

A new politics that addresses the growing fluidity of the British electorate, where macro-economic issues are more settled, and where a new type of populism, as vividly demonstrated by Ken Livingstone's winning of the mayoralty race for the multicultural melting pot that is London, is now emerging. The emergence of more localized, single-issue, diversified lifestyle politics are not amenable to party machinery control from the top, with its 'command' type political culture. Few traditional cues indicate how these new electorates will respond, and so they pose a real dilemma for 'traditional' politicians in this new non-party context. Labour needs to be more responsive by developing a newer more 'bottom-up' egalitarian culture, less 'Middle England' in its appeal. As Marr notes, in *The Observer*, there is no longer one national dialogue as: 'Progressive and conservative populism can coexist in the same places and parties, even in the same people' (Marr, 30 April, 2000). American community politics is instructive. In New York there has emerged a trans-national community building 'rainbow politics', where Latinos now form a larger minority than African-Americans. In California, non-party propositional voting of the 'majority–minority' society, where white non-Hispanics now comprise a minority – but one becoming increasingly resentful and discriminatory to newer over-achieving Spanish-speaking urban gentrifiers – offers some clues, but is mindful that some are negative and to be avoided (Davis, 2000). New Labour will equally have to come to terms with this growing fluidity of culture and minority aspiration coexisting within Britain's major cities, as a newer civic politics extending beyond central control and direction takes root. Freedland's analysis recommending adoption of an American-style reinvigorated localism (and regionalism) is fast becoming a reality – a new Third Way solution to offset European-style 'federalism' and powerful central state control, such as is traditionally exercised at Westminster (Freedland, 1998).

## Conclusion

Is American exceptionalism the harbinger of the future, as Foner implied at the beginning of this chapter? The evidence is diverse and contradictory, so that any prognosis lies in a muddle of incompatible tensions. Europe and the United Kingdom are both intertwined by ties of culture and kinship to the USA, but obviously for Britain that is even more the case. The differences however remain profound. The political and economic evolution of the United Kingdom in the years ahead point if anything to the geographical proximity of Europe drawing nearer, and not just because the majority of UK trade is directed to those markets, but also for growing compatibility of outlook. The Third Way in its New Democrat and New Labour formulations, while accepting the broad contours of the capitalist market including globalization, must further seek to moderate the social injustices revealed by market failure. In doing so, this will bring them closer to mainstream European social democracy, which itself is undergoing renewal.

The DLC's influence has been profound, extending beyond the Democrats and even conditioning the way the Republican leadership will fight the 2000 election. It is however, becoming a victim of its own success, as what once seemed fresh and novel has become its own orthodoxy. The case for limited interventionism into the market by the state is no longer viewed with instinctive opprobrium, as conditioned the situation earlier. However, state spending is unlikely to rise as a percentage of GDP. Domestically, this means supply-side changes, fiscal adjustments and a 'small agenda' of progressive sometimes localized reform, to offset the insecurities bedevilling labour markets and family life, which in no way impairs the international competitiveness of the domestic economy. How 'maintaining international competitiveness' can be fairly defined immediately conjures an extension of government regulation. A growing chorus of voices view the free trade option as more a curse than a benefit in its shifting of production overseas, and exerting downward pressure on unions and workers to moderate their demands. Milton Esman's powerful advocacy, supportive of the federal government, is equally anxious to protect the Democratic heritage and reinstate a more traditional Democrat programme. He would, for example, penalize companies shipping production overseas, thereby exploiting free-trade opportunities, by reimporting the produce back to the USA at the cost of domestic workers' jobs and living standards (Esman, 2000).

People often expect more from government than it is usually capable of and so are constantly riled when it fails to deliver. But as long as economic growth is sustained, and jobs generated, the 'crisis' conditions heralding a change of political direction will not be forthcoming. Political trust and governmental competence need re-establishing, with Clinton's record both ambiguous and paradoxical. The former is withheld by the electorate, while the latter has been partially reinstated, but only by tacking rightwards to conjoin with neo-conservative values. Indeed, the growing role of corporate 'soft money' in sponsoring television political advertising for the two main parties, is now crucial to influencing election campaigns and candidate selection, and is even linked by some commentators to cross-party political support for globalization. However, the majoritarian 'culture of contentment' continues to sustain a consensus, and one possibly moving in a more progressive direction, as fiscal conservative orthodoxy, having outlived its purpose, steps aside once again for limited activist government.

## Postscript

At the time of writing (early December 2000), the presidential election is still unresolved despite intensive legal and political challenges to the legitimacy of the Florida vote. The country literally remains a divided nation – geographically, culturally and politically. The popular majority vote just barely lies with Gore despite a turnout of about 100 million people, while control of the House of Representatives is still retained by the Republicans with a reduced majority, the Senate being split 50:50.

The lesson for Al Gore is that, following the Convention in Los Angeles, his embrace of a populistic class-based economic appeal, though securing his trade union and activist base within the party, may nevertheless have lost him centrist aspiring middle-class support. This growing constituency so assiduously built up by Clinton's Third Way agenda should have been easily secured by Gore, given a favourable economy with real increases in wages and living standards since 1997. It may well be that Gore's largely rhetorical excesses, despite his New Democrat background, were ill advised. Furthermore, Ralph Nader's ecological agenda may have deprived him of marginal, but critical support in a few key states. Women, however, voted for Gore by a margin of 12 per cent and the black vote was nearly unanimous.

By contrast, Bush secured the overwhelming support of white males by a margin of 23 per cent, plus the endorsement of small-town and rural America. This was coupled with the strong endorsement of the Protestant religious right, and was even reflected in the normally pro-Democratic Catholic vote which gave him 46 per cent of their vote, perhaps indicative of some unease over Clinton's lax moral standards about which they were determined to demonstrate their disapproval.

The obvious conclusion is that governing from the centre is the only possibility. There is no mandate for any candidate to pursue either a significant cut in taxation, or a commensurate boost to public spending. This is somewhat ironic given the growing budgetary surplus (from 1988) and continuing economic stability so carefully engineered by Clinton and Greenspan at the Federal Reserve since 1992, and one of the President's key economic objectives.

Today, real public policy choices are again on offer. Policy can be assessed on its merits and not distorted through the prism of contributing to or subtracting from the deficit. Projected surplus revenues over the next decade, *ceteris paribus*, are forecast at over two trillion dollars, but the gridlocked state of the nation may preclude any forward movement. For the first time since the last recorded government surplus in 1969, an opportunity has arisen for purposeful government, but the political majority to sustain it is still not available.

## References

Amsden, A.H., 'Ending Isolationism', *Dissent* (Spring 2000), 13–16.

Baer, K.S., *The Politics of Liberalism from Reagan to Clinton* (Lawrence: University of Kansas Press, 2000).

Bennett, W.J., *The Death of Outrage: Bill Clinton and the Assault on American Ideals* (NY: Free Press, 1998).

Bergsten, F., 'American Politics, Global Trade', *The Economist* (London, 27 September 1997), 25–8.

Bok, D., *The State of the Nation: Government and the Quest for a Better Society* (Cambridge, MA: Harvard University Press, 1996).

Buchanan, P.J., *The Great Betrayal: How American Sovereignty and Social Justice are Being Sacrificed to the Gods of the Global Economy* (NY: Little Brown, 1998).

Burnham, W.D., '"Whole Lotta Shakin' Goin' On": a Political Realignment is on the Way', *The Nation* (NY: 17 April 2000).

Burns M.J. and G.J. Sorenson, *Dead Center: Clinton–Gore Leadership and the Perils of Moderation* (NY: Scribner, 1999).

Chait, J., 'The Slippery Center: the Self-contradictions of the Third Way', *The New Republic* (16 November 1998), 19–21.

Davis, M., *Magical Urbanism: Latinos Reinvent the US City* (London: Verso, 2000).
Easterbrook, G., 'America the OK: Why life in the U.S. has never been better', *The New Republic* (4 and 11 January 1999), 19–25.
*Economist, The*, 'The New Americans', a Survey of the US (London, 11 March 2000), 3–16.
——, 'Poverty in America' (London: 20 May 2000), 31–4.
Epstein, B., 'The Marginality of the American Left: the Legacy of the 1960s', in L. Panitch and C. Leys (eds) *The Socialist Register, 1997* (Rendlesham: Merlin Press, 1997), 138–59.
Esman, M.J., *Government Works: Why Americans Need the Feds* (Cornell University Press, 2000).
Fallows, J., 'The Invisible Poor', *New York Times* (19 March 2000).
Faux, J., 'Lost on the Third Way', *Dissent* (Spring 1999), 67–76.
Firestone, D., 'Population Shifts in the SE Realign Politics in the Suburbs', *New York Times* (3 June 2000).
Foner, E., *The Future of Socialism: Perspectives from the Left*, W.K. Tabbed (ed.) (NY: Monthly Review Press, 1990).
Freedland, J., Bring Home the Revolution (New York: Fourth Estate, 1998).
Friedman, T.L., *The Lexus and the Olive Tree* (NY: Farrar, 1999).
Giddens, A., *The Third Way and its Critics* (Cambridge: Polity Press, 2000).
Gray, J., *False Dawn: the Delusions of Global Capitalism* (London: Granta Books, 1998).
Greider, W., 'Unfinished Business: Clinton's Lost Presidency', *The Nation* (NY: 14 February 2000), 11–20.
Henwood, D., 'Clinton's Liberalism: No Model for the Left' in L. Panitch, and C. Leys (eds), *The Socialist Register, 1997* (Rendlesham: Merlin Press, 1997), 159–75.
Hitchens, C., *No One Left to Lie to. The Triangulations of William Jefferson Clinton* (London: Verso, 1999).
Hitchens, P., *The Abolition of Britain: from Lady Chatterley to Tony Blair* (London: Quartet Books, 1999).
Hyland, W.G., *Clinton's World: Remaking American Foreign Policy* (NY: Praeger, 1999).
Judis, J.B., 'Beyond National Interest: GOP isolationism reborn', *New Republic* (21 June 1999), 22–5.
——, 'Independents Day', *New Republic* (13 March 2000), 22–4.
Lewis, A., 'Nearly a Coup', *NY Review* (13 April 2000), 22–8.
Lipset, S.M. and G. Marks, *It Didn't Happen Here: why socialism failed in the United States* (NY: W.W. Norton, 2000).
Marr, A., *The Day Britain Died* (London: Profile Books, 2000).
Massing, M., 'The End of Welfare?', *New York Review* (7 October 1999), 22–6.
Peter-Martin, H. and H. Schumann, *The Global Trap: Globalization and the Assault on Democracy and Prosperity* (London: Zed Books, 1997).
Petras, J. and M. Morley, *Empire or Republic? American Global Power and Domestic Decay* (London: Routledge, 1995).
Rochman, B.A., 'Cutting *with* the Grain: Is There a Clinton Leadership Strategy?', in C. Campbell and B.A. Rochman (eds), *The Clinton Legacy* (NY: Chatham House, 2000), 274–94.

Rogers, R. and R. Teixeira, 'America's Forgotten Majority', *The Atlantic Monthly*, Vol. 285, No. 6 (Boston: June 2000) 66–75.
Rorty, R., *Achieving Our Country: Leftist thought in twentieth century America* (Cambridge, MA: Harvard University Press, 1998).
Siedentop, L., *Democracy in Europe* (London: Allen Lane, 2000).
Skocpol, T., *The Missing Middle* (NY: Norton, 2000).
Stephanopoulos, G., *All Too Human: a Political Education* (London: Hutchinson, 1999).
Walker, M., *The President They Deserve* (London: Fourth Estate, 1996).
——, 'No Argument', *Prospect* (March 2000).
Wolfe, A., *One Nation After All* (NY: Viking, 1998).
Yergin, D. and J. Stanislaw, *The Commanding Heights* (NY: Simon & Schuster, 1998).

# 10
# The Promise of the Third Way

At the mid-point of New Labour's first term, the Third Way has made scant progress, if any. There is little evidence of social exclusion having abated, of inroads having been made on inequality, of advances in education or indeed accelerated modes of modernization. Discussion regarding the Third Way is muted, the media having turned their attention to other considerations and what matters even more, the public at large remains sublimely indifferent. For many, the movement seems defunct. Proponents have stilled their advocacy, while antagonists have visibly ceased to advance refutations. Already in 1998, *Marxism Today* in its special issue on the Third Way printed the slogan 'Wrong' across Tony Blair's picture on its front page. Wrong in analysis, intellectually sterile, subversive in putting the onus for past mistakes more on the Left than the Right, blind to the destructive forces unleashed by globalization and wrong in deluding Labour followers with promises that New Labour in office had no mind to fulfil (Hall, 1998). The previously referred to 'pleasing all comers' charter makes the Third Way both superficially attractive yet equally an unusable tool in promoting social change.

Significantly, in his May 2000 post-poll setback interview (coinciding with the Livingstone mayoral débâcle), Prime Minister Blair does not once refer to the Third Way. Though several times making reference to New Labour's mission and stressing specifically the priorities of full employment, strong public services and the reduction of inequality plus poverty as the focal points of continued radical reform, no mention whatever is made of it (*The Times*: 'Blair Interview', 8 May 2000). One may well come to the conclusion that New Labour has lost interest in championing the Third Way. Strategically, it appears that the momentum has shifted: that social democracy itself is undergoing renewal; that the Third Way is also undergoing regeneration; that, from the very onset, the Blairite version appeared too anodyne; or more plausibly still that, linking itself with the Third Way, New Labour as such is undergoing a process of re-evaluation. Tony Giddens's – the intellectual mainspring of the Third Way – new book sets out to dispel these assumptions (Giddens, 2000). As Giddens reiterates, far from being unable to deal with inequalities of wealth and power, the Third Way offers the only feasible approach to these issues in the context of the New Age.

We will, in this final chapter, firstly review the main arguments put forward in opposition to the Third Way. We will next turn to Giddens's new book as the exemplar of its current intellectual status. And finally, seek to put forward a modified version of the Third Way – a model incorporating much of the Blairite model and better equipped to translate its aspirations of social equality and inclusion into reality in the future ahead.

## Third Way critique

A recent dialectical exercise attempts an interesting point-by-point rebuttal of the Blair/Schröder manifesto (Barkan, 2000). The Third Way is characterized as a transparent device to lure the Left into the capitalist camp. The tenets of Social Democracy have been abandoned in favour of an unfettered market economy. Equality of opportunity is falsely held out as attainable under conditions where vast divergences in income, wealth and life chances are allowed to persist. Though public expenditure is downgraded as wasteful, the claim is made that policies will add strength to democracy. The fact that private capital has persistently shown itself disinclined to clean up its own mess or to pay its share towards the maintenance of social capital is conveniently left aside. Flexibility is portrayed as a panacea for progress and modernization, when for millions it implies an involuntary decline into contingent employment and the loss of income as well as career prospects. Workplace conflicts are downplayed as a residue of a past age whereas in fact, 'as long as ownership, control, and profits belong to one group that employs the other' (ibid: 55) there can be no end to conflict. Globalization – to which 'there is no alternative' – is welcomed with open arms despite the evidence of its deleterious effects on the effectiveness of the nation state. The question as to 'who governs' thus becomes paramount. If it is to be corporate capital, the time has come to see the manifesto in its true light. If it were to be civic society, then much would need to be changed in regard to the context of the Third Way (Barkan, 2000).

As a polemic the article makes some pertinent points. Analytically however one needs to elaborate. We identify three major strands of Third Way critique.

- In its attempt at inclusivity the Third Way has become excessively vague, incoherent and a questionable instrument for implementation.
- Ideologically starting well to the Right while confident of its own party's consistent allegiance, the Third Way has, in its quest to rally support from the opposite side, found itself engaged in a step-by-step pull to the Right.
- Selecting its agenda from amongst the two principal parties' traditional beliefs, the Third Way finds itself beset by a plethora of mutually contradictory views. In 'facing two directions at once – courting the Right while trying to relegitimise government' (Hutton, 2000: 30), it creates confusion and indecision, inhibiting pragmatic implementation. Thus, the simultaneous emphasis on self-interest and public altruism invokes relentless entrepreneurship together with social compassion for those at the losing end. A stress on globalization coexists with continued commitment to the role of the nation state. While, projected as an instrument for self-realization, 'flexibility' in practice imposes added constraints.

**Inclusivity**

Since its emergence in the mid-1980s, the Third Way has widened into a virtually open ideological tent. Whereas initially it deviated only slightly from the socialist agenda, it has now expanded into a social philosophy that excludes only the radical Left or Right wing. Thus, President Clinton's triangulation gyrations, the political programmes of both American presidential candidates, the Brazilian, Portuguese and French prime ministers' policies – well to the Left of the Blair/Schröder axis – can shelter under an identical wing. Even Austria's notorious Jorge Haider manages to lay claim to be following the same path as the Blairite Third Way.

To accommodate such an extensive spectrum, a political theory needs to be highly eclectic – open enough to attract widespread support, while vague enough to offend only a few. The current Blairite Third Way matches that specification. As it has evolved, it is claimed to represent a catch-all rhetoric applicable to all situations and pleasing everyone instead of being a coherent body of thought and a potential for political action. Little wonder that after three years in office, New Labour's Third Way has neither achieved its stated ends nor attracted any identifiable enthusiasm at grass-roots level. Supporters will plead the constraints of social consensus and electability. It is no more prudent to defy the 'one nation' concept than to put forward a programme that has little chance of succeeding. Critics however argue that the quest for the safe middle has gone too far, inducing the leadership to look over their shoulders, shying away from innovative initiatives out of fear of alienating supportive sections, and more gravely still allowing public opinion polls, together with focus groups, to dictate policies rather than retaining a consistent vision of what ought to be and needs to be done. At best these provide snapshots of ad hoc fluctuations of public opinion, not social philosophies or even a programme coherent enough for steering the country towards a clear goal. It is a volatile 'message' that, as Miles declares, 'changes weekly, or daily, and can vary in relation to different policies' (Miles, 2000) rather than the 'mission' that Blair arrogates to New Labour's Third Way.

A mission is different. It concentrates instead on long-term goals while providing a consistent strategy designed not to follow but lead public opinion. Programmatically this implies tightening the agenda to present a coherent framework for change, while setting aside a platform that is sterile enough to satisfy all and threatens no interests. The new agenda while inevitably controversial in certain ways is directed to social improvement and structural change. It does not need to be radical or indeed consistent with the socialist 'dogma' of earlier days. Fighting the last war, within any perspective, has shown itself to be a futile exercise. Circumstances have altered too much for this to be feasible in the 'New Age'. The proletarian vanguard of solidaristic working-class masses – has dissolved under the impact of social reform plus technological change. The nation state has ceased to be 'master of all it surveys'. Democratic institutions, as such, impose limitations on too drastic change. The combined effects of mass consumption, the media and free time democratization – in many ways the outcome of left parties' activism – make past utopias seem obsolete, while the socialist record itself hardly inspires much confidence. Thus for the sake of retaining credibility, the effort to redefine the Third Way seems inescapable (as we will attempt to do in the final section), the form and direction this takes is bound to be neither a simple nor consensual exercise.

**Internal contradictions**

In one way or another, it is reasonable to describe all systems as subject to inherent inconsistencies: 'internal contractions', in the sociological sense. The Third Way is no exception, as the fault-lines that exist inhibit its progress. Identification, one hopes, might be the first step to re-evaluation. The following appear as predominant.

- The momentum of political change has now been reversed. Capitalism's structural proneness to crisis has been an axiomatic presumption of left-wing critique. Be it through overproduction or underconsumption, the failure of productive investment, impoverishment, immiseration, the united resistance of the oppressed working class or ultimately the ballot box – the sheer numerical weight of the deprived masses, the system would ultimately self-destruct. Though, once deposed, it was taken for granted that the newly liberated would not be foolish enough to turn the clock back, democratic continuity allowed for reversal. The swing of the pendulum might conceivably follow upon the loss of popular support due to failures of the Left-wing regime, for parties of the Right to resume power yet again.

Now paradoxically, the trend is reversed. The very success of the post-war European Social Democracies has proved their undoing. The social progress made thanks to Keynesian economics plus the welfare state raised expectations that could not be fulfilled. 'The future that did not work' caused by excessive pay demands, industrial unrest and chronic inflation put the neo-Right governments back into power. The monetarist strategies of the Thatcher/Reagan era while reversing social reform in return restored the basis of governability once considered lost. The resulting employment changes and renewed prosperity, once again allowed the luxury of a renewed social consciousness, more recently reinstalling centre-left governments subscribing to market capitalism and elected on platforms of moderate social reform (Callaghan and Tunney, 2000).

Blair's Third Way is sensitive to the precarious balance. The dilemma that faces proponents is manifest. The room for manoeuvre is circumscribed. Any step in the wrong direction – pay rises in excess of productivity growth, higher taxation, hints of major redistributive intent, let alone active interference in the free market – is liable to set up a backlash that once again might unseat a Labour government and set back the hopes of the Third Way. The parallel need to keep supporters content with a meagre diet of actual social reform, brings the internal contradiction of capitalism's reversal well to the fore.

- The Third Way is strong on civil society. It is equally resolute on the competitive market economy. Though not entirely mutually irreconcilable, the two concepts do not easily gel. Giddens, in particular, is eloquent on the imperative of civil society and elaborates a new version appropriate for new times. Traditional community life – often romanticized and idealized – has dissipated under the impact of rapid change. Neighbourhoods have broken up, work patterns changed, lifestyles diversified, and inner cities fallen into decay. Suburbanization however, together with prosperity, free time plus a stronger sense of social awareness have interacted to lay the foundations for a civil society that is more effective and durable than ever before. Community renewal through the harnessing of local initiative, protection of the local public sphere together with the new democratic family structure are ushering in an era where civic participation will rise to new heights (Giddens, 1998: 79). Already: 'small groups are doing a better job than many of their critics would like to think. People feel cared for. They help one another even amidst the dislocation tendencies of our society, we are capable of banding together in bonds of mutual support' (Wuthnow, 1994: 12).

One would hesitate to charge Giddens with being naïve, but the evidence he relies upon is far too selective. Firstly, it entirely derives from the United States, where conditions are markedly different. And more seriously, it focuses upon a population segment that is typically privileged and affluent, with lifestyles clearly divergent from the larger majority, professedly the major concern of the Third Way. True enough, the interest groups implied in Giddens's reference, have perfected the art of organizing and forcefully pleading their cause. Yet their campaigns typically are single-issue, sectionally oriented, professionally led efforts to preserve or improve their position, which is alien to the issues affecting the greater majority and irrelevant, if not antithetical, to the supposedly grass-roots-oriented perspective of the Third Way.

The problem goes deeper. The competitive achievement-oriented capitalism that Giddens and other spokespersons project, appears structurally irreconcilable with a social democracy concept of civic society. Post-industrial capitalism may well not be the zero-sum game of Marxist critique, but it equally does not exhibit the 'win-win' outcome that supporters project. Competition is harsh, often predatory, with losers left to their fate. High achievers, corporate tycoons may well support charities or less frequently donate some of their scarce free time. But categorically they do not accommodate to the participatory, share-and-share-alike concept of civic society, dwell among the grass roots or identify with goals of the left – of any stripe. To characterize their involvement as 'voluntarism', rely on their value-free munificence to take care of the needy, or equate 'compassionate capitalism' with a vision of social democracy defies plausibility while hampering rather than furthering the ends enunciated by the Third Way.

- Inequality represents the most glaring dichotomy. In fact Chancellor Brown's out-of-the-blue intervention has brought about a tripartite division. Blair and Giddens have never seen eye to eye, the former forswearing an activist role for government, while, however, guardedly, the latter concedes redistributive intervention as a possible need. However, under the blandly reassuring 'equality of opportunity' formula, debate had been virtually stilled. Now Brown's repeated attacks on the 'privileged elite' have brought the issue into the open. The fact that not only John Major but equally Margaret Thatcher and Edward Heath were wont to employ the very same 'equality-of-opportunity' purported approach, is bound to raise doubts regarding the Blair–Giddens progressive intent. A form of words so vague and eclectic and devoid of actual policy measures appears unlikely to find continued appeal.

Though populist-radical rather than socialist, Brown's attack on the 'privileged elite' at least defines target groups at both ends of the scale. The alleged discriminatory Oxbridge admission procedures, later expanded to the medical and legal professions, is a clear clarion call implying that something is wrong in regard to equality policy and that something needs correcting. Though neither spelled out nor specified at this stage, the appeal is predominantly directed at those very 'conservative' core Labour forces whom Blair increasingly excoriates for clinging to outdated notions of class war. It is a numerically dwindling constituency, traditionally the backbone of union eminence (still some 7 million strong), now downsized and privatized and visibly left behind in the competitive achievement race, but still a sizeable social component on which New Labour's future depends.

Blair's middle-ground stance, in response to political setbacks, has perceptively moved to the Right. He has ceded to a palpably hard-headed decision to relocate away from the dwindling old working class and closer to the prospering middle class, now a clear majority of the electorate. Friedlander, a close observer of the Prime Minister's social philosophy, ascribes this not to opportunism but to a sincere conviction that his message has an undifferentiated and equal concern for all. Globalization, modernization and self-regulation in a context of market-led enterprise will, if all pull their weight, provide for a better, more prosperous future (*The Guardian*, 14 June 2000). Sectionalism, translates into clinging to outdated preconceptions or unyielding opposition to change by self-interestedly blocking progress. Hence investing in outdated industries freezes labour forces where demand no longer exists and extends a timeless helping hand to those unwilling to help themselves. Decisive action becomes stalled in sterile debate. The message is stirring and clear in one vital aspect: hands off the economy, let incentive and enterprise freely work, while averting the threat of creeping bureaucratization – a vision that Giddens, if pushed to the point and consistent with his own argument, would probably dissent from. Already in his earlier text he recognizes that, for all the benefits they bring in other dimensions, market forces inherently bring about inequality. Though not spelling out how this is to be done, redistribution is necessary to turn equality of opportunity into empirical reality. Failing that, the head-start of inherited wealth, the network of special connections, ascribed status or endowment with the hidden capital of social skills will for ever tilt the balance in favour of a select minority over the less favoured majority.

It appears likely that the issue, once raised, will not be put to rest. The straw target of 'equality of outcome' once ascribed to dissenting views is now rarely raised. Though fashionable amongst radical minorities in the 1970s, even a residual hard-core no longer give voice to that view. Blair, if committed to the ends of the Third Way as he claims to be, will have to come off the fence some time soon. As far as inequality is concerned, Giddens stands closer to Brown than to Blair. According to Peter Willey, editor of *The New Statesman*, in the six years since election to the leadership of the Labour party, there has been no transfer from the rich to the poor, no splurge of spending on education and health, and no fulfilment of the promise to restore the standards of the National Health Service or abolish the scourge of poverty (*The Observer*: Comment, 4 June 2000). This criticism however, has been partially rectified by the CSR of July 2000, which in essentials offers a 'catching up exercise' bringing public investment (as a percentage of GDP) up to the levels of 1993 by 2003 (Hutton, 2000: 30). To stave off isolation within the mainstream of his own Labour party, Blair appears faced with the option of clinging to the volatile centre-left constituency or associating himself and the Third Way with the cause of progressive reform. Whichever the final choice, the response to the issue of inequality will be a central factor in determining the future of the Third Way.

**Pull to the Right**

From the very first, the Third Way has accepted the premise that: 'The point has to be made unequivocally that socialism is dead, and that none of its variants can be revived' (Dahrendorf, 1990: 38). Thus, from the very beginning, it rested on slippery ideological ground. All reference to 'socialism' was excised from the agenda, the famously contested Clause Four, committing the party to 'the common ownership of production' was jettisoned as obsolete, while for all practical purposes the axioms of the market philosophy were taken aboard. From that position, there was only one way ahead: that is, employ the carrot and stick to ensure their own party's allegiance, and do all you can to entice the opposite side by consensus politics based on compromise plus the commitment to the principles of the 'one nation' state. The avowed aim is to be ever conciliatory, moderate, pragmatic and unencumbered by 'dogma' resistant to change. At all costs, abjure class conflict or a move to the Left, strive for the middle ground in the interests of eclectic appeal, retain freedom of action under the banner of flexibility and modernization, while for ever striving to widen the tent. Co-opt opposition by awarding concession – a small cost to pay for preserving the common front – and then react to their lukewarm response with yet one more move to the Right (Chait, 1998).

When even Perry Anderson, eminent within British Marxist circles, forswears socialism as no longer a viable option in the new age (Anderson, 2000) – adding that American capitalism has 'resoundingly reasserted its primacy in all fields' – it seems churlish to cavil when Tony Blair, responsible for leading a political party, elects to steer a moderate course. As John Gray argues: 'If capitalism means "the free market"', then no view is more deluded than the belief that the future lies with 'democratic capitalism' (Gray, 1998: 17). Having, in other words, chosen the end of competitive accumulation, no matter which party is in power, it follows that this equally predetermines the means. There is no use being squeamish over abandoning workforce protection, yielding the gradual dismemberment of the welfare state, accommodating to rising levels of inequality or closing one's eyes to degrading work practices within low-wage developing states. Irrespective of the rhetorical niceties of the Third Way, the privatization of state-owned enterprises, deregulation of utilities and other industries, a slimmed-down workforce in the industrial and service fields, plus low tax policies that reward and encourage enterprise have become the prevailing trends. Yet despite that, New Labour struggles to engender a culture of investment amongst British business to bring it up to the levels of its competitors. Underinvestment and correspondingly low productivity remain a chronic problem (Hay, 1999).

This does not however imply that the parties essentially are alike. Manifestly, Blair's Third Way is not 'Thatcherism in trousers', nor will it ever be. Emphasis on socialism might have been replaced by social democracy, class conflict by elitist critique, proletarian consciousness by an accent on individuality and steadfastness by flexibility. Above all, the market is enshrined as a natural good, but the divergence between the Left and Right remains. Social justice and social democracy qualitatively differ in emphasis on the virtues of birth and wealth; concern with the victims of social forces is entirely different from a self-help perspective; while the role of the state – with the neo-Right still inclined to view it as the problem and not the solution – though somewhat muted, remains.

Yet it cannot be denied that there is substance to the critique. It seems reasonable to suggest that, for the sake of leaving behind eighteen years in the political wilderness, the Blairite model of the Third Way accommodated too readily right from the start; that it mistakenly puts its faith in the spontaneous social benevolence of corporate interests and self-centred entrepreneurs; that it wrongly interprets social effects as natural forces; and, last but not least, that its vision is too inspirationally pedestrian and analytically vague to mobilize the social forces on which success depends. Critical comments of the order that 'Labour's second term is being defined by Tories' (McElvoy, 2000) are hardly conducive to inspire confidence within the ranks. More recent versions show some signs of progress, but as we will go on to suggest, are still well short of presenting a programme doing full justice to the 'promise of the Third Way'.

## The Third Way revisited

During the course of the past few years there have been several variants of the Third Way at home as well as abroad. None of the latter as yet have congealed into a coherent framework of thought. While the former, predominantly the product of left undercurrents, will be embodied within the final section. As far as the British formal position is concerned, Giddens's contributions have served as the principal guide to the ideas and policies of the Third Way. His 1998 text *The Third Way: the Renewal of Social Democracy*, in conjunction with Blair's *The Third Way* laid the essential framework for Third Way development. It has now been followed by a further exegesis, *The Third Way and its Critics* elaborating the movement's principles as well as arguing a response to its critics. Fundamentally little has changed in regard to the basic assumptions. Neither have any of the principal ideas found themselves abandoned, nor is there any proposal significantly altering the Third Way perspective. Basically, Giddens reiterates the guiding principles of the Third Way: equal opportunity, personal responsibility, plus the mobilization of citizens and the community. 'The advent of new global markets, and the knowledge economy' he argues, 'coupled with the ending of the Cold War, have affected the capabilities of national governments to manage economic life and provide an ever-expanding range of social benefits' (Giddens, 2000: 2). Hence, as a corollary, *laissez-faire* markets within a system of open-ended globalization, with structures more adaptive to changing conditions than rigid statism, need to be embraced. Top-down government in constricting enterprise and inhibiting initiatives has become obsolete. Equality will be assured thanks to an educational system where unequal access and privilege have been replaced by more inclusive policies. Personal responsibility replaces the outmoded dependency culture of the welfare state. Crime and community decay – the prime concern of ordinary citizens – will naturally respond to reform in a positive way. Likewise, in response to the growth of women's employment and dual careers, family life undergoes regeneration within a more diversified context. Flexibility, modernization and individuation provide the motor force to reduce social cleavages and xenophobic constraints, and point towards a New World where progress and prosperity for all can reign.

Giddens is curiously selective in his choice of which Third Way critique to answer. Except for two, not very representative sources, the substantial body of British critique is left out of consideration. Instead, the Giddens' focus is on foreign contributions which, while by no means irrelevant, in view of somewhat divergent social conditions must be regarded of lesser account, while perhaps contributing to a general Third Way theory. Faux's contribution concerns itself with the 1992 and 1996 American presidential elections, making the point that in their quest for success, the New Democrats had crossed the line into the anti-'over-sized government camp' (Faux, 1999). The 'Continental response' – reflecting German, Scandinavian and Iberian viewpoints – repudiate the Blair–Giddens primacy claim, pointing to their nations' more advanced system of welfare and social protection (Lafontaine, 1999; Tuomioja, 1998; Navarro, 1999). Lord Dahrendorf, ex-director of the LSE, makes some highly pertinent points. He fundamentally condemns the British Third Way for chronic timidity and wanting to have it both ways. How, he asks, can the welfare state's retreat from universalistic principles be reconciled with the pursuit of social solidarity; from where is civil society to draw its resources when state provision, falsely equated with statism – is being withheld; and, with the market's notorious quest for quick profits, who is to take care of the whole gamut of social deficiencies? (Dahrendorf, 1999). While Giddens readily concedes that 'the market doesn't create safe neighbourhoods or clean streets and pathways' (Giddens, 2000: 20), the repercussions of this recognition are not pursued.

Though both the cited British sources derive from relatively marginal contributors, their comments are apt. Hall, standing on the left, charges that 'New Labour has been seduced by the gospel that global markets are self-regulating and require no social or institutional framework to function. The sovereign consumer has replaced the idea of the citizen and public sphere' (Giddens, 2000: 12). The fact that the Third Way offers no strategy for securing a more equitable distribution of income and wealth and that the issue of power is barely referred to, makes it a meaningless political document (Hall, 1998). Ryan, closer to middle-ground Labour, (as noted in Chapter 7) perceptively traces the Third Way's ideological roots back to the early 1900s New Liberalism. Both identify the problem of dealing with the vagaries of the market and are chary of state intervention, but offer no remedy except wishful thinking-type exhortation. Confounded with the far more complex reality of informatics and globalization, New Labour's Third Way is even more likely than the preceding effort to fade into obscurity at an early stage (Ryan, 1999).

Giddens' summarizes the criticisms as follows:-

- The Third Way is amorphous and lacks direction. Hence both the traditional Left and neo-liberal Right appear more capable of responding effectively to current political issues.
- Having perceived the prosperous 'middle England' voters rather than the traditional working class as its target constituency, the Third Way is destined to move more and more to the Right. Allocating too little place to individual liberties with its focus on the traditional nuclear family, tougher policing and self-regulation, it has distanced itself from most socialist versions in its ineluctable move to the Right without, at the same time, achieving a dependable political base.
- The Third Way offers nothing to the increasingly isolated losers of the global marketplace. Having discarded major distributionist poli-

cies as a viable option, it lacks the instruments to achieve greater equality.

- As an essentially Anglo-Saxon project directed to societies with weaker provisions for social justice and social democracy, it has little to offer the European mainland's nations with their more highly developed welfare states.
- Limited to an economic policy which allows the market to rule the roost largely unimpeded, the Third Way may well get by in times of prosperity, but has no visible means to cope with the vagaries of an economic recession.
- Sharing its rivals' manifest indifference to ecological issues or the negative effects of modern technology, it misses a unique opportunity to bring to public notice matters of urgency and to assemble the support of popular forces for a primary global cause.

Undaunted, Giddens proceeds to offer a counter-response. Extensively set out in his final three chapters, the principal points can be summarised in the following way:

- Structural pluralism provides a mechanism that successfully overcomes the inherent tensions between state regulation and the free market that bedevilled social and economic progress in the post-war years. The statist zeal of old-style social democracy has shown how stifling and bureaucratic state power can be. Reversing the past decades' nationalization of major parts of the economy to private industry is evidently beyond consideration. What is needed instead is to bring all the agencies of the state apparatus to the superior levels of performance and efficiency of the private sector. Greater transparency, accountability, attention to consumer demands and preferences, and control over expenditure will bring instant benefits. Decentralization, while bringing services closer to source, by clearing the path for grass-roots participation and imposing compliance with performance criteria to the private sector's optimum standards, removes the necessity for central interference or nationalization.

New times, the argument runs, have brought about new social contingencies. People are no longer unaware of their rights or segregated by widely divergent consumption conditions. They have become fully fledged citizens. Endowed with access to information and communication, they are socially better skilled, less hampered by deference and hence better able to express their best interests and aspirations. More significantly still, integration has made them not only more aware of their rights but equally their communal connections and opportunities. Hence they no longer need or want control by the nanny state, are willing to play their part in civic society as well as within the market economy. Both the public as well as the private sector need to be sensitive to citizens' requirements, open to input and alert to changing their products or services in accord with expressed or incipient public demand. Structural pluralism thus feeds on itself. The more there is of it and the better it works, the more inclusive will be the level of participation – with none exerting dominant power and no one being left out.

• Equality, Giddens reminds us, is an elusive and difficult goal. If expressed as equality of outcome – as Walzer terms it, 'the bad utopianism of the old left' (Walzer, 1998: 50), it is attainable only at the expense of personal freedom in a complex society. Only a tyranny can assure and enforce circumstances where differences of income, wealth, life chances as well as lifestyles find themselves perfectly matched. Equality of opportunity, however, Giddens insists, lies well within the Third Way's reach. The very same capacities – 'social capabilities' as Giddens terms them – are able to translate aspiration into reality. It does not require structural change, merely social adjustment. The government must avoid excessive regulation of the market economy, or stringent redistribution by overtaxing the rich to resolve issues of inequality, but instead put resources into providing an equal starting line. The focus must lie on equalization of life chances, not class conflict as in the past. Thus, good universal provision of health, good housing conditions and above all educational facilities constantly upgraded and equalized is the pathway for at last overcoming capitalism's abiding scourge, namely the problem of social inequality.

Once all start from the same line, each can make of it what they will and can. Some may pursue scientific or intellectual excellence, some power and riches, others cultural, artistic or athletic pursuits, others again voluntary activity or a relaxed leisurely family life – the choice is more abundant than ever. Yet for all that, the government must play its share, it cannot stand idly by. Hitches will occur, it will not all be plain sailing as a night watchman's role is insufficient. Whether it be in the traditional context of the nation state, in regional affiliations or maybe eventually as a fully fledged system of globalization extending beyond the economy and into the wider social and political spheres, breaches of standards may occur. Care will always be needed to ensure that all enjoy an equal life chance.

As Giddens's final chapter, 'Taking Globalization Seriously', demonstrates, globalization rates special attention. The proliferation and growing power of the transnationals cannot be ignored. Nor can the disruptive potential of speculative capital, roaming the globe for quick profits, be left out of account. Yet strong as these are, he argues, they are matched by the countervailing effect of 'globalization from below'. There are now more than 10 000 world-wide non-governmental organizations (compared to a mere 200–300 in the 1950s), who have made it their business to monitor the workings of the transnationals and capital flow. With more and more countries on the threshold of being integrated into this dynamic, expansive economy, the impetus for integrating the forces of the informatics revolution into a world system are likely to grow further (Giddens, 2000: 125).

Merging the massive potential benefits inherent in information technology and biogenetics into the ongoing wave of globalization will smooth out the wrinkles of early development. It foreshadows a future of greater regulation of corporate power, surveillance of financial transactions, more equitable debt management, a global war on poverty and last but not least a much needed commitment to preservation of the ecology and vital resources. Globalization alone can ensure that the headlong trend towards destruction of irreplaceable resources will be turned back. Giddens is confident that the already apparent logic of the 'virtuous circle', that recent innovatory experience demonstrates, can combine ecological and economic priorities ensuring that the benefits of technology be positively applied.

For Third Way supporters, Giddens's book must rank as a distinct disappointment. After a most promising start, the Third Way finds itself in the doldrums. Hardly any of the agenda has been achieved after more than three years of New Labour in office. The momentum, such as it is, has shifted across to the Continent where, though some of the agenda has been adopted, the climate is hostile to the concept of a Blairite Third Way. The eagerly awaited Giddens' new book, anticipated as a new clarion call, polished and erudite as it is, contributes little that is new or original. If anything, compared to the earlier text where redistributive policies were emphasized, it is more deeply grounded within the market economy. Statism, as government intervention has come to be called, is excoriated throughout. Redistributive taxes are likened to soaking the rich. While globally, the regulative constraints indicated to keep the transnationals and speculative capital in check, lie in a hypothetical future with global concord achieved and mechanisms in place to which all, without exception, are voluntarily prepared to subscribe.

The conditions of amicable world government that are foreshadowed may well occur – one ardently hopes that they will – but they depend on a chain of remote unlikely contingencies. Were the climate of universal goodwill on which Giddens's projections depend anywhere close to tangible reality, the complex network of regulations he postulates would be redundant in any event. Peace and concord would already reign. As it is, when it comes to intervention in contested circumstances, the United Nations is virtually impotent (Urquart, 2000). How to attain the projected operative conditions, what policies to pursue and actions to take, or whom to empower to act on behalf of the global community, or how to deal with miscreants is nowhere indicated. Lying ahead in a hypothetical quasi-utopia, they provide little help in planning the next immediate steps. Giddens altogether, for all his polished exegesis, is sadly deficient in policy matters. Neither analysis, nor indeed a programme of action is being vouchsafed – an all too common characteristic among the leading figures of the Third Way.

We realize that hard choices need to be faced. It is idle to pretend that contentious issues such as national interest, class, inequality or employer–worker relations can be subsumed by exhortation or patched-up compromise. The Third Way, to have any meaning, represents a dramatic departure and novel response to the opportunities of the New Age. A manifesto however spruced up that attempts to please all the people all of the time, will not fit the bill. If worth attempting, it needs to confront obstacles as they come up even if this involves a measure of dissent and confrontation. In an attempt to offer a positive contribution, we will set out proposals in the sections below.

## The Third Way and globalization

It is becoming increasingly evident that globalization reduces the functions of the nation state. Literally the term implies the surpassing of national boundaries within a world-wide economy; the free flow of goods, services and communication, a move from notional to formal supra-national relationships, widening opportunities for travel as well as employment and ultimately – even if not ever becoming 'one world' – global bodies that carry determinate weight. The United Nations has greatly expanded its brief in the past fifty years. The IMF and WTO routinely command fund-seeking nations on how to run their economies. Transnationals, quite often disposing of budgets exceeding those of most states, are wooed the world over for favourable investment location. The desertion of 'hot money' forces strong governments into abrupt deflation, in the process crashing their stock exchanges. And with defence, law enforcement and popular culture increasingly globalized, the momentum away from state power is gathering apace. Though the at times projected demise of the nation state may never take place, the signals are evident. Ostensibly, the nation states' days of power and glory belong to the past.

Great as the changes are, the momentum does not stop there. Critics assert that globalization has become 'normalized' to an extent where it is hard to perceive any alternative. Sociologically, its power is 'hegemonic' (Gramsci, 1997: 330–1). The culture of globalization is so overwhelming that seemingly nothing can stand in its way. Even moderate dissent is interpreted as subversive intent, converting social arrangements into putative 'facts' (Swanson, 2000). As noted above, politically Giddens embraces this concept, equating the coming of social democracy with expanded globalization. He bypasses the confines of the national state when it comes to the implementation of the goals of the Third Way, relying on the regulative mechanisms of global bodies instead. Desirable or not (we will turn to this issue below), we generally concur with this trend. In the context of ongoing world affairs, it seems less and less likely that we would perceive a scenario in which Britain, all on its own, would be able to implement a plausible version of the Third Way. European ties plus America's counterweight, the strength of financial and corporate capital and the pervasive impact of communications appear too overwhelmingly powerful for this to occur. The memory of the sterling crisis that financier George Soros virtually single-handedly provoked, is a salutary reminder of current reality. The larger canvas of either a new Atlantic Alliance or progressive integration within the EU seems a more realistic contingency. The Atlantic Alliance appears a long shot: a severely unbalanced arrangement that, essentially moving well to the Right would undo the aims of the Blairite Third Way. On the other hand, promoting an updated version of the Third Way within the EU, could prove to be a mutual shot in the arm – for Britain a unique re-establishment within the inner circles, and for the European Union the gain of a vision that it badly lacks.

Globalization, following the Seattle anti-WTO riots, has been regarded with growing ambivalence. 'Hegemony' is widely adduced in diverse critiques, with the political, economic and social dimensions increasingly merged. Both corporate capitalism and American imperialism bear the brunt of the charge. *Laissez-faire* global trade is attacked as provoking an 'age of disposable humanity' disempowered as a meaningful force, hired and dismissed at will and transformed into an impotent pool of casual employees. The marketplace logic legitimates a competitive race to the bottom with losers abandoned to fend for themselves (McMurty, 1999). Simultaneously, corporate control imposes a 'monoculture of the mind' where discourse is trivialized, civic life depoliticized and a culture of vapid consumerism allowed to prevail (Shiva, 1992). Vast wealth and underprivilege exist side by side. Bill Gates owns more wealth than the 100 million poorest Americans. In today's affluent post-industrial world, 1.3 billion people (of whom more than one-fifth will die before they are 40 years old) live on less than one dollar a day, while even in the richest countries 100 million live below the poverty line (United Nations Development Report, 1997). Globalization left in the hands of corporate capital, the argument runs, is bad as it is will further exacerbate dire conditions.

More moderate critics are increasingly echoing the adverse analysis. Riddell – pointing to the fact that the tax base of western governments and hence their spending potential is undermined by globalization and the anarchy of the internet – poses the pertinent question of 'who will collect taxes in a global village?' 'It will be harder for governments', he indicates, 'to tax transactions as a narrowing base will limit what can be spent, yet there will be demands to spend more to cope with the ageing population and to improve education and training' (Ridell, 2000). Carlsson, on a different track, contends that: 'There is hardly a greater danger to the democratic achievement of the twentieth century than the many powerless politicians at the state level, too removed from local realities to know what decision to make, and too far from the real transnational forces affecting the nation for which he or she is responsible' (Carlsson, 1999: 25). Friedman – coining the apt 'golden straitjacket' depicts the dilemma of a simultaneous pursuit of individual riches and communal relationships – while endorsing the view that globalization's worst aspect is the damage wrought by speculative capital. Having multiplied over five-and-a-half times during the 1990s (from $44 billion to 256 billion) it provokes a race to the bottom that outflanks the power of nation states, produces subservience in governments, leads to ecological degradation and, by the practice of child and prison labour in poorer nations, debases workers' living conditions throughout the advanced world (Friedman, 1999). Finally, Jeffrey Sachs, an economist of world-wide repute, issues the warning that today's technologically driven characteristic of the global economy is causing deepening divisions. While the 15 per cent of advanced nations command almost all technological know-how, around one-third of humankind is virtually entirely disconnected. Lagging badly in education, public health, infrastructural standards and market access, they stand in danger of falling further and further behind (Sachs, 2000).

Third Way proponents have until recently given these issues scant attention. Globalization has all too easily been subsumed under the headings of flexibility and modernization. Portrayed as an overwhelmingly beneficent force that brings opportunity, employment and interchange and that will further the cause of democracy throughout the world, it is projected as analogous to concord and progress. Objectively, much of this is true and accurate. A concept such as the Third Way can only thrive in a setting where the foundation stone of a civic culture already exists. At the lowest level it anticipates a network of free speech, political democracy, outlets for enquiry as well as dissent plus an achievement ethic valuing material progress and change. A measure of individualism and competitiveness – not necessarily centred on self-advancement alone – serves as a prerequisite, an agglomeration of values closely associated with the capitalist ethos and thus predominant in the western world. However, recognition in how to make globalization fairer is to be debated at the UN Millennium Summit in New York in September 2000. Blair and other European leaders, following the Berlin Communiqué of a year earlier, argue that an increasingly interdependent global order requires a framework of 'equal worth and social fairness'. By 'widening the winners' circle in the new economy' through investment in education and human capital; by strengthening civic society as a check on global market power, and developing global responses to such issues as debt relief, trade promotion, employee rights, and pollution controls in a new progressive dialogue building an international social compact benefiting all (Blair *et al.*, 2000).

Taking account of the momentum of globalization, times appear to have passed for the Third Way to progress as a parochial project, confined within national boundaries alone. Britain is, in any event, perceptibly evolving into a more federal structure and with deepening regional ties stands at the parting of the ways in several respects. The options seem evident: either the quest for a renewed Atlantic Alliance or alternatively putting concerted effort behind launching the Third Way within the EU. We will separately consider these options below while briefly focusing on a further contingency, introduced under the heading of 'Reclaiming Work'. Though distinctly a minority concern and most likely a far lower-grade option in view of its putative leftist direction, it has some plausibility and offers a projection that should not be ignored.

## Triangulation

There are two competing models of 'the better future ahead'. Both are based on technological modernization. However their social philosophies differ dramatically. The far better known and already well-established model is an extension of the neo-liberal American Dream. While the second model, more socially directed and community conscious relies on the potentially attainable goal of ending scarcity by distributing the benefits derived from hyper-technology in a more productive, equitable way.

The American Dream, although retaining much of its traditional substance, has subtly been modernized. Its attachment to individualist freedom and enterprise remains intact. However, the new reality of the nation's status as sole superpower, its transformation into a post-industrial state, its outstanding leadership position in hyper-technology, acts as an exemplar for emulation by millions across the world. In some ways, the United States can be seen as the early embodiment of the 'virtual state'. Initially coined as a term to refer to the efficient and goal-directed South Asian mini-states such as Hong Kong and Singapore, parachuting in record time from obscurity to economic pre-eminence, the perspective has changed. Corporate capital plus private enterprise are widely perceived as the ideal alternative to the allegedly bureaucratized heavy-handed interventionist state (Rosecrance, 1999). With agriculture and manufacturing pared down to essentials and public services restricted to vital necessities, the stage is set for addressing the openings of the New Age. Concentration devolves on a spectrum of concepts centred on design and communication. Versatility, open-mindedness and brain power count above all. Competitively no favours are asked and few expected. Yet public consciousness and compassion motivate and create expectations that the economically better endowed invest within the public sphere, take care of the infrastructure of civic society and help the less privileged.

Politically, triangulation emerges as the mode to deal with dissenting issues and social emergencies: a pragmatic, level-headed, impartial and forward-looking determination to advance material progress, stimulate enterprise as well as demand, operate under terms of fair play and transparency to the benefit of all who participate, yet retain the effective leanness of the minimal state. The system of low taxes and interest rates, promotion of enterprise, a flexible labour force adapted to the needs of the New Age, opportunities open to all plus a government that guides but does not regulate have created a condition of general well-being historically unmatched. In many ways, the United States is the personification of 'the future that works'. Record levels of low unemployment, an ever-booming stock market enriching investors increasingly embracing the middle class, consumer choice in abundance, close to one-half of young people entering higher education, widening home ownership and even annually declining crime rates help to persuade many millions of the reality of the American Dream (Mueller, 1999). As Johnson notes: 'The US's GDP per head has widened to 54 per cent above the EU average. Its success is due to both high labour input and high productivity' (Johnson, 2000). That an obverse side exists in regard to widening levels of inequality, urban ghettos that shame social progress, low wages coupled with marginal employment for many, child poverty and millions devoid of all health insurance obviously detracts from the dream. Yet the spirit of 'Good Morning, America!' persists and is widening (Teixeria and Rogers, 1999). Even amongst the deprived, the 'rags to riches' presumption remains far more than a dream (Goff and Fleischer, 1999; Fukuyama, 1995; Hood, 1996). In President Clinton's terms, 'America has been on a roll' or, as Harold Macmillan once put it. 'You've never had it so good.'

In such circumstances, triangulation makes perfect sense. With so much to cheer about, conflict and confrontation can be avoided. Responsible governance, enhanced by the wonders of the informatics age, can forestall social emergencies. A virtual 'win-win' situation exists where, while none might get all they contest, none needs to lose out. Pragmatic analysis, deliberation, rational compromise and mutual goodwill triumph over combativeness. Even Ralph Nader, the once relentless scourge of producers and now the Green candidate, 'has learned to triangulate': electing to run on a centre-stage platform that reconciles rather than threatens the status quo (Chait, 2000).

However adept, in contrast to the Third Way, triangulation is a strategy and not a social philosophy. A tacit device to keep conflict away rather than a programme that sets out to make social change. The stakeholding model that Gates presents reflects an emerging progression of the American Dream. With mutual funds notably displacing individual and corporate capitalists, he argues for more 'personalized, localized, "up-close" ownership (becoming) an every day fact of life' (Gates, 1998: 16). A widening base of equity distribution, social goals incorporated into company policy with wider levels of decision-making participation plus employee stock ownership, are evolving into a capitalism with 'a human face'. Property ownership expanding to ever-widening levels, the needy provided with avenues to make their own way, together with an overcoming of social distinctions, will narrow further the base of potential dissent.

## EU initiatives

The Rhenish model that in the past decades characterized the EU's core states is outmoded. Based on the big labour battalions with a statutory union voice, its Fordist mode is inappropriate for the New Age. The collapse of the manufacturing base, the growth of immigrant labour and globalization, plus the cost of social provision in the face of high levels of structural unemployment have gradually led to its decline. Yet the Anglo-Saxon neo-liberal model is equally shunned on the Continent. New concepts of a mixed economy social democracy are evolving in some states, notably Scandinavia and the Netherlands. The main protagonist however is, and remains, France. Determined to preserve the European cultural tradition not least against US encroachment, to protect the EU against the onslaught of corporate capital, vociferously critical of the Blairite Third Way as a sell-out, though bending noticeably to the pressures of the global market economy, it is engaged in measures of social experimentation that may presage a middle new way.

The 35-hour week, still in its formative stages and as yet to prove effective towards reducing unemployment, points to challenging opportunities for the New Age. Its underlying philosophy has not been sufficiently recognized. Closely linked to the post-industrial 'conquest of scarcity' presumption, it is in the eyes of a circle of social researchers considered to be within tangible reach (Gorz, 1985; Newman and de Zoysa, 1999; Rifkin, 1995; Schor, 1991). Gorz's latest contribution, *Reclaiming Work* is markedly apposite (Gorz, 1999). The thesis is simple: social development lags badly behind technological advance. Were it not for the inhibitions imposed by the *laissez-faire* market economy, within advanced nations the current average working week could be cut by one half that is, from the average weekly total of 40 to 20 hours, or over a lifetime a mere 20 000 hours compared to the 40 000 typical total of today. The economy, it is argued, is not a natural phenomenon but a social artifact belonging to a particular system that can be altered at will. Work has become a scarce commodity and hence, within the capitalist system, the wealthy and powerful seize more than their share. Hence the paradox of 'the Overworked American' (Schor, 1991), the absurd conjunction of technological progress having deprived millions of their employment while 'the contented majority', desperately clinging to dissolving jobs are ever more harassed, deprived of free time and increasingly subject to burn-out and strain. Meanwhile civil society declines for want of volunteers.

There is much in the theory that is compelling although it can be easily overstated, as clearly many are satisfied with their work and the opportunities it provides. However, in an age when the imminence of 'robots to get minds of their own' is confidently predicted by scientists (Arthur, 1998), it seems eminently possible to foresee a time when the bulk of work will be done by machines. If that were achieved, at least for the advanced world, the conquest of scarcity, however defined, would be within reach. The dilemma of the transition however remains. Even ardent proponents admit that conceptually the time is not ripe. Memories of statism are too recent, the market philosophy too deeply ingrained. Presumptions differ, but at the most moderate level, a considerable level of central control would be needed for the next step. Even the moderate French 35-hour week has been marked by a wealth of evasion as well as bureaucracy. The much-touted recourse to mutual societies and cooperatives has chronically been beset by dissension and strife. Part-time or work-sharing are notoriously unstable arrangements. How, within a thriving communication/informatics age, is one to enforce compliance with mandatory work limits, avoid moonlighting or ensure that the needed range of work would be done, is nowhere spelled out. What can be done, on the one hand, about overachievers or workaholics and, on the other, shirkers and the work-allergic, remains an enigma. The list could go on – within any perspective, it would involve a fair measure of central control. Even the basic social wage prerequisite to get the scheme off the ground appears beyond the necessary level of public support in the current climate of public opinion.

## An effective Third Way

Three preconditions seem self-evident.

- Pragmatism must stay as a guiding light.
- The Third Way needs an enlarged context in which to function effectively. No single nation state, with the possible exception of the United States, has the capacity to implement the Third Way goals

all on its own. The threat of capital flight, collapse of the currency or funding deficits is too great to be faced by a single nation alone. The European Union with a larger population and a Gross Domestic Product similar to the US, is powerful enough to successfully surmount short-term disruption.

- Neo-capitalism and social democracy need to evolve side by side. There is no credible current rival to the market economy, yet this need not extend to a market society. The political, social and cultural spheres must connect, without merely reflecting each other. Modes of participatory democracy, social inclusiveness and civic society have to evolve, consonant with the market economy, yet with a character all of their own. While enterprise flourishes and incentives remain, social accord and equality are given equivalent rank.

Pragmatism has its own natural boundaries. Successful reformers are motivated by a consistent world view, and as Margaret Thatcher did, pursue a coherent programme of policies. Society resembles a seamless web in which all components balance and interact. Reforms in one – such as family, schooling, work training, employment patterns or social behaviour – will not have their expected effect unless they are linked to corresponding measures in other dimensions. Thus inclusiveness is a vain goal if merely perceived in terms of smaller classes or concern over truancy. Similarly, equality of opportunity cannot be achieved by self-reliance alone (Swanson, 2000). While some will succeed in making the grade, the larger majority will falter in the face of structural obstacles. Where the *laissez-faire* market predominates, power begets power while wealth accrues wealth. Life chances will never be equalized in the absence of state intervention. Policies such as a steeper graduated taxation, capital gains and conceivably also a wealth tax, a Tobin tax on floating speculative capital, firm legislation to make transnationals pay their fair share and closing tax loopholes cannot be shirked. Manifestly all are feasible within a body such as the EU while beyond the capacity of any one single state. The Social Charter, held back by the Blair government, appears a step in the right direction. A liveable minimum wage, a reduced maximum work week – applicable equally to all white-collar grades, 'contractual' labour and remaining sweatshops – the right to union membership, prior notice on redundancies plus workers' enhanced participation in decision-making seem vital for closing the gap.

For the Third Way to recapture the popular imagination, it stands in need of a paradigm shift. Blair's attack on 'the forces of conservatism', first voiced at the 1999 Labour Party conference, proved a major mistake. At one swoop, it almost denigrated a century of social democratic achievement and isolated him from his sociological base. Yet for all that, 'the Thatcher in trousers' epithet is undeserved. He is certainly not in the Tory mould, but instead far closer now to the Liberal utilitarian (Gladstone) Lloyd George/Beveridge tradition. Globalization is welcomed with open arms, with the state becoming one actor amongst others, while self-reliance is directly linked to workfare. Social exclusion, once ranking high, has taken a back-seat as priorities switch to mainstream health and education, on the back of an economic upsurge boosting employment and tax revenues. This is regrettable as this is an issue which Britain shares with the Continent. 'A new specter haunts Europe', Manuel Castells warns in his magisterial survey of *The Rise of the Network Society*: 'the emergence of a jobless society under the impact of technology in factories, offices and services. The new social and economic organization based on information technologies aims at decentralizing management, individualizing work, and customizing markets, segmenting work and fragmenting society' (Castells, 1996: 269). It manifests itself in different ways. In Britain, already in 1993 as many as 38 per cent of the workforce were not employed on a permanent full-time basis, while within the EU euro11 unemployment averages just below 10 per cent, but is falling. The phenomenon of the underclass is becoming normalized, while educational goals remain unfulfilled, thus little momentum is left to the Third Way.

One would not wish to downplay the achievements of the Blair administration. Devolution, House of Lords reform, city mayors and experimentation with proportional representation, are significant steps in the direction of a more participatory system of government, while the New Deal and introduction of the minimum wage mark important social advances. Social Democracy need not imply statism or nationalization. There is definite scope for reviving the ideals of the Third Way through widening educational opportunity, adopting the goal of gradually shortening the working week, lessening inequality throughout all levels of social existence plus a concerted effort towards progressive cooperation with the EU. Under volatile labour market conditions, it will be as effective to emphasize social awareness and life skills as well as vocational training. The disappointing results of the work-training schemes, where one-quarter of young people were found to be losing their jobs within thirteen weeks, lend weight to the assumption that 'action zones' within unemployment black spots plus curriculum change towards variable skills with lifelong learning will prove a better investment. Convergence between the private and public sectors in regard to resource allocation, equipment and facilities, staffing levels and class sizes should provide for better educational results throughout. Though it is probably too much to hope for the restoration of student grants that contributed greatly to the opening up of higher education, one looks to the easing of interest-free student loans as well as to a more open-ended policy on college admission to achieve more equal outcomes.

The widening inequality of recent years is clearly incompatible with the ideal of social democracy. It is unlikely that a well-timed monitored return to more progressive taxation would have a negative impact on innovation and enterprise. Portable pension schemes need to be generalized, and the contingent workforce brought within the benefits system. Enterprise zones should help restore some viability to industrial wastelands and decayed inner cities – all schemes which, in return for limited investment, promise to bring early rewards, not merely economically but equally for inclusiveness and social cohesion. Additional measures of privatization of public services appear unlikely to contribute to greater efficiency or the enhancement of the quality of social life.

The crunch issue concerns Britain's role within the context of the European Community. We consider that questions of widening and integration are subsidiary to other concerns. Britain's membership of the common currency is a complex issue, clearly lacking current public support, and better deferred until other matters are clarified, notably the question of tax harmonization which could seriously imperil key British interests. It should not be beyond collective ingenuity to devise arrangements allowing Britain's exceptionally buoyant sterling economy to run parallel to the euro for the time being without this impinging upon its place at the top table. It might well prove a conceivable model for other incoming candidates.

Ultimately we consider the social sphere as determinate. Britain's role could be crucial, and adeptly handled, its future status assured. The European Union, once more, finds itself at a parting of ways. France, the champion of the 'European tradition', has visibly moved towards privatization and tax reform. In Germany, in the face of fierce opposition, Chancellor Schröder has also passed tax measures favouring the large corporations in an effort to build upon their improving prospects. With the leading powers setting the pace in the direction of the Anglo-Saxon model of free trade, others who are likely to follow will be encouraged. Countervailingly, within Britain some trends point in the reverse direction. As Pierce reports (Pierce, 2000), in Blair's own Sedgefield constituency, 'local activists defect to traditional socialism'. Confronted by a dying manufacturing base, the car industry in its terminal stages and high levels of persistent unemployment in Labour's heartlands, activists plead for a return to traditional values: market intervention to protect the weaker and rectify irregularities; a tax system that helps by levelling off inequalities; a government less concerned with courting its foes and instead focusing on its stable constituencies, a concern for social justice free of compromise and above all, a citizen's right to a job as long as work is essential to provide for one's needs while establishing a place in society at the same time.

The dilemma could not be more vividly highlighted. Workers of all grades and competence increasingly are aware that their very existence is under threat. Work has become for some a scarce commodity, with mechanical labour increasingly displacing its human counterpart. In the get-all-you-can economy, inevitably the lion's share will go to the holders of power and possessors of valued skills. The Blair/Giddens mantra of self-regulation will not do the trick. Those lacking requisite skills will be marginalized and left to struggle against each other for what remains. The 35-hour week could thus be symbolic of where the future beckons and what could be achieved. Arguably already today, 'only 20 per cent of the workforce is needed to provide the necessary material goods for society as a whole under current productive conditions' (Gysi, 1999: 75). It may not be too fanciful to conceive of a New Age where work, as currently defined, has greatly diminished, free time is opened up to allow for self-growth and social development, and exploitation and poverty have been overcome within a context of common effort and social accord.

As it happens, at the time of writing (summer 2000), the Labour administration is suffering a definite slump, a victim of policy drift and disenchanting performance. Though by no means all of its own making, the Third Way is similarly affected. With the next election now well in the offing, the situation is crucial. Were Labour to lose office – unlikely as this contingency may be – it would equally doom the Third Way. Complex as the grounds for decline may be, outstandingly the government's firm inclination to try to please all at the same time and to put content below presentation bear part of the blame. Ross McKibbin in *The London Review of Books*, suggests that 'they make enemies and influence people', and rather than preach the unalloyed virtues of the British Third Way should instead adopt the Dutch model: liberal, secular, with advanced welfare provision coupled with entrepreneurial flair (20 July 2000). Dismissive left-wing analysis however, is often marked by nostalgia for an apocryphal 'Golden Age', in many ways socially unattractive and inappropriate for the realities of the New Age. People are now educated and materially far better off with higher realistic expectations than ever before. The Third Way, suitably modified, can play its part in ensuring that progress will be maintained.

By itself, the social philosophy underlying the 35-hour week can obviously not be a panacea for all social ills. However the general problem it addresses – the depletion of the wage-based society and the possibility of the not too far distant 'workless revolution' – remain distinct forces, concealed by low and falling unemployment rates that are based on questionable statistics. According to Went, the true EU unemployment total is not the putative 18 million but closer to 30 million taking the early retired and those on government placement schemes into account. The internationalization of capital from the 1970s emphatically began the separation of national economies from effective political control, without putting in place means of adequate redress. Thus the rate of return on capital and its share of income relative to wages has sharply increased in the last twenty years, throwing doubt on the assumption that jobs are destroyed by high wages. It is well to remember that the EU remains a relatively closed economy, with only 10 per cent directly exposed to global competition, 2 per cent less than the USA. Went argues for an alternative approach, namely a shorter working week, involving compensatory hiring without loss of pay, to help in job creation at all levels (Went, 2000) – a proposal that illustrates the potential repercussions of the French 35-hour week, while positively addressing the issues raised by communitarians earlier (in Chapter 7).

Although muted, basic antagonisms between labour and capital remain. Social divisions still structure society; hence the rhetoric of locating the Third Way above Right and Left, causes unease in critical quarters, especially the assumption that politics can somehow operate within neutral territory. Chantal Mouffe argues that in modernizing social democracy, the illusion that by not defining an adversary one can somehow side-step fundamental conflicts of interest is mistaken. Democracy is about alternatives and open-ended debate, as much about collective identities as to self-regarding individual rationalistic difference. Mouffe calls instead for an 'agonistic' pluralism which acknowledges structural division and rejects the current 'sacralization of consensus' (Mouffe, 2000: 113–14).

Other commentators argue that pessimism is unwarranted and overdone, pointing to such items as the globalization of trade unions and the persisting strength of European welfare states (Callaghan, 2000). Alternative prognosis projects a less optimistic scenario: the continuation of tight monetary conditions, increasing inequalities between paid regular work and the casuals and unwaged, and endemic insecurity amongst ethnic minorities. Although women's autonomy will expand, throughout Europe globalization will ensure that welfare objectives take second place to competitiveness, with social policy ever more market-orientated (Bonoli *et al.*, 2000: 160). Finally Therborn asks, which direction will Europe follow? As a unified economic powerhouse it could become a model social democracy, but never a superpower as its ageing demographic structure and lack of military presence limit its influence. Alternatively, it could turn into the world's 'Scandinavia' – prosperous and united while involved in global regulatory bodies, but competitive solely in niche markets (Therborn, 1997).

Given historic circumstances, one cannot be confident that Britain's approach to the European Union, conceived as a pragmatically feasible step towards widening the prospects of social democracy will be greeted with open arms. We consider Prime Minister Blair's declaration that Britain is 'now ready to take our place in Europe as a leading partner shaping the destiny of the Continent', while establishing 'a bridge between Europe and America at the same time' (Gibb, 2000) to be justified. The Anglo-Saxon model with its slimmed-down labour force, low unemployment and flexible response to modernization – seems better equipped for the New Age than the bulk of its EU peers. In a context of Britain in Europe with a new radical role, even such overriding issues as ecology, nuclear proliferation and immigration – beyond the remit of our text – could be addressed. For now, a Third Way redirected towards deriving the optimal benefits of the techno-scientific revolution for the good of humankind at large, appears worth undertaking.

## References

Andersen, P., 'Renewals', *New Left Review*, Second Series, No. 3 (London: January–February 2000).

Arthur, C., 'Robots Get Minds of Their Own', *The Independent: UK News* (London: 19 November 1998).

Barkan, J., 'The Third Way/Die Neue Mitte: Tony Blair and Gerhard Schröder', *Dissent* (New York: Spring 2000), 51–65.
Blair, T., *The Third Way* (London: Fabian Society, 1998).
Blair, T., G. Schröder, W. Kok and G. Persson, 'What the Left Has to Offer the New World of Global Economics', *The Independent, The Wednesday Review* (6 September, 2000), 4.
Bonoli, G., V. George and P. Taylor-Gooby, *European Welfare Futures: towards a Theory of Retrenchment* (Cambridge: Polity Press, 2000)
Callaghan, J., *The Retreat of Social Democracy* (Manchester: Manchester University Press, 2000).
Callaghan, J. and S. Tunney, 'Prospects for Social Democracy: a Critical Review of the Arguments and Evidence' , *Contemporary Politics* (London 6(1) 2000), 55–75.
Carlsson, I., 'A Second Century of Social Democracy' in Peter Russell (ed.), *The Future of Social Democracy* (Toronto, Canada: University of Toronto Press, 1999).
Castells, M., *The Rise of the Network Society*. Volume I of: *The Information Age: Economy, Society and Culture* (Oxford: Blackwell, 1996).
Chait, J. 'The Slippery Center: the Self-Contradictions of the Third Way', *New Republic* (New York: 16 November 1998), 19–21.
——, 'Nader Learns to Triangulate', *New Republic* (New York: 10 and 17 July 2000), 12–14.
Dahrendorf, R., *Reflections on the Revolution* (London: 1990).
——, Ein neuer Dritte Weg? (Tübingen, Ger: Mohr Siebeck, 1999).
Faux, T., 'Lost on the Third Way', *Dissent* (New York: 46/2, Spring 1999), 67–76.
Friedman, T.L., *The Lexus and the Olive Tree* (New York: Farrar, Strauss and Giroux, 1999).
Fukuyama, F., *Trust: the Social Virtues and the Creation of Prosperity* (New York: Free Press, 1995).
Gates, J., *The Ownership Solution: towards a Shared Capitalism for the Twenty-First Century* (Reading, MA: Addison-Wesley, 1998).
Gibb, F., 'We are a Bridge to America, Says Blair', *The Times*: Politics & Government (18 July 2000).
Giddens, A., *The Third Way: the Renewal of Social Democracy* (London: Polity Press, 1998).
——, *The Third Way and its Critics* (London: Polity Press, 2000).
Goff, B. and A.A. Fleischer, *Spoiled Rotten: Affluence, Anxiety and Social Decay in America* (Boulder, CO: Westview Press, 1999).
Gorz, A., *Paths to Paradise: on the liberation from work* (London: Pluto Press, 1985).
——, *Reclaiming Work: beyond the Wage-based Society* (London: Polity Press, 1999).
Gramsci, A., *Selection from Prison Notebooks* (New York: International Publishers, 1997).
Gray, J., *False Dawn: the Delusions of Global Capitalism* (London: Granta Books, 1998).
Gysi, G., 'Twelve Theses for a Market Socialist Policy: a Response to the Blair/Schröder Manifesto', *Review of European Affairs* (London: 64/1999), 65–86.

Hall, S., 'The Great Moving Nowhere Show', *Marxism Today* (London: November/December 1998), 9–14.
Hay, C., *The Political Economy of New Labour* (Manchester University Press, 1999).
Hood, J., *The Heroic Enterprise: Business and the Common Good* (New York: Free Press, 1996).
Hutton, W., 'Gordon's Given you the Ammo, Tony', *The Observer* (London: 23 July 2000), 30.
Johnson, C., 'UK Economic Boasts Have a Very Hollow Ring', *The Independent* (29 August, 2000), 14.
Lafontaine, O., *Das Herz schlägt links* (Munich: Econ, 1999).
McElvoy, A., 'Labour's Second Term Being Defined by Tories', *The Independent* (London: 2 June 2000).
McMurty, J., *The Cancer Stage of Capitalism* (London: Pluto Press, 1999).
Miles, A., 'How Blair is Making his Mission Impossible', *The Times*: Opinion (London: 10 May 2000).
Mouffe, C., *The Democratic Paradox* (London: Verso, 2000).
Mueller, J., *Capitalism, Democracy and Ralph's Pretty Good Grocery* (Princeton, NJ: Princeton University Press, 1999).
Navarro, V., 'Is There a Third Way?' (Barcelona: Pompeu Fabra University, Mimeo paper, 1999).
Newman, O. and R. de Zoysa, *The American Dream in the Information Age* (London: Macmillan, 1999).
Pierce, A., 'Blair Local Activists Defect to "Traditional" Values', *The Times* (London: 11 May 2000).
Ridell, P., 'Who Will Collect Taxes in a Global Village?', *The Times*: Opinion (London: 10 April 2000).
Rifkin, J., *The End of Work* (New York: Putnam, 1995).
Rosecrance, R., *The Rise of the Virtual State: Wealth and Power in the Coming Century* (New York: Basic Books, 1999).
Ryan, A., 'Britain: Recycling the Third Way', *Dissent* (New York: 46/2, Spring 1999), 77–80.
Sachs, J., 'A New Map of the World', *Economist* (London: 24 June 2000), 81–3.
Schor, J., *The Overworked American* (New York: Basic Books, 1991).
Shiva, V.H. 'Monoculture of the Mind', Hooper Inaugural Lecture (Guelph, Netherlands: University of Guelph, 1992).
Swanson, J., 'Self-help: Clinton, Blair and the Politics of Personal Responsibility', *Radical Philosophy* (London: May/June 2000), 29–38.
Teixeria, R. and J. Rogers, *America's Forgotten Majority: Why the White Working Class Still Matters* (New York: Basic Books, 1999).
Therborn, G., 'Europe in the 21st century: the World's Scandinavia?' in P. Gowan and P. Anderson (eds), *The Question of Europe* (London: Verso, 1997), 357–84.
Tuomioja, E., 'Blairism May Not Work Elsewhere in Europe', Newsletter to the Finnish Institute in London (July 1998).
United Nations Development Report 1997, cited by Victoria Brittain and Larry Elliott, 'World's Poor Lose out to Corporations', *Guardian Weekly* (London: 22 June 1999).

Urquart, B., 'In the Name of Humanity', *New York Review of Books* (New York: 27 April 2000), 19–22.

Walzer, M., 'Pluralism and Social Democracy', *Dissent* (New York: Winter 1998), 47–53.

Went, R., 'Making Europe Work – the Struggle to Cut the Working Week', *Capital and Class*, No. 71 (London: Summer 2000), 1–10.

Wuthnow, R., *Sharing the Journey* (New York: Free Press, 1992).

# Select Bibliography


Ackerman, B. and A. Alstott, *The Stakeholder Society* (New York: Yale University Press, 1998).

Alberti, M., *Capitalism vs. Capitalism* (New York, NY: Four Walls Eight Windows, 1993).

Ansell, A.E. and K.O. Moene (eds) *Unraveling the Right* (Boulder, CO: Westview Press, 1998).

Armstong, P., A. Glyn and J. Harrison, *Capitalism since World War II* (London: Fontana, 1984).

Atkinson, A.B., *The Economic Consequences of Rolling Back the Welfare State* (Cambridge, MA: MIT Press, 1999).

Baer, K.S., *The Politics of Liberalism from Reagan to Clinton* (Lawrence: University Press of Kansas, 2000).

Bauman, Z., *Globalization: the Human Consequences* (NY: Columbia University Press, 1998).

Beer, S.H., *Britain against Itself: the Political Contradictions of Collectivism* (New York: W.W. Norton, 1982).

Benjamin, W., *The Arcadian Project* (Cambridge, MA: Harvard University Press, 1999).

Bennett, W.J., *The Death of Outrage: Bill Clinton and the Assault on American Ideals* (NY: Free Press, 1998).

Bernstein, E., *Evolutionary Socialism* (New York: Schocken Books, 1961).

Blair, T., *The Third Way, New Politics for the New Century* (London: Fabian Society, 1998).

Brandon, R., *Surreal Lives* (New York: Grove Press, 1999).

Brittan, L., *A Diet of Brussels: the Changing Face of Europe* (New York: Little Brown, 1999).

Brittan, S., *The Role and Limits of Government* (London: Temple Smith, 1983).

Bideleux, R. and I. Jeffries, *A History of Eastern Europe: Crisis and Change* (London: Routledge, 1998).

Bobbio, N., *Left and Right: the Significance of a Political Distinction* (Cambridge: Polity Press, 1996).

Boggs, C., *The Socialist Tradition: from Crisis to Decline* (London: Routledge, 1995).

Bok, D., *The State of the Nation: Government and the Quest for a Better Society* (Cambridge, MA: Harvard University Press, 1996).

Bonoli, G., V. George and P. Taylor-Gooby, *European Welfare Futures: towards A Theory of Retrenchment* (Cambridge: Polity Press, 2000)

Bourdieu, P., *In Other Words* (Cambridge: Polity Press, 1990).

——, *Acts of Resistance: against the New Myths of our Time* (Cambridge: Polity Press, 1999).

Brown, A., *The Gorbachev Factor* (Oxford: Oxford University Press, 1997).

Buchanan, P.J., *The Great Betrayal: How American Sovereignty and Social Justice Are Being Sacrificed to the Gods of the Global Economy* (NY: Little Brown, 1998).

Burns, M.J. and G.J. Sorenson, *Dead Center: Clinton–Gore Leadership and the Perils of Moderation* (NY: Scribner 1999).
Callaghan, J., *The Retreat of Social Democracy* (Manchester: Manchester University Press, 2000).
Callinicos, A., *The Revenge of History: Marxism and the East European Revolutions* (Cambridge: Polity Press, 1991).
Campbell, C. and B.A. Rochman (eds), *The Clinton Legacy* (NY: Chatham House, 2000).
Castells, M., *The Rise of the Network Society*. Volume I of: *The Information Age: Economy, Society and Culture* (Oxford: Blackwell, 1996).
Castoriadis, C., *Political and Social Writings*, ed. by David Ames Curtis (Minnesota: Minnesota University Press, 1998).
Chryssochou, D.M., *Democracy in the European Union* (London: Tauris Academic Studies, 1998).
Conquest, R., *The Great Terror: a Reassessment* (New York, NY: Oxford University Press, 1990).
Cowling, K. and R. Sugden, *Beyond Capitalism: towards a New Economic Order* (New York: St. Martin's Press, 1994).
Coyle, D., *The Weightless World: Strategies for Managing the Digital Economy* (Cambridge, MA: MIT Press, 1998).
Crosland, C.A.R., *The Future of Socialism* (London: Cape, 1956).
Dahrendorf, R., *Reflections on the Revolution* (London: Chatto, 1990).
——, *Ein neuer Dritte Weg*? (Tübingen, Germany: Mohr Siebeck, 1999).
Dangerfield, G., *The Strange Death of Liberal England* (London: Cox and Wyman, 1935)
Daniels, R.V., *The End of the Communist Revolution* (London, Routledge, 1993).
Davis, M., *Magical Urbanism: Latinos Reinvent the US City* (London: Verso, 2000).
Ellmann, M. and V. Kontorovich, *The Disintegration of the Soviet Economic System* (London: Routledge, 1992).
Elster, J. and K.O. Moene (eds) *Alternatives to Capitalism* (New York: Cambridge University Press, 1989).
Esman, M.J., *Government Works: Why Americans Need the Feds* (Cornell University Press, 2000).
Etzioni, A., *The Limits of Privacy* (NY: Basic Books, 1999).
——, *The New Golden Rule; Community and Morality in a Democratic Society* (NY: Basic Books, 1996).
——, *The Spirit of Community: the Reinvention of American Society* (NY: 1994).
Finnegan, W., *Cold New World: Growing up In a Harder Country* (London, Picador, 1999).
Foner, E., *The Future of Socialism: Perspectives from the Left*, Tabbed, W.K. (ed.) (NY: Monthly Review Press, 1990).
Freedland, J., *Bring Home the Revolution* (NY: Fourth Estate, 1998).
Friedman, D., *The Machinery of Freedom* (New York, NY: Arlington House, 1978).
Friedman, M., *Capitalism and Freedom* (Chicago, IL: University of Chicago Press, 1962).
Friedman, T.L., *The Lexus and the Olive Tree* (New York: Farrar, Strauss and Giroux, 1999).
Frum, D., *Dead Right* (New York, NY: Basic Books, 1994).

Fukuyama, F., *The End of History and the Last Man* (London: Macmillan, 1992).
——, *Trust: the Social Virtues and the Creation of Prosperity* (New York: Free Press, 1995).
——, *The Great Disruption: Human Nature and the Reconstruction of Social Order* (London: Profile Books, 1999).
Gamble, A., *An Introduction to Modern Social Political Thought* (London: Macmillan, 1982).
Gates, J., *The Ownership Solution: toward a Shared Capitalism for the 21st Century* (Reading, MA: Addison-Wesley, 1998).
George, S., *An Awkward Partner: Britain in the European Community* (Oxford: Oxford University Press, 1990).
Geras, N., *The Legacy of Rosa Luxemburg* (London: New Left Books, 1976).
Gerber, C. (ed.), *Radical Politics in the Post Communist Era* (Amherst: 1995).
Giddens, A., *Beyond Left and Right: the Future of Radical Politics* (Cambridge: Polity Press, 1994).
——, *The Third Way: the Renewal of Social Democracy* (London: Polity Press, 1998).
——, *The Third Way and its Critics* (London: Polity Press, 2000).
Goff, B. and A.A. Fleischer, *Spoiled Rotten: Affluence, Anxiety and Social Decay in America* (Boulder, CO: Westview Press, 1999).
Goldblatt, D. (ed.), *The Stakeholding Society: Writings on Politics and Economics* (Cambridge: Polity Press, 1999).
Gorz, A., *Paths to Paradise: on the Liberation from Work* (London: Pluto Press, 1985).
——, *Reclaiming Work: beyond the Wage-based Society* (London: Polity Press, 1999).
Gould, P., *The Unfinished Revolution* (London: Little Brown, 1998).
Gramsci, A., *Selection from Prison Notebooks* (New York: International Publishers, 1997).
Gray, J., *The Moral Foundation of Market Institutions* (London: IEA 1992).
——, *False Dawn: the Delusions of Global Capitalism* (London: Granta Books, 1998).
Green, D.G., *The New Right* (Brighton: Wheatsheaf Books, 1987).
——, *Benefit Dependency: how Welfare Undermines Independence* (London: IEA, 1998).
Hay, C., *The Political Economy of New Labour* (Manchester University Press, 1999).
Hayek, F.A., *The Constitution of Liberty* (London: Routledge and Kegan Paul, 1960).
Henderson, K. and N. Robinson, *Post Communist Politics: an Introduction* (Hemel Hempstead: Prentice Hall, 1997).
Himmelfarb, G., *The De-Moralization of Society: from Victorian Virtues to Modern Values* (London: IEA, 1995).
Hitchens, C., *No One Left to Lie to. The Triangulations of William Jefferson Clinton* (London: Verso, 1999).
Hitchens, P., *The Abolition of Britain: from Lady Chatterley to Tony Blair* (London: Quartet Books, 1999).
Holmes, L., *The End of Communist Power* (Cambridge: Polity Press, 1993).
——, *Post Communism: an Introduction* (Cambridge: Polity Press, 1997).

Hood, J., *The Heroic Enterprise: Business and the Common Good* (New York: Free Press, 1996).
Hutton, W., *The State We're In* (London, Jonathan Cape, 1995).
——, *The State to Come* (London: Vintage, 1997).
——, *Stakeholding and its Critics* (London: IEA, 1997).
Hyland, W.G., *Clinton's World: Remaking American Foreign Policy* (NY: Praeger, 1999).
Jeffries, I., *Socialist Economies and the Transition to the Market: a guide* (London: Routledge, 1993).
Joll, J., *The Anarchists* (London, Penguin Books, 1964).
Jones, T., *Remaking the Labour Party: from Gaitskell to Blair* (London: Routledge, 1996).
Kavanagh, D., *Thatcherism and British Politics: the End of Consensus?* (Oxford: Oxford University Press, 1987).
King, D.S., *The New Right: Politics, Markets and Citizenship* (London: Macmillan, 1987).
Kitschelt, H., *The Transformation of European Social Democracy* (Cambridge: Cambridge University Press, 1994).
Kolakowski, L., *Main Currents of Marxism*, Vol. 1. The Founders (Oxford: Clarendon Press, 1978).
Krieger, J., *Reagan, Thatcher and the Politics of Decline* (Oxford: Blackwood, 1986).
——, *British Politics in the Global Age: Can Social Democracy Survive?* (Cambridge: Polity Press, 1999).
Kuttner, R., *Everything for Sale: the Virtues and Limits of Markets* (New York, NY: Knopf, 1997).
Lafontaine, O., *Das Herz schlägt links* (Munich: Econ, 1999).
Leadbeater, C. and I. Christie, *To Our Mutual Advantage* (London: Demos, 1999).
Levitas, R., *The Inclusive Society? Social Exclusion and New Labour* (London: Macmillan, 1998).
Liddle, R. and P. Mandelson, *The Blair Revolution: Can New Labour Deliver?* London: Faber, 1996).
Lindbeck, A., *The Swedish Experiment* (Stockholm: SNS Forlag, 1997).
Lipset, S.M. and G. Marks, *It Didn't Happen Here: why socialism failed in the United States* (NY: W.W. Norton, 2000).
Lloyd, J., *Rebirth of a Nation: an Anatomy of Russia* (London: Michael Joseph, 1998).
Luttwak, E.H., *Turbo-Capitalism: Winners and Losers in a Global Economy* (New York: Simon & Schuster, 1998).
MacDonald, R. (ed.), *Youth, the Underclass and Social Exclusion* (London: Routledge, 1997).
Mair, P., *Party System Change* (Oxford: Clarendon Press, 1997).
Marr, A., *The Day Britain Died* (London: Profile Books 2000).
Marshall, T., *Citizenship and Social Class* (NY: Anchor, 1965).
Marx, K., *Capital*, Vol. 3. (London: Lawrence and Wishart, 1972).
Marxism Today, *New Times* (London: October 1988).
McLellan, D., *Marxism after Marx* (London: Macmillan, 1979).
McLennan, G., D. Held and S. Hall (eds), *State and Society in Contemporary Britain* (Cambridge: Polity Press, 1984).
McMurty, J., *The Cancer Stage of Capitalism* (London: Pluto Press, 1999).

Miliband, R., *Socialism for a Sceptical Age* (Cambridge: Polity Press, 1994).
Miller, J., *Egotopia: Narcissim and the New American Landscape* (Tuscaloosa, AL: University of Alabama Press, 1997).
Miller, L.H., *Global Order; Values and Power in International Politics* (Oxford: Westview Press, 1998).
Moore, B. Jr., *Social Origins of Dictatorship and Democracy* (Boston, MA: Beacon Press, 1966).
Mouffe, C., *The Democratic Paradox* (London: Verso, 2000).
Mueller, J., *Capitalism, Democracy and Ralph's Pretty Good Grocery* (Princeton, NJ: Princeton University Press, 1999).
Nettle, P., *Rosa Luxemburg* (Oxford: Oxford Univerity Press, 1969).
Newman, O., *The Challenge of Corporatism* (Macmillan: London, 1981).
Newman, O. and R. de Zoysa, *The American Dream in the Information Age* (London: Macmillan, 1999).
Northcott, J., *Futures: Issues and Choices* (London: Policy Studies Institute, 1999).
Novak, M., *Is There A Third Way? Essays on the changing direction of socialist thought* (London: IEA, 1998).
Nove, A., *The Economics of Feasible Socialism* (London: Allen & Unwin, 1983).
Nozick, R., *Anarchy, State and Utopia* (London: Blackwell, 1974).
Offe, C., *Contradictions of the Welfare State* (London: Hutchinson, 1984).
Olasky, M., *The Tragedy of American Compassion* (Washington DC: Regency Gateway, 1992).
Oppenheim, C., *The Inclusive Society: Tackling Poverty* (London: IPPR, 1999).
Panitch, L. and C. Leys (ed.), *The Socialist Register, 1997* (Rendlesham: Merlin Press, 1997).
Paterson, W. and A.H. Thomas, (eds), *The Future of Social Democracy; Problems and Prospects of Social Democratic Parties in Western Europe* (Oxford: Clarendon Press, 1986).
Peter-Martin, H. and H. Schumann, *The Global Trap: Globalization and the Assault on Democracy and Prosperity* (London: Zed Books, 1997).
Petras, J. and M. Morley, *Empire or Republic? American Global Power and Domestic Decay* (London: Routledge, 1995).
Pierson, C., *Socialism after Communism: the New Market Socialism* (Pennsylvania, PA: The State University Press, 1995).
Piore, M.J., *Beyond Individualism* (Cambridge: Harvard UP, 1995).
Pipes, R., *Communism, the Vanquished Specter* (Cambridge, MA: Scandinavian University Press, 1994).
Plender, J., *A Stake in the Future: the Stakeholding Society* (London: Nicholas Brealey, 1997).
Prins, G. (ed.) *Spring in Winter, the 1989 Revolutions* (Manchester: MUP, 1990).
Putnam, R., *Bowling Alone* (NY: Simon & Schuster, 2000).
Rand, A., *The Virtue of Selfishness* (New York, NY: Signet, 1964).
Rifkin, J., *The End of Work* (New York: Putnam, 1995).
Rorty, R., *Achieving Our Country: Leftist thought in twentieth century America* (Cambridge, MA: Harvard University Press, 1998).
Rosecrance, R., *The Rise of the Virtual State: Wealth and Power in the Coming Century* (New York: Basic Books, 1999).
Rothbard, M., *For a New Liberty: the Libertarian Manifesto* (London: Collier-Macmillan, 1978).

Sakwa, R., *Postcommunism* (Buckingham: Open University Press, 1999).
Sassoon, D., *One Hundred Years of Socialism: the West European Left in the Twentieth Century* (London: Fontana, 1996).
——, (ed.) *Looking Left: European Socialism after the Cold War* (London and New York: I.B. Tauris Publishers, 1997).
Schor, J., *The Overworked American* (New York: Basic Books, 1991).
Schrecker, T., (ed.) *Surviving Globalism: the Social and Environmental Challenges* (London: Macmillan, 1997).
Schumpeter, J.A., *Capitalism, Socialism and Democracy* (London: Unwin University Books, 1943).
Schuparra, K., *Triumph of the Right: the Rise of the California Conservative Movement 1945–1966* (Armonk, NY: M.E. Sharpe, 1998).
Schwarzmantel, J., *The Age of Ideology: Political Ideologies from the American Revolution to Post-Modern Times* (London: Macmillan, 1998).
Selbourne, D., *The Principle of Duty: an Essay on the Foundations of Civic Order* (London: Sinclair-Stevenson, 1994).
Seldon, A., *Capitalism* (Oxford: Basil Blackwell, 1990).
Sennett, R., *The Corrosion of Character: the Personal Consequences of Work in the New Capitalism* (New York, W.W. Norton, 1998).
Shevtsova, L., *Yeltsin's Russia: Myths and Reality*, Carnegie Endowment for International Peace (Washington, DC, 1999).
Siedentop, L., *Democracy in Europe* (London: Allen Lane, 2000).
Skocpol, T., *The Missing Middle* (NY: Norton, 2000).
Smith, A., *The Wealth of Nations* (London: Dent, 1776).
Smith, D. and S. Wright (eds), *Whose Europe? The Turn towards Democracy* (Oxford: Blackwell, 1999).
Soetendorp, B., *Foreign Policy in the European Union* (London Longman, 1999).
Stephanopoulos, G., *All Too Human: a Political Education* (London: Hutchinson, 1999).
Tabb, W.K. (ed.), *The Future of Socialism: Perspectives from the Left* (New York: Monthly Review Press, 1990).
Teixeria, R. and J. Rogers, *America's Forgotten Majority: Why the White Working Class Still Matters* (New York: Basic Books, 1999).
Third Way (3W), *The Third Way* (London: 1998).
Thurow, L.C., *The Future of Capitalism* (New York, NY: William Morrow, 1996).
Turnock, D., *The East European Economy in Context: Communism and Transition* (London, Routledge, 1997).
Vallely, P. *The New Catholics: Social Catholic Teaching for the 21st Century* (London: SCM Press, 1998).
Vandenbroucke, F., *Globalisation, Inequality and Social Democracy* (London: Institute for Public Policy Research, 1998).
Walker, M., *The President They Deserve* (London: Fourth Estate, 1996).
Waller, M., *The End of the Communist Power Monopoly* (Manchester: MUP, 1993).
Wallerstein, I., *Utopistics* (New York, NY: Free Press, 1998).
Wallis, J., *The Soul of Politics* (London: Fount Paperbacks, 1995).
White, S., *After Gorbachev* (Cambridge: Cambridge University Press, 1993).
Wolfe, A., *One Nation After All* (NY: Viking, 1998).
Woodruff, D.M., *Money Unmade: Barter and the Fate of Russian Capitalism* (Cornell: Cornell University Press, 1999).

Wuthnow, R., *Sharing the Journey* (New York: Free Press, 1992).
Yergin, D. and J. Stanislaw, *The Commanding Heights* (NY: Simon & Schuster, 1998).
Zepezauer, M. and A. Naiman, *Take the Rich Off Welfare* (Tucson, AZ: Odonian Press, 1996).

# Index